Fighting
the Current

Fighting the Current

The Rise of American Women's Swimming, 1870–1926

LISA BIER

McFarland & Company, Inc., Publishers
Jefferson, North Carolina, and London

LIBRARY OF CONGRESS CATALOGUING-IN-PUBLICATION DATA

Bier, Lisa, 1971–
    Fighting the current : the rise of American women's swimming,
1870–1926 / Lisa Bier.
      p.   cm.
    Includes bibliographical references and index.

    ISBN 978-0-7864-4028-3
    softcover : 50# alkaline paper ∞

    1. Swimming for women — United States — History.
    2. Swimming — United States — History.   I. Title.
    GV837.5.B54   2011
    797.210820973 — dc23   2011022793

BRITISH LIBRARY CATALOGUING DATA ARE AVAILABLE

Front cover image: jumping in for a race at Shelter Island,
New York, 1904 (Library of Congress)

Manufactured in the United States of America

McFarland & Company, Inc., Publishers
  Box 611, Jefferson, North Carolina 28640
  www.mcfarlandpub.com

Table of Contents

Introduction

This book was first conceived of as a biography of Gertrude "Trudy" Ederle, the first woman to swim the English Channel. I had heard Trudy's name when I was growing up because she was the closest thing my family had to a celebrity. My grandfather's cousin was married to one of Trudy's brothers. The brother had died young, so the marriage was brief and there was no longer a connection between the families, so I never actually met anyone who knew Gertrude. Out of curiosity, I typed her name in the *New York Times* online database, and was astounded at just how much of a celebrity she had been in her time. She had appeared in hundreds of articles in the *New York Times*, even long before her famed Channel swim. I was astounded that this had occurred when she was only 18 years old, and I was also impressed by some other facts — that no books had ever been written about her; that she is relatively unknown today, and that her fame had been turned sour by many who wrote about her. Perhaps the most notable thing about her was that sports writers often painted her as a tragic female pioneer.

Sadly, I am such a slow writer that three other books about Gertrude were published as I was working, including one by her niece. But, by then, I was so enmeshed in my research and had discovered so many other interesting swimmers that I decided to highlight the women who had preceded Gertrude. I learned that there was a tradition of women swimming competitively in New York City dating back to the 1870s. These women were breaking barriers 50 years before Gertrude Ederle, and they have been all but forgotten. Some of their names are known, but many more go unnamed because of the number of women who were involved in the sport. It was not just a few celebrity swimmers. Many women swam for sport, for health, and just for fun. The competitive achievements of Gertrude Ederle can be directly traced to the women of New York City who sought out natatoriums or learned to swim in the ocean in the 1860s and 1870s.

More importantly, these swimmers did not keep a low profile. They received extensive attention for their performances in the newspapers. I initially expected that their stories would be hard to come by, but newspapers revealed the opposite. They were, for the most part (with some notable exceptions), well accepted in their day, popular and appreciated, although they were not treated equally as male athletes. Interestingly, their achievements appeared in the sports pages, not the special sections of the paper set aside for ladies' interests, such as society news and homemaking. Yet, they and their impressive activities have been forgotten.

I would like to thank the librarians and archivists at the Cantigny Foundation, the Museum of the City of New York; the Dover Museum; the International Center for Olympic Studies at the University of Western Ontario; the Herbert Hoover Presidential Museum; Lake Forest College Library; the New York Public Library; and the Brooklyn Public Library (who sent me materials, answered questions, and connected me with hard-to-find items). I would like to thank Jeff Bridgers at the Library of Congress and Ivonne Schmid at the International Swimming Hall of Fame for assisting with locating photographs. I especially wish to thank the staff of the wonderful International Swimming Hall of Fame in Ft. Lauderdale for allowing me to use their archive and library, where I was able to see the personal scrapbooks that had been proudly assembled by these young athletes. That, more than anything, gave me a sense of the lives of these women, and how swimming had opened up the world to them.

I thank my very supportive colleagues at Hilton C. Buley Library and I thank Southern Connecticut State University for providing support in the form of reassigned time for research and travel grants.

I'd like to thank my friends Jessica Kenty-Drane for inspiration and support; Astrid Eich-Krohn for kindly translating some materials; Christina Tam and Rachael Payne for dog-sitting; Carol Skalko for keeping me sane during a tough year, and Mike Ryan for making sure I finished.

1. Safe Waters

Dirty Water

Generally speaking, whenever women in the United States have engaged in an activity that was new to them — be it voting, owning property, or entering the workforce — they have been scrutinized, supervised, and criticized. Women's early participation in sports and leisure activities was likewise resisted and protested. One hundred years ago, opportunities for women to exercise, play sports, and have fun while doing so were few and far between. The very ideas of exercise, health, fun, and recreation as individual concepts were fairly new; combining all four in one activity may have seemed highly perplexing or self-indulgent, if not offensive and even dangerous to a women's health and supposedly delicate body.

As a recreational activity, swimming was slow to reach the masses. It was different from other kinds of activities, especially for city dwellers, for a few very important reasons. One, it required access to safe and clean water that was at least deep enough to float in. Two, when performed incorrectly, it could be fatal. Three, it usually involved wearing fewer, smaller, and more revealing items of clothing than was considered acceptable for the time.

Safe and clean water was first and foremost necessary for swimming, but it was in short supply in the 19th century, especially in cities. Considering the conditions, there are good reasons to ask why anyone would have wanted to go swimming at all. For instance, in 1870, *Frank Leslie's Illustrated Newspaper* reported a most disgusting scandal. The crews who had been hired by the city of New York to remove and dispose of dead animals were not doing their work correctly. They were supposed to be taking dead cats, dogs, carthorses, and remnants from butchers, far out into the wilds of New Jersey and burning them. Instead, they were tossing them into the water not far from Manhattan, where they easily washed back up on beaches or floated close to land. New York was suffering through a heat wave that summer, and the citizens could not ignore the horrible sight and the noxious stench coming from the offshore carcasses. According to the paper, the carcasses drifted "about in the bay, going out and returning as the tide serves, until the effect of water and sun in these seething days renders them so absolutely putrid that human olfactories cannot stand the stench. Such is the condition at present in our bay and along-shore, that it is next to impossibility to breathe. At a moderate estimate, from Fulton Ferry to Coney Island, there are from 50 to 100 carcasses floating about or roasting upon the shore. There are cats, dogs, cows, goats, and horses, with tons of putrid liver and entrails, now slowly floating in and out, or else stranded, and all of them giving forth odors that would sicken the stoutest stomach in Christendom."[1]

When people in cities looked at the rivers, lakes, or ocean around them, they didn't necessarily see a beautiful view or a cool, refreshing place for splashing, frolicking, and other aquatic fun. They saw a barrier to travel, and they saw danger. Often they also saw animal entrails, jagged pieces of lumber, and rotting garbage bobbing along in oil slicks. Waterways were essentially highways for infectious diseases to travel upon, and Manhattan, being an island, was surrounded on all sides by fetid rivers carrying the wastes of upstream industries and the effluvia of the city's own production. These rivers are brackish, closer to salt water than freshwater, and out of necessity the city had decided to bring in its own drinking water from the upstate Croton Reservoir by the 1840s. This improved public health immensely but didn't solve the problem entirely. Even so, the piped-in water could carry illnesses such as cholera and typhoid, and in 1849 New York suffered a cholera outbreak that killed approximately 5,000 people.[2] Of course, bringing fresh water into a city did not solve the problem of removing waste from the city. Most sewage and garbage still ended up in the waters immediately surrounding the city.

New Yorkers recalled the disgusting state of the water in the oral history compilation, *You Must Remember This: An Oral History of Manhattan from the 1890s to World War II*. One man remembered, "When I think about it now, the sweat goes runnin' down my neck. We swam among the condoms, the garbage, and the filth, everything the Hudson was noted for. As a matter of fact, the first intestines I ever seen came floatin' down there once."[3] Another Manhattanite cheerfully recalled, "At 114th Street they had the sewer that went right out there when we went swimmin'. It was a big sewer — maybe six feet in diameter. We used to be on top, because it was encased in a concrete box. We would dive offa that. Every once in a while the sewer stuff would come out. Gheeegh! Everything came out. 'Hey, it's comin,' boys! Move out.' It was a riot. Ya got hit all over. Goddam, we had to push that crap away when we went in there, otherwise ya caught it in the face."[4] Someone else remembered swimming in a virtual abattoir. "We hung out by the river seven days a week.... The slaughterhouses were there, too. They used to kill sheep and cattle. They had a big sewer pipe goin' into the dock, and every now and then there would be a big gush of blood into the river while we were swimmin,' and we'd get caught in it and be covered in blood."[5] Not everything in the water was dead. "The water was clean at high tide, and when the ferry pulled out, we swam around there. The water rats were gigantic, but if we didn't bother them, they didn't us."[6]

For boys and men willing to take the risk, it was possible to swim around the docks on the East and Hudson Rivers. This was usually done stark naked and was illegal, not to mention unclean and dangerous. A great amount of police energy went into chasing naked men and boys away from piers and docks, lest they expose themselves to women on passing boats. Women of all social classes would have avoided swimming in this situation, and the occasional outrage sparking from this improper display eventually helped lead to the creation of more controllable swimming facilities in the city. But for women who were interested in swimming, it was almost impossible to find a clean, safe place to swim.

A crowd of bathers at Atlantic City, New Jersey, 1903. Detail (Library of Congress Prints and Photographs Division).

It was at the beach that most average people received their first introduction to swimming. By the 1860s, resort areas were opening outside the city, where New Yorkers could leave the tightly enclosed city neighborhoods behind and spend a day strolling the shore, watching the amusements, and taking a dip in the sea. Coney Island was reachable by steamboat, train, or horsecar, and it could draw hundreds of thousands of people on a hot day. For those who owned a swimsuit or had the money to rent one, swimming or wading was a wonderful, cooling possibility. In 1868, a reporter for the *New York Times* wrote, "Surf-baths and clam-bakes — for these Coney Island is justly celebrated. The beach slopes rapidly into the sea so that you do not have to go far from the shore to get a full immersion. Almost anywhere along the shore bathing dresses may be hired for twenty-five cents each, and in some places remote from public view even these are dispensed with. Toward sunset, all along the shore, on a Midsummer's day, myriads of people of all ages and both sexes may be seen tumbling about among the breakers. It is an amusing sight to gaze upon and much more entertaining to be part of the spectacle."[7]

Unfortunately, the beaches at the resort areas were not much cleaner than the water immediately surrounding Manhattan. Brooklyn, then not yet part of the city of New York, contained the seaside resort areas of Coney Island, Rockaway, and Manhattan Beach, and it was there that the problems of inadequate garbage disposal had a more visible impact. Garbage dumped off Coney Island almost immediately washed up on shore, including large numbers of dead dogs, cats, and rats. In 1876, Brooklynites testified that "as many as 150 carcasses of animals have been found on the beach in a single day. William Harker, who has charge of the beach from the Brooklyn City line to Fort Hamilton, avers that he finds on an average from thirty-five to forty dead animals per day on the shore." Hotel and bathhouse owners in the resort areas were enraged at the impact on their businesses. No one wanted to make the long trip from Manhattan, rent a bathing suit, and walk down to the shore only to discover the water was disgusting. "Bathers are compelled to leave the surf on account of the stench, and the water itself, encumbered with a mass of putrescent material, is rendered unfit for bathing purposes. In this way it is a cause of serious loss and injury to those who make a living by furnishing bathing-suits."[8]

The following year, the problems continued unabated as the garbage scows moved north of the city. "Capt. Charles Smith, of the Seawanhaka, reports that the beach at Cow Bay, New-Rochelle, Sea Cliff, Hart's and City Islands, and all the other resorts between the points named, is strewn with dead dogs and cats, putrid liver, rotten oranges, and all kinds of similar offal that will float, and that a stench pervades the air which is unbearable. Private summer residences are rendered uninhabitable, the bath-houses are sur rounded with disgusting odds and ends, and unless something be done a pestilence promises to sweep the shore as soon as the regular heated season sets in." The impact of the dumping was such that entire oyster beds were dying out and the river bed was becoming shallower, filled to capacity by the strata of refuse that New York had sent upriver for dumping. Citizens were so disgusted by this that the "more hotheaded are loudly advocating summary measures, such as firing the scows and driving the tug-boats off by musketry and artillery."[9]

Despite laws enacted as to where the scows could drop their loads, illegal dumping continued. This 1880 account of bathing at Manhattan and Brighton Beaches gives an idea of the massiveness and foulness of the problem. "Persons who had gone in bathing when the tide was down, and found the water clear and bright, observed that when the tide came in it brought quantities of decaying straw and hay, floating vegetable cans, rotten lemons and melons, great patches of these offensive things coming ashore, to be dashed upon the bathers as they sported in the surf. It was impossible to avoid the noisome stuff, for it was stretched out in a disgusting mass for miles along the shore, and could be seen floating for a distance of half a mile out to sea. The rollers tossed it upon the beach, where it lay exposed to further decay in the sun, or was dried up and blown away with clouds of sand. Occasionally, small carcasses of cats and dogs would be found with the decaying vegetable matter and miscellaneous refuse, and bathers who ventured out without noting which way they were swimming were disagreeably surprised to find themselves floating besides one of the nauseating objects. Human nature at Coney Island beach is very much like human nature in the City, and it is not particularly partial in either place to unburied dead cats. Troops of disgusted patrons of the large bathing houses freed themselves from the refuse which clung about them, and went in hot haste to complain, and to suggest that something should be done to put a stop to the nuisance."[10]

The illegal dumping continued in spite of the anger of the resort proprietors and the swimmers. Even as beach resorts invested in massive oceanfront hotels, boardwalks, and pavilions, the stench and sight of the garbage continued to ruin vacations. One summer day in August of 1886, the garbage brought business to a standstill. "On Monday morning Manager Schumann, of the Manhattan Bathing House, declined to receive bathers. Four or five hundred came along with quarters in their hands, but he refused to take the money. For twenty yards out from the water's edge there were layers of stuff like a big raft. The substratum seemed to be of straw, hay, and weed. This was cemented with mud, ashes, and sewage. It carried a miscellaneous cargo, in which cut melons, decayed fruit, grease-coated barrel staves, old bottles, and an exhaustive assortment of cats and dogs in various post-mortem stages appealed with staggering arguments to the senses of smell and sight. The breakers came up and lapped this mass, but could not get over, under, or around it."[11] When confronted with this kind of enormous barge of garbage, the beach managers had to wait for it to float ashore, and then were forced to dismantle it physically to cart it away for burial under the sand, which was hardly a long-term solution.

The situation was so serious that in 1891, the Manhattan Beach Hotel, Land, and Improvement Company sued New York City and its New-York Street-Cleaning Department, which was responsible for dumping that city's garbage in the waters off Brooklyn's beach areas.[12] In 1893, responding to the general public's outrage and the knowledge of the more educated citizens that no other world-class cities were so barbaric in their disposal of garbage, the city acquired Riker's Island and began putting the garbage in a landfill. By 1900, the city had created plants for burning the garbage, a solution that sent the trash up into the air and into people's lungs, but at least kept it away from the beaches. When the Barren Island incinerating plant was destroyed by fire in 1906, the problem returned almost immediately. Scows were required to dump at least 50 miles from shore, but trash almost immediately began to wash up on the beaches of Long Island and New Jersey. Illegal dumping from scows continued sporadically into the 1920s, when a vacationer at Long Island's Long Beach sent the following complaint about polluted beaches to the *New York Times*: "It is an uncanny feeling to have a dead body of a dog, sheep, chicken or cat roll against one's leg while in the surf, but a more serious blow to one's nerves to get a crack in the head from a bottle on the crest of a wave."[13]

The putrescence washing ashore may have been the impetus for some of the resort areas to begin installing swimming pools. In 1890, the upscale Hollywood resort in Long Branch, New Jersey, unveiled its newest amenity, a saltwater bathing pool. The enormous concrete tank was enclosed by wooden walls decorated with stained-glass windows, sheltered by a partially open roof. The pool area featured a bandstand and a café and was an immediate success. "Hundreds of persons, not only women and children, but men who love to perform feats in the water, have given up surf bathing and enjoy swimming in the tank. It is so large that it is not crowded even when from 300 to 500 persons visit it in a day, and the nicely graded depths of from three to six feet put danger out of the question."[14]

For those beachgoers who were able to enter the water at the seashore, being in the water was usually more a form of wading as opposed to fully immersed swimming. Many resorts strung ropes from shore out into the sea that bathers could cling to while they bobbed in the water or splashed about. Swimming wasn't the primary goal of a day at the shore; it was just one possible aspect of the excursion.

Barriers for Women

Women's bathing costumes ranged from the rented plain suits to very fancy silk ones, but what they had in common was coverage. These suits provided more skin coverage than today's dresses, with skirts that reached at least the knee, corsets, sleeves, bloomers, stockings, and bathing shoes. They were dark in color for modesty's sake, and often quite heavy when wet. Pressures from society concerning modesty conflicted with issues of safety and function. For women interested in venturing away from the ropes and actually swimming, not just wading, the suits were a hindrance and a danger.

Women's access to swimming was also hindered by attitudes about women's physical capabilities, which were shaped by the dualistic beliefs of the times. Men and women, it was believed, were opposites, each providing one unique and noninterchangeable half, if not an equal half, of the natural whole. What men could do and did do, women were believed incapable of and generally prevented from even attempting to do. Men did what was masculine, females did what was feminine, and everyone was supposed to know which was which.

Just as there were objections when women encroached on the societal

Bathers at Rockaway Beach, 1904. The ropes allowed non-swimmers to immerse themselves in the water safely. Detail (Library of Congress Prints and Photographs Division).

territory of men by becoming educated, having careers, owning property, and trying to gain the right to vote, there were objections to women participating in sports, couched in concern for their supposedly delicate natures. Sporting activities were allegedly too difficult or exhausting for women to handle without causing irreparable damage to the uniquely female aspects of their health, especially the ability to produce and rear healthy children. Some of the earliest and strongest objections to women participating in athletics and sports centered around concerns for women's reproductive systems, which seemed to be, then as now, everyone's business but their own.

There were a number of objections to women participating in sports and swimming over the years, and the objections seemed to change and grow stronger each time the previous objection was disproved or forgotten. First, it was thought that athletic exercise was too difficult for women, that they might injure themselves or deprive themselves of reproductive abilities. Then it was thought that while healthful exercise was acceptable, competition was not feminine, and in fact, had a masculinizing effect on women. Some in the medical field expressed grave concern that women who engaged in athletic activities were headed down a dangerous path on which they would forever lose their femininity and abilities to be mothers.

The idea of play and exercise for girls was not something advocated as natural and fun, as we like to think of it today, or necessitated by cultural norms about extreme fitness or thinness for girls and women. Early physical educators believed that girls and boys were entirely different and, even in matters of play and recreation, needed to be guided to appropriate activities that would train them for the roles they would ultimately hold.

As a result of attitudes such as these, girls weren't entirely barred from participating in exercise and sports, as long as such activities were noncompetitive, not overly strenuous, and ultimately led to their development as better wives and mothers. Despite this, some women were able to ignore these attitudes and do as they pleased, with little negative result and much personal benefit.

Private Pools

In cities like New York, open space was rapidly disappearing as real estate became more valuable by the hour. It was somewhere between difficult and impossible for women to find opportunities and places where they could engage privately and safely in recreation, leisure, or exercise. In a time before public parks and mandated physical education, private organizations stepped in to carve out space in the city for their members.

By the 1880s, working-class and middle-class women were beginning to have a few options for joining private civic groups that promoted physical fitness, many of which were religious or ethnic organizations. The Young Women's Christian Association provided some access to sports, exercise and self-improvement for women. Founded in its earliest form as the Ladies' Christian Association in 1848, it was an entirely separate organization from the Young Men's Christian Association, the YMCA, although the two mirrored each other in many ways. Both were founded to keep the young people who had been drawn to cities looking for work from being lured into the dangerous, seamy, and sinful aspects of city life. They offered lodging and opportunities for learning, recreation, and worship.

Many Jewish synagogues invested in large community centers that functioned as place of worship, community center, cultural center, and recreation facility, a phenomenon that has been referred to as the "shul with a pool." In 1916, the New York Young Women's Hebrew Association completed the construction of an eight-story multi-purpose building. Located at 110th Street in Harlem and overlooking Central Park, it featured a modern pool and gymnasium, dormitories, classrooms, and a library. Importantly, this was not a men's organization that offered use of its facilities to women a few hours a week — this was a facility created especially for the recreational needs and betterment of Jewish women.[15]

Ethnic organizations, including the German Turnvereins, provided thousands of women with recreational opportunities that would never have been available otherwise. The first American Turnverein was founded in Cincinnati in 1848, and soon thereafter many more were established in cities up and down the East Coast and all over the Midwest. The Turnvereins were athletic and social clubs founded on the teachings of the German father of gymnastics, Friedrich L. Jahn, who had created a system of gymnastics as a means of restoring his countrymen's lost morale after Napoleon's occupation of Germany. Jahn's methods incorporated calisthenics, marching, running, dancing, swimming and work on apparatuses like the balance beam and pommel horse. Jahn had wanted his gymnastic programs to provide Germany with an army of strong, able, and agile citizens ready to defend the fatherland, and this belief came to America with the Turnvereins. Vast numbers of Turners, as they came to identify themselves, joined the Union Army during the Civil War; there were at least four regiments whose membership consisted solely of Turners. By 1896, there were at least 24 Turner societies in Chicago alone, where they were active in pushing public schools to teach physical education and in the development of public parks.[16]

Some factories and textile mills sponsored athletic organizations for their workers. In addition to keeping workers fit and entertained, these programs were thought to bond the workforce, improve morale, and create better relationships between workers and management.[17]

There were also more exclusive private athletic clubs founded by and for the wealthy. These generally excluded women from participating in most sports, although they did provide some of the earliest opportunities for women to play a few activities, specifically golf and lawn tennis. Many of these clubs gradually evolved from athletic facilities to competitive athletic clubs to country clubs, with an emphasis on socializing rather than athletics.

Some women were interested in learning to swim for social reasons, such as those who might spend the summers at a resort or aboard a wealthy husband's yacht. But for many others, knowledge of swimming was a matter of life and death. In a world where people commonly traveled by boat, and women wore large, voluminous clothing that could drown them if waterlogged, any swimming skill to speak of was a needed advantage in the fight against a watery grave. Whether for safety or health, by the mid–19th century there was a demand for women's swimming lessons.

Private baths provided a place where, for a fee, women could learn to swim in privacy for educational, recreational, or health reasons. Some of these early swimming pools were little more than small tanks in the basements of buildings, while others were privately owned floating baths. The floating baths were large wooden cages that were anchored to the ends of piers or docks. The slatted woodwork of the pool enclosure allowed water to enter and exit the pool, freeing the employees from having to clean the water as they would in an enclosed tank of water. The floating pool was surrounded by a tall enclosure that provided privacy to the clientele from prying outside eyes. The floating baths were occasionally the source of confusion for city authorities who couldn't decide whether to treat them as boats or as buildings.

One of these early private baths, Benton's Warm Ocean Swimming Bath, was just opposite Brooklyn's City Hall, and opened in 1861. Their facilities were advertised this way: "At this novel and unique establishment may be found a swimming lake, from three to seven feet deep, large enough to accommodate hundreds of people at one time, into which cascades and jets of perfectly filtered ocean water are constantly flowing. Steam pipes have been so arranged as to keep the immense body of water summer heat during the winter. A commodious and completely furnished dressing-room provided for each bather. Also, hot or cold salt or fresh shower and private baths for both ladies and gents. Competent teachers, male and female, in constant attendance, to teach the art of swimming. The luxury of a bath in a lake of pure ocean water, with a perfectly smooth and even bottom, free from shell and other annoying construction, in a fairy-like grotto, protected from sun, wind, and the gaze of the multitude, in the very heart of a great city, was never before offered to the public in any country. Change of hours for bathing. Gents' swimming, warm, and shower baths open from 8 A.M. to 9 P.M. Hours for ladies' swimming bath from 10 A.M. to 2 P.M. Private baths 9 A.M. to 5 P.M. Ladies entrance on Adams st."[18]

A single admission was 40 cents, a lesson was one dollar, and a three-month ticket was 12 dollars, not a price that a working-class person could afford on a regular basis, if ever. This, as was clearly stated in the advertisement, was a place of sport, health, recreation, and amusement, rather than hygiene. The intended audience was upper-class ladies and gentlemen with leisure time, money, and a concern for health. Its opening was sufficiently exciting an event that the *Brooklyn Eagle* sent a reporter before opening day, who filed this detailed report.

As this institution, which in all its departments is the conception and design of Mr. B. T. Benton, the proprietor of the Park Theatre, is destined to become one of the most agreeable resorts in this city; we sent one of our reporters this morning to examine and give a brief sketch of the new institution. The idea of a salt water swimming bath situated in the centre of a large city, is sufficiently novel in itself to create interest in the man who had brought it to completion and the manner in which it is to be maintained.

The Academy is located in the Park Theatre building, running through from Fulton to Adams street, and in making an examination this morning, our reporter started at the foot of Adams street, where is located the steam pump by which the water is supplied to the bath. The pump used is one of Campbell and Harlick's steam pumps of forty horse power, and capable of discharging 741 gallons per minute. The suction pipe, which is six inches in diameter, extends over four hundred feet into the river, which at this point is entirely free from sewers, and from the pump a 6 inch pipe leads to the foot of the hill from whence a 4 inch pipe extends to the top of the hill at Concord St., where there is a reservoir capable of holding 3,000 gallons of water, from this point there is a fall of twenty-six feet to the bath, and as the reservoir will always be kept full, in case of any accident to the pump there will always be sufficient water in this reservoir to keep the bath supplied. Entering at the Adams street entrance the visitor finds himself in the ladies' department, fronted by a richly furnished parlor, 19 × 16 feet from which are twenty bathing and dressing rooms. Seven of the rooms are furnished with bath tubs where hot and cold water either fresh or salt can be had at all times. At the end of the hallway is a nicely fitted up sitting-room, communicating by an open window with the Park Theatre Ice Cream saloon, where ladies may obtain such refreshments as they desire, and from this room a handsome staircase leads to THE SWIMMING BATH, which is believed to be the finest institution of the kind on this continent. It is 40 feet wide by 60 feet in length and has a depth of water varying from three to seven feet. The bottom and sides are formed of cement, making a hard smooth surface. The water forced from the river by the pump above alluded to passes, before going into the bath through an immense filter out of which it goes into the bath as clear as amber, while its saline qualities are retained in all their force. Around the bath are seventy dressing rooms, and the platform in front of them is made of rounded slats about two inches thick and a quarter of an inch apart, through which all the water, &c., is carried to a sewer below and carried into the street sewer without having any connection with the bath. The water in the bath is kept constantly fresh, as a current is continually flowing by the water from the river constantly flowing in, and a discharge pipe carrying off a corresponding quantity. There is nearly 100 feet between the bath and the ceiling, and midway is a handsome gallery lit by over a hundred gas jets, and hung around with rustic baskets. On this gallery there are private baths, refreshment rooms, &c., for gentlemen. The gentlemen's entrance is on Fulton street, where a handsome barber shop has been fitted up. For warm water two immense tanks have been placed under the sidewalk in Adams street, each capable of holding 1,000 gallons of water. One holds salt water and the other fresh. These are heated by steam, which is obtained from the iron works of Supervisor Howell, opposite, and around the Swimming bath also runs a steam pipe which is for the purpose of keeping the water at an equal temperature. The entire cost of the construction of this bath has been of $40,000, and there is no doubt that when opened next week, Mr. Benton's enterprise and liberality will be duly appreciated by the public.

The bath has been placed under the superintendence of Mr. Gray, formerly of the Fulton Ferry baths, a man whose large experience and excellent judgment in these matters promise well for the establishment, everything about which has been fitted up in a style of the most lavish expenditure.[19]

Not all were happy with the policies of the Benton's Bath and its part-time admittance of females, and in 1870 the *Brooklyn Eagle* published an editorial that laid out two main complaints about the bath. One complaint was that men should be allowed to swim in the nude. "Any man who can swim at all can swim more easily and comfortably without garments. No swimmer likes, after paying for his bath, to be charged ten cents more for donning an uncomfortable garment that has been worn promiscuously by hundreds of other people, and which, for aught he knows, may entail risk of contagious disease, and which at least will encumber his movements in the water." But worse still than the ban against nudity was the ban on smoking. "Every swimmer is a smoker, as a general thing, and any man who likes to smoke at all, likes his smoke best of all directly as he comes out of the water." The writer maintained that the rule against smoking was so that women, swimming during their own hours, would not have to smell the stale tobacco stench. He proposed making it a gentlemen's club entirely, so that the men could smoke freely, in the nude, and not concern themselves with offending female customers.[20]

2. Swimming Schools and Kate Bennett, New York's Swimming Instructor Extraordinaire

One of the earliest and most influential figures helping women make the leap into the world of swimming was Miss Kate Bennett, a swim teacher and proponent of water safety for women. In 1870, she opened a swimming school in Manhattan. Over the years, the school would move from indoor tanks to floating baths and back, from Manhattan to Brooklyn, but her influence in swimming circles was permanent. Kate Bennett almost singlehandedly made swimming fashionable and was personally responsible for teaching two generations of New York women to swim.

Kate's reasons for choosing swimming as a vocation were personal: she had lost her father to drowning.[1] Initially, her swimming students were middle to upper class. Of one of them, Kate said, "We had a lady from Staten Island yesterday who learned the motions and swam very nicely in one lesson. This lady's husband has a yacht and there is quite a bet pending as to her daring to jump out from the yacht and swim off with him, but I think she can do it. Anybody can learn in four lessons."[2]

Kate was a genius at self-promotion. She advertised her tutelage in the same section of the newspaper classifieds as excursion boats to the beaches. One advertisement, appearing directly below one for the steamer *Morrissania*'s schedule for Coney Island, reads, "Learn to swim at Prof. Van Glovne's Swimming Academy, 7th Ave. and 59th St., before going upon an excursion. Ladies are under the immediate supervision of Miss Kate Bennett and her sisters, the most accomplished swimmers and successful teachers in the world, ably assisted by a competent corps of assistants. Gents are under the care of Prof. Van Gloyne, whose improved method and ability to impart confidence and instruction is not surpassed. No lady or gentleman ever attended the school without learning to swim. Learn to swim. None too old, none too young."[3]

Kate was a confident promoter of swimming for women and of her own skills as a teacher. She often hosted performances of her students to which friends, family, the press, and the public were invited. The students would demonstrate their aquatic skills by racing, swimming underwater, diving, jumping, and more. Kate would narrate the program, often announcing the number of lessons a student had completed, emphasizing how easy it was to become a proficient and confident swimmer. From little toddlers to married adult women, the impressive abilities of the students were always well received by audiences.

Kate hosted a "water party" in September 1877. Guests were invited to her school, which at that time was located at a floating bath moored at West 23rd Street on the Hudson River, and seated on a platform where they observed Kate's female swimmers appearing in a series of "sudden plunges and much upheaving of water."[4] Students demonstrated swimming underwater and diving from a springboard. Eliza Bennett, Kate's sister and the assistant instructor, dove from the roof of the bath house. Medals and trophy cups were given to the participants.

Another of her exhibitions was written up in great detail. Kate first gave a lecture on the benefits of swimming, concluding by saying that "a young woman is more likely to catch a husband by saving his life than by spending his dollars." The students then performed. "Three maidens would dive together and swim with the 'steam-launch' stroke, which must be seen to be understood, under the surface across the bath. Then they would float on their backs, locked together lengthwise with their feet under the arms of the girls in front and simultaneously through their arms upwards and backwards, and swim exactly like a six-oared boat's crew. They could also manage to get through the water with hands and feet lashed together, and Miss Olive swam on her back, holding about the water a tray, from which she ate a piece of pie and drank a glass of water while en route.... Miss Lizzie Simmons stood on the shoulders of Annie Gober, who in turn balanced herself upon the fair champion Olive, and the three dove together, avoiding broken necks with apparent ease." In all, said the reporter, "It was wonderful to see with what utter abandon and fearless grace the girls, big and little, let themselves fall into the troubled pool."[5]

Kate's school continued to grow. In 1878, she was teaching in a natatorium in the Central Park garden that was 80 feet long by 20 feet wide, with a depth graduating from four feet to six. The pool was outfitted with ropes, harnesses and pulleys used to help some of the more timid swimmers develop confidence in the water. The pupils demonstrated their swimming skills during an exhibition that year, clothed in bathing costumes from shoulder to knee, exhibiting diving, swim strokes, and endurance. Girls as young as five dove from eight feet and swam underwater until "the spectators were fully convinced that one neither be old, strong, or masculine to become an expert swimmer." Kate herself was described as a "powerful and wonderfully expert swimmer."[6]

By 1884, Kate and another of her sisters, Teresa, had opened a summer school in Fort Hamilton, Brooklyn, where the floating bath was located at the end of a long pier in the Narrows between Brooklyn and Staten Island. They held a contest in which two teenage girls were rowed a quarter mile from the pier and then swam back. "The tide was running in pretty strong, and there was considerable swell on, but the girls did not hesitate. They plunged boldly into the water and started back for the baths. The tide was so strong that it threatened to carry them far above the baths, but they buffeted against it and reached them in as good form as the half-dozen men who accompanied them in the water."[7] Following the open-water swim, one girl demonstrated swimming underwater, while another performed a number of comedic stunts, including swimming about with a cracker "without getting so much as a drop of water on it," pretending to doze in the water, and artfully catching a bouquet tossed to her, after which she blew kisses to the crowd. She finished up this performance by swimming with her hands and feet tied, and then, with a fake cigar for a prop, proceeded to "put her fingers in the armholes of her costume to represent Gen. Grant."

Kate's exhibitions straddled a line between athleticism and crowd-pleasing theater. An August 1889 exhibition seems to have been half a demonstration of legitimate aquatic skill and half variety show. Kate started the show by diving into the water with her three-year-old niece on her back. Next came a catamaran chariot race, with girls playing both the catamarans and the chariots, then a rendition of a famous scene from the popular play, *A Dark Secret*. "Miss Bertie Souther, who represented Flora, was thrown overboard, tied hand and foot, to be rescued by Miss Agnes McGilken. Miss Frankie King swam the entire length of the bath with a cup poised upon her forehead. Miss Evelyn Edgerly did some very clever fancy swimming. Little Adele Wishlade, a little tot, swam all around the bath. Miss Kate Bennett, the proprietress, did some wonderfully clever swimming, jumping, diving, swimming under water and performing other feats."[8]

Bathing dress was less of an issue at the private schools, where function was more important than modesty, than at the beaches, where the clothing of both men and women was an issue of public policy. Kate described the suits that would be best for actual swimming:

> The short suit is the best for a swimming dress. Presumably ladies don't feel so comfortable in them, but there is no reason why they should not carry as little

weight as possible in the water. Cut short and leaving the muscles of the arms and lower limbs free, they prevent chafing, which comes with too much clothes. It can be readily understood that a lady in skirts is handicapped in the water. Some facetious individual has suggested that in lawn tennis the gentlemen, to be on equal terms with the ladies, should also wear skirts. If gentlemen wore them in the water they would be quick to appreciate the inconvenience under which the other sex labors when attired in the costume fashion dictates as the proper one for the swimming baths.[9]

3. Swimming for All

Early Public Baths and Swimming Pools

The earliest public pools to which women of all social classes had access were originally intended as bathing facilities. They were a response to the fact that lower class city dwellers, packed into airless tenements buildings, often had no running water or anywhere to bathe other than a communal tub in the hallway or backyard; New York City did not mandate running water on all floors of tenement buildings until 1901. As early as 1858, New Yorkers were asking for public places to bathe, understanding that the cleanliness of the working class was linked to the public health of all.[1]

In 1866, the *New York Times* complained that while the Board of Health was publishing and distributing circulars about the importance of staying clean, the city was providing no facilities at which people could actually get clean.

> Men and boys will have their swim, and as there are no proper places provided for this healthful and purifying exercise, they do it in a manner which is neither conducive to good morals or public decency. In the cool of the evening thousands of swimmers are seen sporting in the water along the docks and wharves, conforming in their attire to the fashion set by Adam and Eve, and in plain view of all passers, and the many thousands who cross the various ferries. Even in midday surreptitious urchins, dodging about the wharves, suddenly shake off their outer shells, like crabs, and recklessly plunge into the stream, regardless of all propriety and expostulation. Frantic policemen rush wildly into their midst, seizing now and then one, but usually they slide into the water like a mud turtle off a log, and escape quite as dexterously. Every little pondhole in the suburbs has its swimmers, and not infrequently many wander out from the City to participate in the water sports. We saw on Sunday last at one of these ponds at least fifty persons bathing at once, while congregated around the pond were quite as many spectators. Among the latter were many women, who seemed delighted with the antics of the mermen, and to envy them their refreshing recreation. But this style of thing is hardly proper for the moral and virtuous City of New York. Let us have our baths — swimming baths, shower baths, douche baths, hot baths, cold baths, baths for one

19

and baths for all — but let us have them in private and pay a proper regard to the proprieties.[2]

Clearly the demand was there for both kinds of baths — the kind for cleansing and the kind for recreation.

New York City established free municipal floating baths in 1870 and placed them under the control of the newly created Department of Public Works. Two baths were initially purchased; the West Side bath was installed at a pier at the end of 14th Street and the East Side bath at 5th Street. The pools were 85 feet long by 65 feet wide, and equipped with 68 changing rooms and gas lights for nighttime swimming. The pools were open to each gender on different days; initially, Mondays, Wednesdays, and Fridays from five in the morning to nine at night were reserved for women.[3] On Sundays the baths were open to men, but just from five A.M. to noon, and there were complaints about this since Sunday was the only free day that most working class people had to themselves.

The rules were fairly strict: the pools were free, but bathers had to give their names and addresses and pay three cents for the use of a towel. No

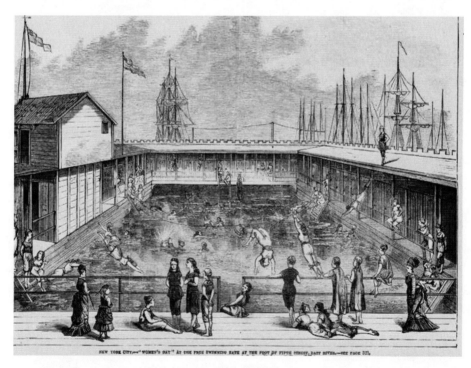

Etching depicting women's day at the floating free bath at the foot of 5th Street, East River, New York City (New York Public Library Print Collection).

swearing or pushing people into the water was permitted. Bathers could only spend 20 minutes in the pool and had to return their dressing room key within 30 minutes. No spectators or dogs were allowed. Women and girls were required "to furnish suitable bathing dress."[4] The Commissioner of Public Works assured the public that no lewd, suspicious, or disorderly characters would be permitted to enter the baths or to observe the women as they swam.

The baths were immediately and immensely popular. People waited in line for hours to use them, and they were quickly recognized as places to have fun and to socialize. The first open day for women at the baths was sparsely attended due to poor weather, but even so, the 300 or so attendees had so much fun that a newspaper remarked that "such screaming and splashing about has not been heard in that vicinity for years."[5] The second open women's day, the Fourth of July, 1870, attended by almost four thousand women, was "a grand charge of females of every age, color, and condition."[6] They were described as the "wives and daughters of working men," and it was suggested that upper-class women would be too shy to use the baths for awhile. "It will be two or three weeks before ladies residing in the center of the City will venture — if at all — to test the merits of the bath." In 1871, Brooklyn followed New York's lead and authorized the construction of floating baths for the public.

An article from 1872 illustrated just how much the baths were valued by women and girls. The public floating bath at Charles Street drew about 1,500 women on a women's day. "The dark-eyed daughters of Israel, the yellow-haired children of Teutonic parentage, the smiling immigrant from the Green Isle, and the rollicking Americans" all used the bath. The female pool attendants provided lessons, and soon timid mothers were following their daughters in imitating the teachers "in the most diverse antics, throwing somersaults, backward and forward, diving in head foremost, side swimming, floating, and diving for sunken shells." As evening came, the gas lamps were lit and the newly arrived horde of recently freed factory girls dove into the water in groups. "Merry laughter, interspersed with faint shrieks, rung out continuously as these daughters of toil disported themselves, mermaid-like, in their agreeable and healthful pastime."[7]

The popularity of the baths was indisputable. During the month of August 1873, 189,882 people used the Manhattan baths, and 38,629 of them were women.[8] Working-class women and girls were now able to attend free swimming lessons at the pools.[9] Races for women at the floating baths were arranged in 1880 by Mr. James McCarthy, the superintendent of the free floating baths, who announced, "These swimming matches are gotten up for the purpose of encouraging young girls and women to learn how to swim, and it would astonish you to witness one of these matches, and see how gracefully and well the young girls can swim." In 1880, the free public bath at the Battery held races for 34 girls divided into age groups. They competed for a range of prizes including a knife, fork, spoon and napkin ring set, a Maltese cross, a goblet, a medal, and a butter dish, all of silver. A separate race for "fat women" attracted five competitors.[10]

It seems that as long as there have been bathing suits, there have been ways to make women feel bad about wearing them in public. A male reporter, visiting the Gouverneur Street Bath in 1881, made several observations about the women at the bath. The reporter took great pains to analyze and rate the physical appearances of the women, joining the long and ongoing journalistic tradition of making women feel self-conscious in bathing suits. "Most of the persons visiting the baths are of the working classes, and it is proof of the prosperous condition of the laborers in the country that the bathers generally have the appearance of having enough to eat. The men present much finer physiques than the women. The bathing dresses do not prevent one from judging of the development of the latter, though they do increase the ugly looks of the ill-favored ones. Here and there may be seen a well-formed, and well-preserved woman, who has escaped the blight of hard work, sorrow, poverty, of ill-tempered husbands, which has given her sisters a woe-begone look. Naturally the fine forms belong to the younger women and girls, but it is noticeable how few carry their good looks beyond womanhood."[11]

The reporter concluded, "The women and girls who frequent the pay baths, as would be expected, show a finer physique on an average than the harder-worked women in the free baths, though both show extremes of beauty and ugliness."

Having gotten the required degrading physical description of the women out of the way, the reporter went on to describe the fun the women were having. "Probably no place in the city shows people having such a good time while benefiting their health and acquiring proficiency in an art which may be needed any day to save themselves or someone else from drowning. They are all in the water now: white arms gleaming, white feet splashing, and bright eyes, both old and young, sparkling with excitement." Describing one woman's neat dive and long underwater swim, he wrote, "No boy could have done it more neatly.... Many others are doing the same feats, or swimming hand-over-hand, floating, playing 'leap frog,' or swimming straight ahead in the orthodox way." One of the Bennett sisters was the keeper of the bath at that time, and "she certainly had apt pupils or was very successful in imparting her own confidence and skill."

One pool attendant said, "The women are a lot more troublesome than the men. Each set is supposed to stay in just twenty minutes, but they just won't come out, and the women attendants can't do a thing with them. We

Girls and women wait in line at a floating free bath in New York City. The girls at the door are holding up their suits for inspection by the attendant (Library of Congress Prints and Photographs Division).

have to call a policeman in now and then. When once they're out of the pool, there's not much trouble, although they've been known to steal each other's shoes. The women come to bathe oftener than the men, and there's some of them — girls mostly — that swim like dockrats."[12]

Ethnicity, Class, and Neighborhood Differences at the Pools

Class and ethnicity differences were notable at the different baths. Upper-class women reportedly came from Jersey City and Brooklyn with servants in tow to use the Battery baths. The clientele at Gouverneur Street, Fifth Street, and 19th Street were reportedly Germans and Jews, while the 27th Street baths clientele was "Irish and Americans of the middle classes." This generally reflected neighborhood composition, but the fame of some instructors, like Kate Bennett, attracted patrons of better means to particular baths even when they did not live nearby.[13]

In 1877, a reporter described the different clientele at the different baths, focusing on economic status rather than ethnicity. The bath at 113th Street in Harlem saw between 200 and 500 women on each of its women's days.

"This part of the city is mostly composed of houses built of brick and rented in floors, but with none of the signs of extreme poverty which are conspicuously apparent in the tenement houses in some parts of the city. There are no evidences here of carelessness or indifference to appearance, but on every hand are to be observed indications of neatness and respectability. Those of the female sex who patronize the bath are mostly women who work during the day in stores, factories, etc., with quite a number of cottage-residents, who are generally persons of comfortable circumstances, but, having pure air in this locality, prefer staying in their homes and take advantage of the bathing here to going to the seaside."

The bath at 51st Street was "extensively used by the females employed in the factories in the vicinities, one of which has 1800 operatives of the feminine sex. The attendant, Mrs. Graves, does not find this mass of well-behaved young women as great a care as the schoolgirls, who require constant watching, as they are continually playing tricks upon each other."

The bath at 37th Street saw between 2,000 and 3,000 women per day, and tracked the different women who came at different times of the day. Many housekeepers and schoolgirls came to swim early in the morning. From 9 A.M. to 3 P.M., there were fewer bathers, and these women were "mostly of the better classes, who can command their own time. These are the people living in the more aristocratic neighborhoods, but who are democratic and sensible enough to take advantage of these valuable public institutions. Many come a distance of thirty or forty blocks for the purpose." After 3 P.M. came the school girls, and then from 6 to 9 P.M. came the factory girls.

The Bethune Street bath was noted because it attracted many of the better swimmers. "These women all belong to the working classes, and their development of muscle gives beauty of line, elasticity, and grace to their forms. Most of those frequenting the free baths supply their own bathing dresses and towels. They are not allowed to wear skirts. The favorite dress is a single garment, with openings for the lower limbs, arms, and head to pass through, reaching about half way to the knees, with arms and neck bare, and a button fastening the garment at the back of the neck. Those who do not bring their own suits are charged a moderate fee for the use of those to be obtained at the bathing-houses. It is generally the case that the young women and girls, who have no extra clothing to impede their progress, learn to swim in much less time than those who are robed in the full bathing-suit."[14]

Swimming Lessons

The swimming classes that were offered at the public baths were extraordinarily popular. Over 3,000 children learned to swim the summer of 1899, with 450 achieving scores of one hundred percent in the examinations. The baths continued to be wildly popular with all ages and types of women, including the "foreign tenement house population." Many of these women were good swimmers, and happily attributed their skills to the free classes at the baths. During a 1900 visit to a floating bath, a reporter watched as "an extremely stout woman in the free swimming baths at the foot of Corlears St. threw her wet arms around Miss Grace Blankley, one of the swimming teachers yesterday and exclaimed, 'I just love you. I should never have known how to swim if it hadn't been for you. I learned by looking at you and the children.'"[15]

The reporter also observed a competitive tendency among the girls. "There is a good deal of rivalry among the children as to who shall become the best swimmer. 'Teacher, did you say that Tessie Devine was the best swimmer in the class?' asked a black eyed little girl. 'I can swim just as well as Tillie Levy, can't I, teacher?' was heard on the other side. Meanwhile, another girl who had conquered the breast stroke, was trying to dive, as she had seen her teacher do, from the step, and another was attempting somersaults in the water. Both struck the water like pieces of lead, after each effort, but it was evident that peace would never be restored in their minds until the feat was accomplished. Others were swimming back and forth, enjoying the newly acquired art, while more advanced ones were practicing side strokes, swimming on the back and floating. Rescues were being made at one side, and a land drill going on on the platform."[16]

At some point during the 1870s, Kate Bennett was hired as a pool attendant and swimming teacher for the city baths as well as at her private school. In 1880, she was the attendant at the Gouverneur Street pool, and she arranged an event that was attended by both her private students and her students from the free baths. The wealthy patrons watched as the students from the free baths performed, clad in their makeshift swimsuits. "Any old clothes that were past duty as every-day raiments were utilized as bathing suits, and the bright-eyed, happy faced children cared not for cut, fit, or quality so long as they had the privilege of a plunge." Miss Bennett's goal was to convince some of the wealthy patrons to supply new swimsuits for the students at the free baths. Indeed, the private school students began throwing coins into the water, and the little girls from the public baths dove for them, coming up with silver coins and handfuls of pennies. Ever the entertainer, Kate ended the show by joining the girls in the water and swimming about the pool with only her feet above the water, to everyone's amusement.[17]

Women who worked as swim teachers came from a variety of neighborhoods and classes. One source was the Blankely family of Brooklyn. In 1902, four sisters — Mabel, Agnes, Grace, and Adeline Blankley — were hired by the city Board of Education to teach swimming at different public baths. William Blankley had raised all eight of his daughters to be powerful swimmers from a young age. As young girls, they swam the Narrows between Brooklyn and Staten Island and were recognized as great athletes by the local newspaper. "A six year old Blankley girl could put to shame many of the strongest men along the water front. Over to Staten Island and back again without a rest was a hard task for anyone, but they did it easily. The fame of the girls grew until they were regarded as the best swimmers around New York City. They were not afraid to do anything in the water that could possibly be done. Their exceptional ability as swimmers attracted attention from the city authorities, and four years ago four of the girls were employed as teachers of swimming in the public baths — Mabel and Grace at Corlear's bath, Adeline at the Battery, and Agnes at the Duane street baths."[18]

Teaching swimming to hordes of excitable children was not easy. The baths were incredibly busy in warm weather, and groups of hot children were constantly cycled in and out of the pools in half-hour periods. Swimming teachers had to control and discipline the excitable girls, while simultaneously maintaining their attention long enough to teach swimming strokes and watching to make sure they were all safe.

Indoor Options for Swimming

As authorities grew more aware of the dangers of pollution, they began to question the wisdom of swimming in the floating baths. In 1904, the superintendent of the Department of Docks and Ferries said, "These floating baths are not a permanent thing. What we want is to have plenty of public baths on land. When you think of it, it doesn't seem very healthy to bathe in the rivers where hundreds of sewers are emptying. One reason we didn't get started earlier this year was because of the trouble to find suitable locations for our floating baths. The Board of Health was careful that we wouldn't have a station at the mouth of a sewer."[19]

The *New-York Tribune* stated, "The best authorities seem to be feeling more and more than these baths are pernicious. The boys enjoy them, but while the average East Side boy does not mind sewage in the water he sports in, doctors say that the same is bad for him and for the general health." The article quoted an unnamed city commissioner who said, "Not long ago someone gave me a bath ticket and wanted me to go down and try the floating bath at the Battery. Now, you'd suppose that down there in the bay with the strong tides there are there, the water would be pure. I assure you, it was filthy. Just watch the water there when the current sets certain ways, and you'll see dead dogs, dead cats, masses of the refuse of a big city drifting around the bath, typhoid fever germs and their various cousins you can't see, but depend on it they're there."[20]

Nonetheless, the floating baths remained popular because people went to them for swimming, for fun, and for relief from the heat, not necessarily for hygiene. They were willing to ignore the dirty water because there was no place else to have that much fun.

By 1911, New York had created some more hygienic options for those interested in swimming. The city now had 12 public baths, which offered showers and tubs for the public. Two of those facilities had indoor swimming pools, allowing for year-round swimming for those able to travel to the two pools. One was on East 23rd Street, and the other was at West 60th near Amsterdam Ave. The baths employed five men and five women for cleaning the building and admitting the public, plus a team of two engineers and three firemen who operated the mechanicals of the plumbing system and kept the boilers running around the clock. It was no easy feat to regulate water temperatures, attend filtration, and monitor the steam heating of the baths. The pools were filled with filtered fresh water from the Croton Reservoir that was changed three times per week, and heating that massive quantity of cold water required constant heat.

In addition to the indoor baths, there were 11 free floating baths which were open from June to October. The Public Works Department reported attendance numbers that showed the popularity of the pools, especially among women. In August of 1911, 812,952 people visited the floating baths; 492,753 were male and 320,199 were women. In October, when the weather in New York was decidedly chilling, 6,296 men visited the floating baths and 3,225 women did as well. By then there were 12 additional free indoor baths where women could get clean in tubs or showers, and it has to be considered that these women were visiting the floating baths for swimming and recreational purposes, not just to get clean. These were women who enjoyed swimming and were willing to brave the October waters in order to do so.[21]

Improprieties

Although men and women did not share the baths at the same time, improprieties could and did occur. In September of 1883, Kate Bennett and her sister were reassigned from the Gouverneur Street free baths to an uptown bath. Instead of accepting the reassignment, Kate and Teresa resigned from their jobs, refusing "to be subordinate to such indecent and unprincipled management as the Department of Public Works permits." Kate had been employed as a teacher and a bathkeeper at the bath for eight years, and something drastic had caused her to leave. For a while, she had been noticing something about the behavior of one of the male bathkeepers, Julius Simon. She watched him suspiciously as he wandered too close to the women's changing rooms, and she suspected him of inviting other men, including policemen, to the upper level of the baths where they could watch the women swimming and changing. Simon had even barged in on Kate as she was changing, and she suspected that he was allowing men and "women of bad character" to swim together at night after hours.

Kate was initially prevented from speaking to the press, but she eventually broke her silence and told her story to the *National Police Gazette*.

> On the 6th of July things came to a climax. I employed a girl of about 13 in the bath. On the evening of that date I sent her upstairs to get a taper. Simon followed her and attempted to take improper liberties with her. She ran away from him to Teresa. An hour afterwards, while he was outside, I sent her to the room for some tea. He saw her and followed her, and attempted to assault her. She ran down stairs. Running after her, he seized her and threatened to throw her out of the house. Then my patience gave out. I had a cane — I'm sorry it was split rattan, and not a club. I hit him over the head with it. He let go of the girl, called me a trollop, and struck me on the chest. Then I took him and caned him until my arm was too tired to lift the stick again.[22]

Deputy Commissioner Hamlin of the Public Works Department hastened to reassure the public that there were no such improprieties occurring at the baths, saying that the commissioner himself visited every bath every day, the two assistant commissioners visited all the baths twice a day, and that, according to them, there was no reason to believe that Miss Bennett's charges were substantiated. They had noticed the "bickering" between Kate and Julius Simon, and claimed that was why they had decided to reassign the sisters. Further, because Mr. Simon was a married man, Hamlin did not wish to dismiss him. Instead, he said, "We felt it necessary to censure Miss Bennett for some departmental irregularities and Simon, for having perhaps hustled the girl too rudely after she refused to leave the bath at his request. I do not wish to get into a controversy with Miss Bennett. She is a good teacher and we will be sorry to lose her services."[23]

4. Swimming as Spectacle

As early as the 1870s, people were realizing that swimming was entertaining. It combined stamina, speed, danger, and the opportunity to see women wearing fewer clothes than usual. Swimming races in particular became extremely popular. They were often part of a day-long series of events that were part excursion and part spectacle. The matches were advertised or announced in the papers, usually with a description of the impressive athletic histories of the racers and the purse or prize money clearly spelled out. They occurred between individuals, as functions of the various swimming schools, or at demonstration events. Newspapers covered the races, turning in long, colorful, and suspenseful reports of the outcomes. Wagering was expected.

In 1875, the English Channel was swum for the first time, an event that made swimming races even more of a public obsession. The English Channel had emerged as the ultimate test for a swimmer, and people had been trying to cross it for years. The first recorded non-boat crossing occurred in 1862, when William Hoskins of England kick-paddled across on a bale of straw. In May of 1875, the charismatic Captain Paul Boyton of Atlantic City, New Jersey, decided the channel would be the perfect place to promote his "life-saving suit," a rubberized coverall equipped with a paddle, a sail, and inflatable air pockets. Accompanied by a steamer loaded with seasick witnesses and reporters, he left France at three in the morning and paddled his way across on his back, taking breaks only to smoke cigars and eat. Slightly less than 24 hours later, a crowd of thousands cheered as he waddled ashore near Dover in his suit.[1] The fact that he survived over 23 hours in the cold water probably said more about the suit than it did about Boyton. Neither of these episodes can legitimately be considered swimming, of course, but Boyton's crossing provoked the first real channel swimmer, Britain's Captain Matthew Webb, into action.

The 27-year-old Webb had spent most of his teen years and adulthood either on a boat or in the water, working on trading ships, as a salvager of wrecks, and on the ships of the Cunard Mail Service. He made a name for himself as a man who simply did not recognize danger, winning prestigious awards from the Royal Humane Society when he endangered his own life after he leapt off a moving ship into a stormy sea to rescue another man who had fallen overboard. Early in 1875 he began drawing attention to himself and his proposed channel swim with an 18-mile swim down the Thames River and a nine-mile course in the ocean. The attention garnered him the sponsorship of a newspaper that took up a "subscription" to be paid to Webb upon his successful crossing of the channel. On August 11, he made his first attempt, but failed. On the 24th, he set out again, accompanied by a rowboat carrying a referee and a sailboat loaded with crew, coach, pilot and members of the press. Porpoises were spotted in the water, and Webb was occasionally hampered by floating mats of seaweed and made nauseous by the bites of jellyfish, requiring brandy to settle his stomach. He also consumed hot coffee, cod-liver oil, and beef tea throughout.[2] He landed at Calais, France, 21 hours and 45 minutes after he began. He was welcomed back to England by ecstatic crowds, greeted as a conquering hero, and the subscribers handed over several hundred pounds to him in recognition of his astonishing physical abilities. Today, Webb's swim is considered the first valid English Channel swim, and Boyton's voyage is seen as a notable oddity, if it is remembered at all.

After this barrier fell, swimming races of all kinds, especially endurance swimming contests, rose to new heights of popularity. Webb and Boyton even raced each other, meeting in Newport, Rhode Island, in 1879. For a prize of $1,000, Boyton was to swim 25 miles in his lifesaving suit, while Webb swam 20. Webb ended his swim after being seized with cramps after eight miles, but Boyton finished.[3]

The boats and barges that followed the racers were floating parties. A race in 1880 was described by the *New York Times* as being little more than an excuse for the barge owners to float around the harbor, providing gambling tables and serving high-priced beer and food to its captive passengers. The race didn't end and the barge didn't head back to land until all the beer was gone and the passengers had spent all their money.[4]

Exciting things could happen at the races. Mr. J. B. Johnson swam against Thomas Coyle, a shipyard worker from Pennsylvania, in a 13-mile race for the "championship of the world," and a prize of $2,000. Coyle initially led, pausing only for a few refreshing swallows of whiskey, but passed out before he could finish and had to be retrieved from the water. Johnson only managed to swim nine miles, but upon being pulled from the water immediately announced he could swim back to the starting point if anyone was willing to wager $2,000.[5] The next day Coyle said he had been drugged, perhaps by someone who had bet a large amount of money on the outcome of the race.

Races occasionally drew the attention of the police because of the law against Sunday exhibitions. In 1885, a race between Dennis F. Butler, head teacher at Hall's Battery Baths, and Gus Sundstrom, a teacher at the New York Athletic Club, ended unexpectedly when the police intervened. Observers paid 50 cents to follow the race onboard the excursion barge *Coxsackie*, lunching on sandwiches and beer. The men were racing for "$250 a side and barge receipts."[6] The men's physical appearance was impressive. "When the swimmers appeared at the edge of the barge, there was a shout of applause. Neither wore anything but a very trifling pair of trunks, and their bodies glistened like polished copper from the effects of the Vaseline." The barge and scores of smaller boats followed the men up the East River, when a police boat spotted the race and moved to intercept it. The men tried to continue the race, but were ordered into the police craft. Both had removed their trunks and were now stark naked. "Sundstrom seemed much embarrassed until someone threw him his hat, when he put it on and recovered his equanimity." While Sundstrom was covering up, Butler dove back into the water and headed back to the barge, not willing to settle for a mere hat to cover himself. He was apprehended getting dressed on the tug boat. Both men were charged with 'violating the law against giving public exhibitions on Sunday.'"[7]

Women's Races

Women's participation in swimming races goes back at least to the 1870s. In 1872, Mr. Richard Allen's Oriental Salt Water Baths and Swimming School at 54th Street held a day of aquatic competition that included races for women. A large crowd of enthusiastic men and women crowded the shores above the East River, waiting for the racers to emerge. A band played throughout, adding to the air of festivity at the event. The women's half-mile race had seven competitors battling for a first prize of $75 or a second-place prize of a gold ring. Their swimsuits were described: "Miss Katie Allen [daughter of the proprietor of the establishment], dressed in blue sailor's suit trimmed with white; Miss Broderick, red plaid suit; Miss Weber, black and white sailor's suit; Miss Siegel, red suit; Miss Cohen, black and white; Miss Westerner, red and black, and Miss Candidus in a brown suit." Katie Allen won the race. The *New York Times* described the "frantic efforts and screams of the competitors," Katie Allen's "powerful trained stroke," and stated that "the competitors evinced great skill in the art of swimming, and were loudly cheered during the contest."[8]

The following year, Katie won a 200-yard race at the school. The race was part of a full day of boating and swimming contests. Katie and her competitors, Mrs. Bertha Walters and Miss Maggie Broderick, wore "blue and gray costumes and deported themselves in the deep waters with admirable courage." The women swam in the open water of the river, racing through the lunging waves created by passing steamships.[9] The same year, another race at Allen's drew a crowd of spectators estimated to be several thousand strong who wagered on the races that offered $50 and $40 gold medals for the male winners and gold bracelets and coral earrings for the ladies. Four women took part in the women's race. Katie Allen, Ellen Allen, Mary Cunningham, and Fredrika Sands swam for "a distance of about 100 lengths, breasting the roughing waters with as much courage as the swimmers of the sterner sex. They were attired in ordinary bathing suits, and when they came out of the water were very anxious to know whether they had betrayed symptoms of fright, or had presented a ridiculous appearance. Upon being assured of the contrary, like all womankind they were greatly pleased."[10] The day of races wasn't over yet, and a band played music by the floating baths while the spectators danced. It was reported that "a force of policemen was present to preserve order, but everything passed off very pleasantly."

In 1874, women were part of a "swimming entertainment" that featured a men's race from Blackwell Island to the natatorium at 66th Street, followed by a match in which four young women raced a half mile. The winner was awarded a "gold prize." The day concluded with a performance by Mr. J. B. Johnson, the self-styled swimming champion of England, who entertained the crowd by drinking milk and smoking a cigar underwater and executing "other surprising feats apparently at variance with the laws of nature."[11]

Another swimming match for women was held in the Harlem River in 1874 and attracted competitors from Philadelphia, Massachusetts, Maryland, Virginia, and Ireland to swim a one-mile race. The victor was Miss Delilah Goboess of Philadelphia, who covered the course in 40 minutes and took home a silk dress valued at $175.[12]

Kate Bennett, the swimming instructor, was one of the great promoters of swimming races. She realized quickly the popularity of her pool-based exhibitions, and soon figured out how to increase the turnout. In 1874, she began offering lessons in the summers at Fort Hamilton, Brooklyn. She held small races throughout the summer and her students raced one another for prizes, such as gold necklaces, lockets, and rings. In August, she placed an advertisement in the New York Sun that read: "Ladies' Swimming Match at Fort Hamilton, Saturday and Sunday, Aug. 22 and 23, will take place at 2 P.M."

The weekend event drew approximately four thousand people from Manhattan and Brooklyn who traveled by horse car to the site of the race. Eager spectators lined the dusty quarter-mile road leading from the bluff overlooking the Narrows down to the shore where the race was to start. A flotilla of police boats and yachts bobbed off shore. Fashionably late, Kate arrived at three o'clock, as ten of her students entered the water. They began with a typical Bennett School exhibition. The girls floated, swam, and dove in the water; they "laughed joyously and ducked each other with screams of merriment. They were amphibious. The water was cold, but this did not seem to interfere with their fun." Kate announced to the spectators, "You can see the value of the knowledge of swimming to the ladies. The grace which they acquire in the water clings to them on the land. Depend on it, the best swimmers always prove the best walkers and best dancers."[13]

Following the exhibition, seven of the girls entered the water for the highly anticipated 500-yard race, the winner of which would receive a gold locket. That race was followed by a 300-yard race, for gold earrings, between two of the girls.

One week later, Kate repeated the stunt, advertising the event as a race between 24 women swimming a 300-yard race, with the winner to take home a gold watch and chain. Unfortunately for the spectators, only four racers showed up, the others having been scared away by rumors that Lily Eldred, who was "popularly believed to be without rival as a swimmer," was to be among the competitors. She wasn't, but the race went on with only four racers. Miss Annie Bogenkamp won the race, finishing in two minutes.[14]

Women's races were organized and sponsored by other organizations as well. The Water Rats, a men's swimming club in Bath Beach, Brooklyn, held a swimming match on Labor Day 1894, that included a series of races for women, including one open to girls under the age of 18, of approximately one mile in open water. In one swim of the Narrows, the Brooklyn Rowing Club organized the event, and gold medal prizes were donated by club members.[15]

Races were generally held between same-sex competitors, but in 1885, a woman named Carrie Falk took part in a race between swim teacher Dennis F. Butler and six other men, all fairly well known athletes who had won races at the various resorts around the city. About 300 spectators paid 25 to 50 cents to join the swimmers on board the barge *Republic*, which then headed out to the harbor between Castle Garden and Governor's Island. Carrie, described as a "pretty little brunette who has executed wonders in the surf at Coney Island," was given a two-minute head start, and dove from the barge into the water to a round of applause.[16] Carrie and the other swimmers headed straight for Brooklyn, but Butler, armed with knowledge of the tides, first headed for Staten Island, which turned out to save him more time in the long run. Half an hour later, Carrie was in third place, with Butler in the lead and Brady in second. By the time the swimmers began giving up the race, Carrie was leading all but Butler by a quarter mile. "Miss Falk was the last to leave the water at two minutes to seven. She had gone seven miles and wanted to continue to Fort Hamilton as she was not, she said, fatigued in the least. Her pluck was heartily cheered and by general consent she was awarded the first prize, a handsome silver cup."[17]

Women's swimming races were very commonly reported on in the newspapers and, judging by the crowd counts given, were enormously popular with the general public. The races were at this time considered, for the most part, a healthy and impressive pastime for women. In 1874, the *New York Times* described swimming races as a "healthful athletic accomplishment," and they noted when races were announced, that "perhaps it is an evidence of the tendency of the times that the first to enter the lists are ladies."[18]

But female competitors could be the target of criticism that was not levied against male racers. In 1874, a newspaper writer took a judgmental view of a women's swimming event. He described the swimmers as being "neatly and prettily attired," but went on to say that "the rowdy element was present in force, and their shouts and jeers quite intimidated the four girls who were the only ones brave enough to put in an appearance; and the affair ended in a fiasco, an angry disappointed crowd, and general dissatisfaction. It is well enough for all women to learn to swim well, and an accomplishment to be able to do so; but giving promiscuous public exhibitions is neither useful nor creditable."[19]

In 1875, the *Brooklyn Eagle* passed the following harsh judgment on women who were vulgar enough to "unsex" themselves:

> There is certainly nothing whatever to be commended in the performance. While there are good ferries and bridges, the necessity for swimming is dispensed with, and even as a matter of choice or a wager, it hardly seems proper for a woman to make such a proper exhibition of herself. If the feat had never been performed by anyone before, it might have been worthy a woman's ambition to try it, but since in its accomplishment she is only imitating and not surpassing man, it seems unfitting for her, to say the least. Women who develop such alarming capacity for muscular exercise and such decided taste for notoriety should discover more original modes of exhibiting both than in merely imitating men. To do poorly what men have always done well is no triumph for women or sign of power in them: it is only another evidence of lack of good taste which, it is hoped, the women of the future will correct. It may be very gratifying to the woman in question to win so much money and to be called a natatrice, but how would it do for a number of women to be seized with a like desire could not be told until the sight of a dozen or more in the water at one time had been seen. Then the utter vulgarity and absurdity of the position for women would be realized, and no more prizes would be offered. It is to be regretted that there are any women at all who bite such bait as prizes of this kind. Any premium offered woman to unsex herself, instead of being accepted under any circumstances, ought to be considered an insult to all women, and should be so sternly rebuked that a repetition would be

impossible. But as long as there are any willing to be trapped, just so long will there be traps set for them, and the pity it is that it is so, prizes and gold medals to the contrary notwithstanding.[20]

Happily, women did indeed continue to enter the races by the dozens. But like all public individuals, their behavior and activities were open targets for the opinions of all. One very common tactic used by commentators was to belittle the appearances of women, specifically, the expressions on their faces as they exerted themselves in activity. "Swimming face" was said to be far worse than "bicycle face." Especially to be found in females, swimming face came to the swimmer through a combination of exertion, determination, and seriousness, resulting in an "agonized expression of painful purpose, which, added to an aimless kicking of legs, waving of arms, and large displacement of water, is extremely ludicrous."[21]

The large swimming contests also drew the ire of more respectable residents of nearby neighborhoods, who resented the crowds, the wagering, the presence of rowdy toughs, and the fact that these contests often took place on Sundays and in violation of the law that prohibited public exhibitions on Sundays. A swimming match at Nelson's Baths, East 55th Street, was described as attracting "several thousands of men, women, and children, mostly of the lower orders" and "several parties of roughs ... who created much disturbance at intervals throughout the afternoon."[22]

In 1884, the Law and Order Society of Fort Hamilton threatened to take action to prevent Kate from holding her swimming contests, but never followed through. Still, the threat was enough for her to publicly remind people that the girls who swam in her races were entirely respectable.[23]

Swimming as Entertainment for the Masses

Both men's and women's swimming matches were hugely popular and could pull in as many as 20,000 spectators along a route. Barges and boats would often follow alongside, carrying crowds of picknickers. In 1894, a half-mile race between Florence Golding, Ethel Golding, Mabel Clark, and Annie Aren drew about four thousand riveted spectators, some of whom functioned as an early form of a fan club. Spectators waved banners embroidered with the contestants' names and chanted rhyming fight songs in the hours leading up to the swim. The 13-year-old Ethel finished first. The long, detailed, and enthusiastic coverage of the event in the *Sun* concluded by pointing out: "After the girls' race there were races between men and boys, but there was no such enthusiasm shown as had been displayed in the earlier race."[24]

When the *Kings County Journal* sponsored its ninth annual half-mile race for women in 1895 at Brighton Beach, over twenty thousand spectators turned out to watch. The swimmers, Ethel Golding, Florence Golding, Lee Hultgren, and Sadie McCormick, were taken to the starting point, a sloop anchored about 300 yards off-shore. None of them wore the skirts on their bathing costumes, having dispensed with them for function's sake. For safety, each entrant was followed by a rowboat, into which they were hauled at the end of the swim. The race was over in 11 and a half minutes, with Ethel winning the gold medal for first place and Lee taking home a silver medal for second place. When they returned to land, "It was with difficulty that they could reach the bath houses, so enthusiastic was the reception accorded them."[25] Following the girls' race, Captain Paul Boyton, the man who had floated across the English Channel in his rubber suit, gave an exhibition in which he shot off "roman candles, sky rockets, and miniature mines."

Swimming races were well established by the turn of the last century. Local "championships" took place. Women's races were routinely covered in the sporting pages of the newspaper. Races could be sponsored by companies, newspapers, bathing resorts, or the various athletic clubs.

Ethel Golding, of Brooklyn, emerged as a star swimmer during this era. By the time she was 14 years old, in 1893, Ethel was racing for prizes before crowds of thousands. For several years in a row, she was the winner of the annual *Kings County Journal* race, and from 1893 to 1904 she was the most famous swimmer in America.

In 1901, Ethel was hired by the *Evening World* newspaper to write a series of articles designed to teach women to swim. The series, entitled "The Champion Woman Swimmer Tells Women How to Swim," began with a discussion of bathing suits, of course.

> To begin with, a good deal depends on the suit. I know a professional swimmer will laugh at that, but I have seen so many people hampered by heavy and badly made bathing suits that I cannot say too much to warn people about the sort of costume to wear, especially when first going into the water. Personally, I always recommend brilliantine. It is far better than flannel, which is heavy and clings to the limbs. Brilliantine is light and sheds water. I think bloomers are especially bad in bathing suits. The bloomers, or full trousers, either fill with water or prevent free motion of the limbs. My own bathing suit consists of rather tight trousers of brilliantine, well above the knee, and met by black stockings. The waist has short sleeves and a low neck and is not made very full. The very short black skirt, made scant, completes the costume. One may stay for hours in this costume without becoming tired.[26]

Tragically, Ethel died in 1904 at the age of 23 of what was then referred to as Bright's Disease, a generic term for diseases of the kidneys. Her funeral was attended by five hundred people. At least one observer took the opportunity to blame her death on her athleticism, idly opining that her physical training may have been too much for her and left her vulnerable to disease, claiming that "this constant training overtaxed her powers is a reasonable supposition."[27]

For some women, swimming offered a means to an income. Besides teaching at a public bath or at the resorts, women with exceptional swimming and diving abilities could work in the entertainment world. Variety shows sometimes included acts in which women would swim underwater or dive into small onstage tanks. The shows were popular because they combined danger, athleticism, and attractive, wet women in a single act. One of these stars was Marie Finney, who was known for a successful dive from the London Bridge and for a later arrest in 1890 in Dublin, Ireland, when she attempted to dive off a bridge into the River Liffey as thousands of spectators watched. In 1901, she was part of a brother-and-sister vaudeville act that specialized in underwater tricks. The two traveled with

Ethel Golding posing for the 1900 Annual Report of the U.S. Volunteer Life Saving Corps of New York (Government Document, State of New York).

a glass swimming tank in which they held their breath for up to four minutes at a time while playing cards, eating eggs, drinking from a bottle, and performing "fancy floating."[28]

Bridges and swimmers seemed to go together handily, and bridge-jumping was, briefly, all the rage for 19th century extreme sport enthusiasts. In 1885, swimming teacher Robert Odlum, assisted by his friend Captain Boyton, leapt over the rails of the Brooklyn Bridge in full view of a group of friends and crowds of supporters. He died shortly thereafter of internal injuries. In 1886, Steve Brodie survived a leap off the bridge, allegedly for a $200 bet. These performances, or dares, along with stage acts like the Finneys, placed some swimmers in a category beyond athleticism and almost into sideshow.

Dora Woolard and Madeline Berlo of Boston, ages 16 and 17, were athletic swimmers who had capitalized on their swimming abilities. Both girls were well-known long-distance swimmers; Woolard had won a cup in a distance-race swimming in Boston Harbor. She also held the record for holding her breath underwater, at four minutes and 28 seconds. Berlo at one point held the half-mile record for women. Performing together as Pattee's Diving Venuses, the girls put on a show of fancy diving, headstands, jackknife dives, somersaults, conjoined leaps, and more, in a 7,000 gallon tank on the stages of vaudeville houses. "The front shoulder dive was a startling act and very risky, because of the narrow compass in which the girls had to work, one having to dive from the shoulder of the other."[29]

In 1914, six "physically perfect girls" known as the Six Water Lillies were performing at Hartford's Palace Theater. They appeared on stage thrice daily for a week, performing stunts and diving into a large tank. A special feature of the week's engagement was the opportunity for audience members to compete with the women. The men of Hartford were challenged to see who could most perfectly replicate the women's dives, with the audience serving as judges. The winner would receive a silver cup. The girls and women of Hartford were given an opportunity to do the same on a separate night. The girls also performed at the riverfront on the weekend, diving from a bridge over the Connecticut River and impressing the crowd with a show of long-distance swimming.[30]

The same year, Pattee's Mirthful Mermaids, Helena Gaudreau and Anna Morecroft, appeared at Hartford Poli Palace. To advertise the show, the girls put on an exhibit from a barge in the Connecticut River, carefully scheduled for lunchtime on a weekday, causing a newspaper to note that "young men whose luncheon hour begins at 12 and ends at 1 o'clock did not dally about but quickly made for the elevator and with hurried steps followed the shortest course to the Connecticut River." They were hustling to the riverfront to see the girls' demonstration of trick dives, swimming in strong river current, and sprinting. Also featured was a lifesaving demonstration in which Anna Morecroft showed the best way to rescue a young man. The crowd of spectators grew to three thousand, lining the shores and bridges as well as crowding around the barge in rowboats and launches.[31]

Perhaps even more exciting, there were opportunities for female swimmers in the burgeoning motion picture industry. A young woman who could swim and row a boat could earn five dollars a day posing as a bathing beauty or a water-logged damsel in distress. It wasn't for everyone, since it required both aquatic skills and the ability to act, or at least pantomime emotion, but it could be a moneymaker for the women who had both.[32]

5. The Rise of the Amateur Movement

The swimming exhibitions and races that appealed so enormously to the general public did not sit well with everyone. Upper-class athletes were realizing that they disliked sharing social, literal, and newspaper column space with lower class athletes, and they rejected the circus-like atmosphere enveloping some sports.

In the 19th century, most sport in the United States was pure entertainment aimed at the masses. From the saloons that held boxing matches, dog fights, and billiard games to the baseball teams that pulled in great raucous crowds at baseball fields all over the country, spectator sport was an affordable, entertaining way for the average working man to occupy what small amount of leisure time he had. It was also big business; the boxer expected to be paid, and baseball players usually received a cut of the gate count or an actual salary. Because few early athletes were of independent means, they needed and expected to be paid. The very best could make a living off of their chosen sport, either directly from the prize awarded, the gate count of the sporting event, through gambling, or by supplementing their incomes by participating in exhibitions or on the stage in variety shows, where manly demonstrations of strength and agility were popular.

The amateur movement sought to end this supposedly degraded athletic atmosphere, of working class athletes who accepted money for their efforts and attracted gamblers and other hooligans. The amateur movement had begun in England and spread to elite American universities and athletic organizations. Private clubs that already had been established to provide a distinct arena for upper-class men rapidly adopted the ethos of amateurism, which redefined sport as the age-old and God-given province of the elite. It was assumed by these gentlemen, in a display of upper-class arrogance, that when the working class engaged in athletics the endeavor was corrupt and impure because of the exchange of money involved, and probably decadent as well.

Workers who had time to engage in sport, instead of working, were assumed to be lazy, shiftless, and neglecting other areas of their lives. In a move to reassign control of sports to their own class, the amateur movement first defined what it meant to be an amateur or a professional, and then declared that amateurism was the true form of sport and that professional, or paid, athletes were merely a corruption of the pure form.

In 1884, Dr. Dudley A. Sargeant, the director of Harvard University's gymnasium, gave an influential lecture entitled "The Evils of Modern Athletics" that defined the amateur philosophy. "The natural tendency of all sports is towards professionalism, and we must regard it as the evil of all evils. A professional athlete in success is praised and paraded before the world until he overestimates his ability, becomes vainglorious and haughty." In great detail Sargeant described how the vainglorious athlete then must turn to "trickery, jockeying, and crooked scheming" to maintain his now-lost prowess. Athletes were controlled by trainers, who were controlled by gamblers, who influenced judges. Managers fixed their games to appeal to their audiences. Sargeant took aim at the newspapers that he held responsible for the state of affairs because they continued to report on professional sporting events. "What a tremendous amount of harm a newspaper can cause when it devotes three columns to a fistic encounter, and describes minutely every motion in a sensationalistic way." This coverage, he claimed, was only encouraging the crooked dealings of the professionals, and he encouraged the papers to join with the "regular sporting papers" and "the religious press" to condemn such debauchery.[1] Some of his criticism may have been valid, but the redefining of amateur and professional was to have profound effects.

Whether an athlete held amateur status or turned professional was important for a number of reasons. For one thing, the athlete's status determined everything an athlete could do or not do. An amateur athlete could only appear in competitions and demonstrations for which they were never paid. They could not appear in advertisements of any kind, or accept paying work as teachers or coaches. Once an athlete claimed professional status, they could be paid for appearances, performances, competitions, races, appearances and coaching. To certain people, turning professional also said a lot about the individual. In the eyes of the amateurs, amateurs were those who practiced their sport for the pure joy of physical exertion and competition. Professional athletes, on the other hand, were those crass folk who would accept money in exchange for their physical talents. Amateurs were those who could afford to engage in sport for no remittance. University athletes were counted among the amateurs, and most of them were from upper-class families.

According to Yale University's Walter Camp, the father of American football, "A gentleman against a gentleman always plays to win.... A gentleman does not make his living, however, from his athletic prowess. He does not earn anything by his victories except glory and satisfaction." Camp criticized those athletes who played for money or sold their medals for cash, and even decried the giving of medals. "Perhaps the first falling off in this respect began when the laurel wreath became a mug. So long as the mug was but the emblem, and valueless otherwise, there was no harm. There is still no harm where the mug or trophy hangs in the room of the winner as indicative of his skill, but if the silver mug becomes a silver dollar, either at the hands of the winner or the donor, let us have the laurel back again." A gentleman never competed for money, directly or indirectly, he said. "If he plays, he plays as a gentleman, and not as a professional; he plays for victory, not for money."[2] Clearly, according to Camp and the elite community he appealed to, there wasn't any such thing as a gentleman who competed for money.

Walter Camp was very clear on his message that a gentleman did not need or want money. "If a man comes to you and endeavors to affect your choice of a college by offers of a pecuniary nature, he does not take you for a gentleman, or a gentleman's son, you may be sure." This attitude extended throughout elite America, creating a clear division between the lily-white gentleman athletes who competed for the joy of honest competition and the lower-class worker who would accept money for racing, fighting, playing baseball, or diving into a swimming pool.

And so, in what could nowadays be pointed out as the supreme in unsportsmanlike behavior, the upper-class creators of amateurism sought to exclude professional athletes, many of whom were working class, from participating in legitimate sport. This allowed the upper-class amateurs to compete without the intimidating presence of the lower-class professionals and to avoid the raucous fan base drawn by these athletes. The wealthy simply removed from the game many of the best competitors and declared themselves the only true athletes.

The upper classes were claiming sport for themselves, as if the lower classes had no right to it anymore. In doing so, they set the rules for athletic clubs throughout the country, and by defining what an amateur athlete was, controlled who was able to compete in their games.

The locus for the amateur movement in the United States was the New York Athletic Club, founded in 1868 by and for upper-class men who wished to engage in sporting competition with men from their own social class. By 1885, the NYAC had built itself a grand building with a swimming pool, gymnasium, bowling alley, dining room, and much more. Although women attended occasional social events at the Club, they were not allowed to use the athletic facilities or to become members.

In 1883, the New York Athletic Club hosted the first amateur swimming championships, with competitors from throughout the U.S. and England. Women did not compete, but specific note was made of the many "pretty girls that inspired the swimmers to make their best efforts." There was no mention of prizes, of course, but the winner was treated to the "shrieks of all the pretty girls and the howls of their brothers."[3]

The Amateur Athletic Union

The NYAC tired of organizing the amateur championships after a few years, so members of that and other athletic clubs formed the Amateur Athletic Union (AAU) in 1888. The Union was made up of athletic clubs from around the country. All clubs were required to adhere to the AAU's code of amateurism, which defined an amateur as "one who has not entered in an open competition; either for a stake, public or admission money or entrance fee; or under a fictitious name; or has not competed with or against a professional for any prize or where admission fee is charged; or who has not instructed, pursued, or assisted in the pursuit of athletic exercises as a means of livelihood, or for gain or any emolument; or whose membership of any athletic club of any kind was not brought about or does not continue, because of any mutual understanding, express or implied, whereby his becoming or continuing a member of such club would be of any pecuniary benefit to him whatever, direct or indirect, and who shall in other and all respects conform to the rules and regulations of this organization, will be considered an Amateur."[4]

One of the primary functions of the AAU was to make sure that all of its athletes were true amateurs. All athletic clubs that were members of the AAU were required to scrutinize their membership rosters and purge anyone who did not meet the exacting standards of the AAU. Because the rules were applied retroactively to anyone who had ever been in a professional event, they allowed the AAU to control exactly the kinds of men present at the competitions. Any club that wanted to be part of a competition had to be absolutely certain that its entire membership fit the definition of amateur. In addition, the AAU declared that all amateur and collegiate athletes had to register with them. They also had to pay a registration fee. In effect, the AAU was able to tax athletes for the right to participate in athletics.

The distinction between professional and amateur athletes had been made very clear. No longer were the papers providing exciting accounts of swimmers racing for money, jewelry, or other prizes while spectators gambled on the outcome. Instead, they wrote about "trim looking, clean-cut athletes" of the private athletics clubs, or the quaint activities of women of the leisure class. The *New-York Tribune* wrote about a "delightful" day of sport at the

New York Athletic Club's Travers Island that was thankfully devoid of lower-class types, saying, "As admission was obtained by invitation only, that cheap and undesirable element which patronized sports and recreation simply to appease its longing to be 'sporty' was missing."

The amateur-professional divide was solidified by 1896, when Pierre de Coubertin, an aristocrat and minor nobleman of France, established the modern Olympic Games. Coubertin had long dreamed of recreating the glorious games of ancient Greece. Coubertin was a great supporter of sports in their amateur form, and he saw the games of Olympia as the ultimate in athleticism for the simple joy of pure sport. He wanted to establish a modern Olympics, which he envisioned as a beautiful, dignified event where young men could compete with one another, protected from the crass and vulgar taint of commercialization. He treasured the idea that the Olympic athletes were "young men, who, imbued with a sense of the moral Grandeur of the games, went to them in a spirit of almost religious reverence." In his view, the Games produced something "grandiose and strong which dominated Hellenic civilization, influencing happily and gloriously the youth of the country and through them the entire nation."[5]

The men's athletic clubs that adhered to AAU rule excluded women from all athletic events. Instead, to entertain the wives and daughters of their male members, they held Ladies' Days, when the clubs would open their doors to women for the day to dine, listen to music, and watch exhibitions by men, but not actually use any of the equipment or facilities. Although women were not allowed to take part in the athletic contests, they were treated to performances of female impersonation known as harlequin races. The club men would dress up in women's clothing and jump into the water, to the great enjoyment of the crowds.

An 1893 Ladies Day event included a lifesaving exhibition performed by male club members dressed as women. "The lifesaving exhibition was much enjoyed. W. E. Dickey, dressed as a woman, stood at the edge of the tank, and as he toppled over he gave a great scream. F. L. Slozenger then jumped in and saved him."[6]

A Ladies' Day at the Larchmont Yacht Club, just outside of New York City, featured a harlequin race, in which male members dressed in women's bathing costumes and then raced. A photograph in the *New York Daily Tribune* showed four tall and well-built men, looking amused and breathless, wearing soaking-wet dresses with puffy sleeves and hosiery. One appears to have ripped open a sleeve and the more muscular men seem ready to explode from the dresses.[7]

Although the AAU had further fortified its rule over men's athletic events, women like Kate Bennett's students and Carrie Falk were still taking part in serious swimming events outside the AAU's reach. Although some male athletes had been forcibly pushed out of amateur athletics, women had never been part of it in the first place and in a way were unaffected by the changes. This provided women swimmers with a semi-invisible means of continuing right along as they always had. They continued to enjoy swimming for pleasure, competition, and sometimes also as employment, at least for the time being. Women were still able to participate in independently organized races, advocate for swimming education, and earn a living as swimming teachers or working in entertainment, moving among defined categories in ways men could not.

6. International Waters

Throughout the U.S. and Europe, there were many women pursuing swimming competitively or in solo efforts. In 1875, Agnes Alice Beckwith of England swam five miles from London Bridge to Greenwich in one hour and seven minutes. A week later, another young British woman, Emily Parker, swam even further along the same route. Agnes Beckwith became a self-promoting star swimmer in her own right and became known for longer swims and other aquatic endurance feats. She spent 30 straight hours swimming and treading water in a tank at the Royal Aquarium "clad in her *costume du bain* of black silk, trimmed with crimson" for crowds of interested Londoners. Before entering the water she was examined by a group of female officials who made certain she wasn't wearing anything that would help her float. To entertain herself during the 30 hours of "ornamental swimming," she read a book while floating on her back, holding the book above her head. She also drank coffee from a floating table and sang to keep herself awake during the night.[1] She authored a book on swimming techniques and traveled to America where she made an unsuccessful attempt to swim from Sandy Hook, New Jersey, to Rockaway Beach, a course of almost 20 miles.

In 1900, Countess Walpurga von Isacescu of Austria made headlines by attempting to swim the English Channel. She had started her swim from Calais, France, entering the ocean discreetly from a bathing box after a breakfast of eggs and port wine. The weather had been fair when she began, but an easterly wind arose, and after three hours she was actually east of where she had started. After almost ten hours, the weather worsened further and she gave up the attempt, having swum an estimated 20 miles in 60-degree water, consuming only tea and lumps of sugar throughout.[2]

In 1906, a nine-mile race down the Seine River in Paris attracted three female entrants.[3] A 15-mile race down London's Thames had 15 female competitors in a field of 49. Seven of the 27 who actually finished were women, and a woman finished in fifth place.[4]

In 1912, 23-year-old British swimmer Lily Smith made an attempt at crossing the English Channel and failed after six hours. The next year she made her second attempt on the Channel, but withdrew after five hours. Lily had tried in 1911 to make a round-trip swim of the Solent, the strait between the English mainland and the Isle of Wight, whose waters are narrower but faster than those of the English Channel. Lily made the first half of the swim successfully, but struck a submerged barrel on the return trip and eventually had to give up because of blood loss. Lily's goals were political as well as athletic, and she stated, "I am going to swim the Channel in order to demonstrate that woman is the physical equal of men. I am going to put a stop forever to all this twaddle about the weaker sex. Yes, I am a firm believer in woman suffrage."

All of these events, and many more, were covered in American newspapers with regularity, and the American public was fully aware of the aquatic feats being attempted and accomplished by women in other countries.

Annette Kellerman

The best-known international swimmer during this time was Annette Kellerman, a young Australian swimming champion. She was a serious athlete intent on having a professional career, and she probably did more to make swimming appealing to women than anyone else, bringing it a glamour it had heretofore been missing. Glamour came naturally to Annette; she had been raised among salons, artists, and performers of all kinds. Her mother was a concert pianist who had been born in Cleveland and raised in Paris before moving to Australia, while her father was a violinist and music teacher. Annette learned to swim at a young age to counter physical weakness brought on by a childhood illness. Her teachers were soon encouraging her to swim professionally, but her father initially resisted the idea of his daughter earning a living in that fashion. But Mr. Kellerman was ill and the family was facing severe financial problems, and he soon changed his mind, becoming Annette's chaperone and biggest supporter.

In 1904, 17-year-old Annette and her ailing father arrived in England, looking for professional swimming opportunities. They were more interested in making a living as opposed to setting records, and Annette first set out to "make the English people take notice" by swimming down the Thames River. She swam 26 miles of the "flotsam and jetsam of London, dodging tugs and swallowing what seemed like pints of oil from the greasy surface of the river."[5] Annette's swim was greeted with excitement, and part of the enthusiastic response can be attributed to her bathing suit. She swam in a sleek, close-fitting men's suit with tight leggings attached, which provided an unprecedented opportunity to look at the female shape and silhouette. To eyes unused to the lines of the female figure, it was an astonishing departure from the bulky, baggy, and concealing swimsuits that women were supposed to be wearing to the beach. Within weeks of the Thames swim, she was a media star, appearing in newspapers and attracting thousands to watch her practice.

Annette caught the eye of a sports editor from the *Daily Mirror*, who said his paper would sponsor Annette and her training for the English Channel attempt for eight pounds a week. Annette spent several weeks in Dover, swimming from shore town to shore town, attracting crowds while she acclimated herself to the Channel water. She and her father had so little money during this time that Annette subsisted on bread and vegetables, and journalists were quite shocked to hear that her diet was almost meatless, although by necessity rather than choice. She also consumed chocolate, having acquired another sponsorship from the Cadbury candy company.

Annette made her first attempt at swimming the English Channel the same night as six other rivals, all of whom were male. Each swimmer started from a different point along the shore, based on each camp's research, knowledge of the tides, and opinions of the respective sponsoring newspapers. Annette left from Dover while the others left from various other points along the southeastern coast of England, each accompanied by a steam tug and a rowboat. The famous British swimmer Jabez Wolffe was one of the competitors, along with another well-known swimmer, Thomas Burgess. The men were able to swim naked for the sake of comfort, but Annette wore a swimsuit that chafed painfully. She became seasick after four hours, which she attributed to the Cadbury cocoa she had been drinking throughout the swim. The amount of money that the *Mirror* would pay her was dependent on how long she swam, so she forced herself to spend another two-and-a-half hours swimming as best she could, vomiting all the while. She recalled, "Dad and I were desperately poor — we must have money. And I kept saying to myself, 'The longer you stick, the more you get!'"[6] The swim earned her about 30 pounds. None of the other swimmers finished the Channel swim.

She tried and failed to swim the Channel two more times, and then wrote off the entire endeavor by claiming that while women may have endurance, they did not have the strength of men. "I think no woman has this combination; that's why I say none of my sex will ever accomplish that particular stunt," she said.[7] Annette wasn't being negative; she was simply stating what she believed to be a fact. Annette was an excellent swimmer and she knew it. Her Channel attempts had been methodically planned with success in mind, and still hadn't been successful. She moved on to bigger and better things with barely a backwards glance at the Channel.

Later on, she revised her opinion about women's long-distance prospects,

Annette Kellerman poses in her revolutionary swimsuit, 1919 (Library of Congress Prints and Photographs Division).

saying, "It's no use for a woman to try and beat a man at short distances. That is a question of brute strength. But for long distance I certainly favor my sex, because we have more patience. I am willing to swim any man in the world at any distance over 10 miles. I do hope I will be able to get some of your American champions to try a long distance match with me."[8]

She traveled to Paris and was the sole female competitor in a race down the Seine River, tying for the finish with Thomas Burgess. Thousands of thrilled spectators watched the race, and Annette was welcomed with open arms as a daughter of France, given that her mother was French. She raced Countess Walpurga von Isacescu on the Danube. Annette continued to perform in exhibitions in London, and was even invited to meet the Queen while performing at the Hippodrome. In 1906, she was invited to perform in Chicago at the White City amusement park, where she performed in a grueling 55 shows per week. By then, she had made enough money that she was able to purchase a house for her family in Paris. Her father returned there and died three months later. That same year, she moved to Massachusetts to work at an amusement park in Revere Beach, where she was paid the spectacular salary of three hundred dollars for only 14 shows per week.[9]

Upon arriving in Revere, Annette tried to go for a swim in the ocean. When she approached the water in her tight swimsuit, she was stopped by a policeman and arrested for indecency. The swim may have been planned as a publicity stunt, and it got Annette a lot of attention. The form-fitting bathing suit immediately became known as an "Annette Kellerman." From there Annette was hired to perform her show on Broadway, diving into a small onstage pool before an entranced audience. The show toured vaudeville theaters all over the country, and the star was making $1,500 per week. She also appeared in some short silent films and in 1914 she proposed a film that would take place almost entirely in the water, with herself as the star. *Neptune's Daughter* was filmed in Bermuda, and Annette was involved in all aspects of its production. While filming an underwater scene through a glass tank, the glass broke and Annette was so severely injured that she spent six weeks in a hospital. The film was a spectacle like no one had ever seen before, with underwater cameras and 20,000 extras. It was a huge hit, making Annette a true star and a movie pioneer. In Jamaica she made *Daughter of the Gods*, in which she was not only the star but was responsible for teaching scores of starlets to swim with their feet tied together in their mermaid costumes. Annette did all of her own stunts, including diving off a waterfall and being thrown into a pool with crocodiles. Annette's performance was groundbreaking: she appeared nude in some scenes, with her long hair strategically concealing certain parts.

Although Annette Kellerman was the perfect example of an unabashed professional athlete, the biographical movie *Million Dollar Mermaid*, released in 1952 and staring Esther Williams as Annette, distinctly tried to portray Annette as an amateur, rather than a professional. The film depicts Annette and her father coming to England so that he could open a conservatory and she could practice ballet, and Annette only taking money for her swimming and diving after a series of other failed enterprises. But *Million Dollar Mermaid* does show Annette selling her championship trophies for grocery money, something at which Walter Camp would surely have been aghast. But as Annette said frankly, they came to England specifically to find paying swimming work and almost starved while doing so. She progressed very deliberately from amateur swimming to paid swimming and diving appearances, to stage shows, and finally to Hollywood movies.

Annette's influence on female swimmers was immense. While touring, she also gave lectures on the benefits of swimming for women. With her stage performances and movies, she made swimming glamorous without losing any of her serious athleticism. In 1918, she published a book, *How to Swim*, in which she advised female swimmers in every aspect of the sport. She laid out a clear argument in favor of her functional swimming suit: "Not only in matters of swimming but in all forms of activity woman's natural development is seriously restricted and impaired by social customs and all sorts of prudish and Puritanical ideas. The girl child long before she is conscious of her sex, is continually reminded that she is a girl and therefore must forego many childhood activities. As womanhood approaches these restrictions become even more severe and the young woman is corseted and gowned and thoroughly imbued with the idea that it is most unlady-like to be possessed of legs or to know how to use them."[10]

She advised her readers, "Perhaps you will say that in your locality the one-piece tights will not be tolerated. In that case get one-piece tights anyway and wear over the tights the lightest garment you can get. It should be a loose sleeveless garment hung from the shoulders. Never have a tight waist band. It is a hindrance.... There is no more reason why you should wear those awful water overcoats — those awkward, unnecessary, lumpy 'bathing suits,' than there is that you should wear lead chains. Heavy bathing suits have caused more deaths by drowning than cramps ... anyone who persuades you to wear the heavy skirty kind is endangering your life."[11]

How to Swim included Annette's story of the early years of her life and discussed the beauty and health benefits of swimming, and she advocated for large issues such as women's right to vote and swimming pools for all. She critiqued America for being slow to encourage its citizens to swim, and complained about the lack of decent swimming facilities, saying, "Many of the so-called pools I have seen in America are but dank and gruesome tanks, which remind one of the barn cellar after a flood."[12] The book was also packed with photographs of Annette modeling different suits and swimming capes.

By the first years of the 20th century, women had proven themselves in the world of swimming as teachers, athletes, entertainers and promoters of the sport. A number of powerful female swimmers emerged, many of them associated with lifesaving organizations.

7. The Water-Safety Movement and the Volunteer Life Saving Corps

Deaths by drowning were far from uncommon in Victorian America. In the days before subway, bus, and bridge, ferries were a major means of transportation in cities like New York. Ships sank, people fell off docks, and there were no government standards for safety equipment such as life preservers or lifeboats. Women were at a distinct disadvantage if they fell into the water because their thick and multilayered clothing could quickly become waterlogged, weighting down and exhausting the wearer. Voluminous skirts could sweep over a woman's head in the water, and a pinching bone corset could impair a desperately struggling woman's ability to breathe.

In the summer of 1874, drowning deaths at the beaches near New York seemed to be happening on a daily basis. "Hardly an excursion leaves New York, full of fun and frolic, but returns, saddened and agonized, with the corpse of one who, but a few hours before, was full of hope and glad anticipation," noted a reporter, who attributed some of the frequent deaths to the popularity of swimming races, as men and boys swam to distances far beyond their ability trying to emulate Webb, Boyton, and other celebrity swimmers.[1]

Lifesaving and water safety were novel ideas at the time. Neither was provided by the city, and inventive private citizens had to step in to fill in the gaps. Out of necessity, neighborhoods provided their own essential services. For example, the earliest New York City firefighting companies consisted of gang members who would respond to fires in their own neighborhood and those concerned with water safety followed a similar path, without the criminal affiliation.

One of the earliest attempts at organized lifesaving was that of Nan the Newsboy. Nan, real name William O'Neill, worked as a bootblack and a newsboy on the Lower East Side. In 1878, Nan and three friends formed the New-York Amateur Life-Saving Association, and began nighttime patrols along the docks and the waterfront of lower Manhattan. They pooled their money to buy some hemp ropes, but that was the extent of their equipment. Since they had no boat, their main technique of rescue was jumping after the drowning person and hoping someone else would haul them back in.[2]

The four young men attracted the attention of Captain Paul Boyton, the man who had floated across the English Channel in his famous rubber suit. In December of 1878, he took the lifesavers under his wing and began a fund-raising campaign on their behalf. He invited the boys out for a "high pie" dinner at the Fifth Avenue Hotel, where he induced them to discuss their work. Nan, who had by then rescued 15 people from the water, talked about his lifesaving methods and the general ungratefulness of those he had saved. "The other night we rescued a sailor, and when we got him out he swore like anything at us. It's my opinion that he wanted to commit suicide. But the funniest thing I ever know'd was a little rooster — a little fellow what fell over-board. I went after him, and he caught me by the arms, and we went down together twice. Then I got loose and hit him, and held him off. Two men pulled him up on a derrick, and there that little rooster stood and swore at me for hitting him. Whenever anybody catches hold of me in the water I always mash him in the nose. It's the best way I know."[3]

Boyton began raising money for the squad by pressing New York's mon-eyed men for subscriptions to support the work. In January of 1879, Nan was present when Boyton made a frigid nighttime swim from the Battery to Staten Island to test an improvement to his rubber suit. The suit now had a winter feature of thick rubber cladding designed to protect the wearer who might be bumping into ice floes and rocks. Boyton and his companion did not make it to Staten Island; the water was so cold that they were almost able to climb over the miniature icebergs that gripped them. The two finally landed and stumbled about for an hour before bursting in on a startled cook opening his restaurant in the pre-dawn hours who was surprised to see the two bubble-suited adventurers.[4]

The relationship between the practical Nan and the showman Boyton soon soured. Boyton had convinced the squad members to give up their day jobs and focus on lifesaving fulltime; he had secured a rickety, fume-filled boathouse near a sewer for them as a headquarters and promised salaries for the men, although he also required all their expenses to come out of their salaries first. When the boys found outside work accompanying ferry excur-sions, Boyton required them to turn over half their earnings to the accounts he had created. Nan accused Boyton of using the squad to advance his own interests and to advertise the famous rubber lifesaving suit. Boyton accused

Nan of being ungrateful. The rift could not be healed, and the squad disbanded. Nan took a full-time job with the ferry company.[5]

Nan's ideas were slightly ahead of their time, but other individuals and organizations sprang up to meet the need for water safety. At the neighborhood level, individuals and organizations stepped in to police the waterfront. Local lifesaving crews kept an eye on dangerous neighborhood spots known to be tempting places for children to swim. Some of these efforts were informally organized, but others were much more elaborate.

A typical lifesaving crew organized at the 91st Street Pier in 1903. The neighborhood had lost a number of children to drowning, so neighborhood parents, dockworkers, and fishermen organized the volunteer association. The volunteers organized in a military fashion, naming a captain, first lieutenant, and so forth, and followed a schedule of shifts so that the pier was always protected. The crew had a female member, Annie Donahue, who had saved a boy and a girl from drowning, and had once leapt off of an excursion boat to rescue a woman who had fallen overboard.

In an interview, the crew's Captain Sam Dunn talked about his experiences in the line of lifesaving: "Now, these fellows that write books about saving people tell you that when you're rescuing a drowning man you ought to first smash him in the face so he'll quit struggling. To my way of thinking that's all wrong. Let the fellow struggle all he wants to." Dunn described the method of rescue used by all members of the crew, which was to come behind the person, get a grip under the armpits, and swim backwards, pulling the person along.[6]

> Women and children are the hardest to save. You see, a woman can't do much on account of her dress, and she is inclined to sink in despite of her struggles. Then it takes a lot of strength to keep her afloat. When you try to pull a kid out of the water, he'll grab you around the neck every time. It's almost impossible to get a hold under his arms like you would with a man, and it's a mighty tough job all around.
>
> To save my life, I couldn't keep track of the kids I've hauled out of that river. It's just like the one I took out this morning. They're tumbling in all the time. I pull them out, give 'em a spanking sometimes and send them home without asking their names. What we need most of all on this pier is a policeman. If an officer was stationed here he could keep the kids off the pier, and that would prevent 'em from falling overboard. The police department, however, has refused to help us out.

Many of the crews organized under the umbrella of the United States Volunteer Life Saving Corps. The Corps was not to be confused with the United States Life-Saving Service, whose members were often based at lighthouses and were trained to rescue people and cargo from doomed ships that had run aground or capsized in high seas. The Life-Saving Service was a forerunner to the United States Coast Guard, while the Volunteer Life Saving Corps sprouted up at the neighborhood level, organizing itself at beaches and piers, rather than at the open ocean.

The Corps was founded in 1894 by Colonel J. Wesley Jones and originally based in New York City as an entirely volunteer organization that tasked itself with establishing expert lifesavers at every beach in the state. The national organization worked to supply local crews with lifebuoys, medicine chests, and life boats, and also campaigned to convince their state legislatures to fund these goals. They promoted training of crew members in rescue and resuscitation methods. The local crews organized volunteers who taught swimming and patrolled beaches, looking for swimmers who might be endangered.

By 1897, 581 local corps with almost 6,000 members had been organized throughout the state of New York. Women were participating in all public activities of the group. That year, women took part in a Corps event in Brooklyn that featured lifesaving demonstrations, simulated rescues, and performances of resuscitation methods. There were races for men and women and demonstrations of high dives. One of the female divers was described as "less nervous than any of the men."[7]

The Life Saving Corps and its messages of water safety and personal aquatic empowerment were popularized by Commodore Wilbert E. Longfellow of Rhode Island, who conducted a charismatic one-man lifesaving campaign that began around 1900 and lasted almost a half century. Longfellow, a reporter for a Rhode Island newspaper, was struck by the fact that he wrote about far too many drowning deaths and became passionately interested in water safety. After joining the United States Volunteer Life Saving Corps, he soon rose to become head of their activities in Rhode Island as Commodore. He campaigned for more places where people could engage in healthy and safe swimming. He tied together the lack of hygienic bathing places to the need for pools, beaches, and public baths and incorporated the public in his quest for clean swimming sites.

Longfellow quickly determined that women were the campaign's key to success, recognizing immediately that women not only desperately needed to be educated about swimming, but that they could be integral to his plan of spreading the gospel of water safety. The 1904 annual report of the Rhode Island Volunteer Life Saving Corps described extensive involvement of girls and women in the Corps. An article written by Commodore Longfellow was illustrated by photos of Clara Olweiler and Dora Howe, active members of the Rhode Island Girls Crew. Longfellow said of the girls, "Both young women are strong swimmers and good divers and they are proficient in the resuscitation work of the corps, being members of a girl's crew recently organized in the Washington Park district."[8]

The Corps sponsored an essay contest for the children of Providence, offering a five-dollar prize to the youngster who could best address why most girls never learned how to swim. The overwhelming answer was that there simply weren't enough places to swim. One respondent wrote, "The saltwater near the city is not overclean. The places are overcrowded on hot days, and many of the girls do not care to assay the task before the hoodlums, who in some cases are under little restraint and have little regard for the feelings and rights of girls and small boys learning to swim."[9] The astutely class-conscious essay winner, Lillian Syner, pointed out that Providence girls couldn't learn to swim because "many Providence girls that live in the cities are too poor to afford to go to the bathhouses," and "because poorer girls have no time or vacation to learn in."

Rhode Island's first summer's programs were a success. At the start of the summer of 1904, women were reluctant to compete, but by the fall Longfellow was able to report that "a healthy increase of interest in swimming by both men and women is already noticed, and by another year there will be a much larger number of swimmers of both sexes whose skill will compare favorably with the residents of other states on the waterfront."

The Corps practiced lifesaving in a number of ways. They taught swimming at beaches and baths, no easy task as it took great effort to convince overexcited children to learn proper swimming techniques. In the summer, swimmers were admitted to public baths in groups of two to three hundred for approximately 20 minutes of swimming before the next group was admitted. Teachers had to maintain order, control exuberant children, and teach swimming to anyone whose attention they could hold.

The Corps also patrolled beaches and resort areas and actively looked for swimmers in need of assistance. They gave well-publicized awards to citizens who rescued others from the water. They played an enormous role in educating the masses about swimming and water safety, and one of their most powerful means of education was to hold events called water carnivals throughout the summer. The carnivals included races, lifesaving demonstrations, diving, and more, much of it performed by women. A carnival in Boston featured something called a hurry-scurry race, in which "the contestants will start from the headhouse, run down the beach, dive into the water, swim out to the raft, dress in grotesque costumes, eat a pie and swim to the shore and run to the headhouse."[10]

The exhibitions also sometimes featured the same kind of harlequin races that the men's athletic clubs featured. At a demonstration in Newport, Rhode Island, "Surfman Jack Angilly of Providence, [posing] as a girl, and Clarence Hebb did some lovemaking in a rowboat and were overturned and rescued in fine style, to the delight of the big crowd assembled."[11] Sometimes these harlequin swims were for entertainment purposes, but often they served to educate the public on the extreme strength needed to swim in waterlogged clothing.

As Longfellow had predicted, the presence of competitive, confident Corps women taking part in races attracted so much positive attention that they served as advertising for the Corps and educated by example. "The spectacle of the perfectly healthy young men and women participating in these exhilarating contests has undoubtedly done much to encourage young men and boys to learn to swim and to perfect themselves in this best of sports and most necessary accomplishment for a Rhode Islander. This is particularly true of the women and girls who witnessed the sport, and not only will a larger number of the fair sex take up swimming, but an increased number will enter contests from present indications. This is due largely to the spectacle of the healthy and well-posed young girls who show themselves perfectly able to take care of themselves in the briny deep."[12]

Although not all lifesaving crews accepted women as full crew members, a few did, and many others had auxiliary units made up entirely of women. Miss Florence West of Brooklyn was an early member of the Fort Hamilton Volunteer Life Saving Corps in 1902. The *Brooklyn Eagle* said of her, "The Fort Hamilton life savers do not bar from membership in their corps the fair sex, as some other corps do. In fact one the most efficient members in the Volunteer Life Saving Corps at Fort Hamilton is a young woman who is master of the art of swimming and counts her rescues with the best of the men." She was not the only woman in her crew. "Miss West and her women companions are the life of the corps and do not hesitate because of their sex to take any of the chances required by the rules of the corps."[13]

One very serious aspect of the Corps' work was the suppression of the "rowdyism" and roughhousing that kept timid people away from the water. "One service which the corps performed, and it was an important one, was the prevention of a large amount of the rowdyism on beaches which has heretofore prevented interested persons from acquiring a knowledge of swimming. Boys and men far from gentlemanly in their action, seemed to delight in 'ducking' or splashing the timid learners just starting to swim, and thereby destroying all the confidence in themselves and, instead, creating a fear and distrust of the water and of persons really desirous of assisting them to learn. There is very little police protection on the beaches near Providence, and such policemen as are detailed are not amphibious, and such control as they have stops within a few feet of the water's edge."

Rowdyism was very much a fear for some beachgoers. Women were not always safe from verbal and physical assaults at the beach, even in crowded places with lots of witnesses. Two incidents a week apart at Manhattan Beach in Brooklyn indicate the very real threat of harassment faced by women. In August 1901, the *Brooklyn Daily Eagle* reported that a young woman who was at the beach by herself, wearing a "deep red bathing suit with white trimmings and red stockings and a red cap," was chased into the water by a gang of toughs when she ignored their catcalls. She was thrown into the water multiple times, and then a crowd of men and women stood around her, pelting her with handfuls of sand. The newspaper went to great lengths to note that her suit was in no way immodest and that the hoodlums were entirely improper and that the crowd was operating under some kind of mob frenzy that the hooligans had whipped them into.[14]

A few days later, two chorus girls from the musical *Floradora* were visiting the beach with several male friends. One of the women, Miss Vidal, rented one of the beach's bathing suits in order to go swimming and was soon surrounded by a group of ogling men. According to the *Brooklyn Eagle*, Miss Vidal attracted attention even in her plain rented suit because she was wearing a feather boa. First, the men catcalled, then they "got up from the sands and moved over towards the Floradora girls. The girls moved away and the men followed. The men strolled along with the girls making complementary remarks such as 'Ain't they fine! She can have me!' and others of about the same degree of refinement and intelligence." Eventually a policeman noticed what was happening and came to the girls' defense.

Miss Vidal later said, "If I had had my revolver I would have shot some of those hoodlums. I always carry a pistol, but of course, I couldn't carry it into the water. I think it was an outrage."[15] Miss Vidal had done nothing more than wear a feather boa with her bathing suit, but she had probably learned the frightening lesson that even in a rented woolen swim suit, she could at any moment become a target for men's unwanted attention.

The Volunteer Life Saving Corps had many branches throughout New England, New Jersey, and New York. They were necessary not just in beach towns and resort areas, but in all neighborhoods that had river access. In hot weather, children were constantly sneaking into the water to cool off.

In 1912, a swimming teacher at the East 135th Street Baths, Marie L. Ramsperger, made headlines when she rescued two boys and a man from the East River. The boys had been intending to swim at the free public baths, but the bath was filled to capacity, so they headed down to the docks rather than wait in line. Playing on a floating raft of lumber, they drifted out into the river and capsized. A dockworker swam out to help the boys, but when it became obvious he couldn't help both panicked boys out of the water, he tried to cling to the raft and keep the boys from slipping under the water. Marie then swam out and held onto all three until help arrived.

Taken by itself, this story is a single incident. But on the very same page of the *New York Times* that carried this article were five more stories about the dangers of water. First, a "fancy diver" giving an exhibition at the 25th Street Pier drowned in full sight of a crowd of several hundred people. In separate incidents at beaches near Far Rockaway, one man drowned in rough seas while two more were rescued, one of them not regaining consciousness for two hours. And at Clason Point in the Bronx, a 15-year-old-girl drowned at a beach full of picnicking families. No one had even noticed. The threat of the water was a constant.[16]

There was also danger from ship accidents, and one disaster in particular impacted city dwellers like no other. In June of 1904, the *General Slocum*, a sidewheel paddle boat used for local excursions, was chartered to take members of a German Lutheran church, mostly women and children, from lower Manhattan up the East River to the north shore of Long Island for a day of picnicking. Not long after leaving, a fire started on board, but instead of heading to shore, the captain continued north. Terrified passengers grabbed for life preservers that were so old that they fell apart in their hands. Lifeboats were unusable, having been painted to the deck. Many passengers leapt overboard and drowned; others died in the blaze. When the ship was finally beached at North Brother Island, an isolated island by the Bronx populated only by a hospital for victims of infectious diseases, the captain and crew deserted the ship. Rescue was left to passing ships and nurses from the hospital who ran to the beach to help. In all, 1,021 passengers perished, and only 321 survived. Locally, the *Slocum* disaster was devastating to New York City's German community and made an enormous impact on the progress of water safety in the United States. Even Germany's Kaiser Wilhelm was appalled, and wrote to the German consul of New York City, asking for lists of the dead and the heroes, making a special request for the names of the three bravest nurses. The Corps was assured that one of them would have to be Miss Smith, Superintendent of Nurses at Riverside Hospital, who "stood knee deep in the water and passed the bodies of the dead and dying to the eager arms of those ready to receive them."[17]

The Volunteer Life Saving Corps of New York was able to verify that four of the children who survived had been taught to swim at Life Saving Corps stations. Following the disaster, the Corps offered to provide additional instructors at the city's baths, and the offer was accepted.[18]

8. Women and the Volunteer Life Saving Corps

The lifesaving crews provided the greatest source of organized competitive swimming for girls and women during this era. Every summer, women raced at the water carnivals and in the longer endurance races arranged between the crews. Many were affiliates with the local Volunteer Life Saving Corps organizations, independent lifesaving crews, or other swimming clubs. When the *Brooklyn Eagle* wrote about an impending women's race off of Coney Island, they identified the girls' trainers, who were affiliated with other local lifesaving crews. "Alice and Maggie Ward have been swimming daily from Manhattan Beach to the pier, under the coaching of Alfred Girard, of Doyle's Life Savers, and Maggie expected to win. Maggie Hogan has developed strength under Life Saver Johnson's tuition and will make a struggle for first place."[1]

Often, the girls had to pass a qualifying exam in order to gain membership in a crew. In 1901, 13-year-old Julia Timpany swam the Narrows between Brooklyn and Staten Island to qualify to become a member of one of the Brooklyn crews. Also attempting the swim were two teenage boys and Julia's 11-year-old sister, who dropped out half a mile from shore. Julia completed the four-mile swim in an hour and a half.[2] In 1904, Linda Hough and Maud Hauff, probationary members of the Long Beach crew, were tested for endurance swimming and rescue methods before a crowd of 500 observers in order to gain crew membership.[3]

Norma Hamilton, described as a "beautiful young society girl," related how she was invited to join a crew. "I swim at Long Beach all the time and sometimes stay in the water all day. One day the inspector for the Volunteer Life Saving Corps asked me to go through some tests and then he asked me to join. First I had to swim in the breakers — but that was easy. Then I took out the lifeboat and catamaran without upsetting it."[4] The article effused over Norma's beauty and the outfits she wore to the beach, including "white duck

Two of the independent lifesaving crews. Devlin's Life Boat and Doyle's Life Boat, New York City, 1892 (Library of Congress Prints and Photographs Division).

sailor suits, with rolling collars, turned back from a well-moulded throat, tanned brown by the wind and sun." Unfortunately, just a few weeks later, she was forced to stay home from a qualifying event because her mother did "not sanction any notoriety for her daughter in the swimming line."

The Corps held an annual endurance race. Women from crews all over the state were early participants in the race, which was highly publicized and received extensive coverage in newspapers. In 1904, Florence West and Eleanor Weber, along with 30 men, raced from Brooklyn Bridge to Coney Island, a distance of about 13 miles. The two women were among only seven people to finish the race. Florence, Eleanor and the five male finishers were presented with medals during an award ceremony at the Young Men's Christian Association of Brooklyn.

Augusta Gallup and Clara Hurst made headlines in August 1908 when they participated in the annual endurance race, which drew thousands of spectators at the starting point and the finishing point, as well as a flotilla of boats that followed the swimmers as they dodged ships and other traffic in the harbor. Augusta earned extra praise for continuing the swim even after having slammed her head into submerged lumber as she dove into the water at the start of the race. She said, "I like to go into water head first. Diving from the pier, all of us had to swim through a sea of vegetable refuse, sticks, logs, and other river rubbage. I struck an obstacle and cut my lower lip. The salt water made it smart fearfully, but I wasn't going to quit. It pained all the way down, and my eyes seemed to be burning as well."[5]

Augusta and Clara were forced by officials to quit the race early. Augusta, who worked summers teaching swimming to children in the public baths and winters in a millinery shop, told a reporter, "Why, they dragged Miss Clara T. Hurst and myself out of the water when both of us were as fresh as when we started. You see, we made Norton's Point in fine shape, when the tide turned, and it's a bit hard making way against a good stiff tide. I wanted to go on. The doctors all said we were in far better condition than the men. Oh, it was just jolly. I never knew what real fun there is in long-distance swimming. I felt so good when I got dressed that I just wanted to go in again."[6]

To avoid being pulled from the water again, she vowed to try the swim solo. "I'm going to swim to Coney Island alone some afternoon. I can do it, you just see. I could hardly expect to beat the young men whom I swam against yesterday, but I'll bet any one of them won't beat me at twenty-five miles. I've made arrangements today to swim to Far Rockaway and it can be done if I'm lucky enough to escape that turn of tide. No one can buck a tide and make real headway."

As a swimming teacher, Augusta also had an opinion on the swimming abilities of women. She was clearly exasperated by what she saw as women pretending to be weaker than they were. "Women nowadays are cowards in the water. They're afraid of wetting their puffs or rats, besides lacking courage to place their heads under water. Ever try to teach a woman to float? Well, the moment she knows you're not holding her, down go her feet and up come her hands. They hang on life ropes all day and then say how fine swimming is. Women could outswim men if they had the courage. That's all that's needed."

"I'm so glad Miss Hurst and myself finished so well. We just showed people that women can do things, too, didn't we?"

Like most female swimmers, Augusta also had strong opinions on swimwear, saying, "It is difficult enough for the average woman to make progress in the water without the useless handicap of yards of heavy water-soaked cloth, whereas with a rational bloomer suit and a removable skirt she can get along very well indeed after entering the water. The skirt can be replaced on leaving the water, if one chooses. Even in the bath where women are alone permitted the use of the pools, some will come with a long skirt or a flimsy wrapper which keeps them so busy managing it that they can give little help to the swimming instructor. In many of our public baths in New York, the

The August 1908 long distance race from Manhattan to Coney Island, passing under the Brooklyn Bridge (Library of Congress Prints and Photographs Division).

women make combination suits of bloomers and waist that do so splendidly, are wonderfully sensible, and give free scope to the limbs."[7]

This really was one of the most pressing issues facing female swimmers. Bathing suit style was often dictated not just by the larger society or by fashion designers, but by police or local officials. For example, in 1907, George Titcomb of the Rockaway Beach Taxpayers Association demanded that police address the problem of women wearing revealing swimsuits. "The scandalous disregard of modesty and the shocking suits or lack of them worn by women on Rockaway beach when the bathing season is in full swing have endangered the morals of the children," he charged. "The skirts worn by women while in bathing have been altogether too short. In fact, they have been mere apologies for skirts."[8]

The same year, the Atlantic City police department declared that women who attempted to visit the beach without stockings would be forced to wear some, and they linked the problem to women who were swimming at baths and pools. "This practice of refusing stockings at the bath-house while introduced by a few careless or super-bold young women, promised to become the most daring fad of the season. But we quickly stopped it. We are dress censors in so far as compelling bathing girls to wear hosiery."[9]

In some places, women were told to cover up, had the length of suits measured by beach monitors, or were even taken in by police. Many beaches employed beach censors who closely examined the bathing suits of women and, less frequently, men. Some beaches required women to wear stockings, a proviso that extended well into the 1920s.

A 1911 lifesaving competition featured races for both men and women from the lifesaving stations at Coney Island, the Bronx, and Sheepshead Bay, among others. Women participated in races, dives, simulated rescues, and boat-tipping contests that afternoon. One young woman, Adeline Trapp, was singled out for specific mention in a newspaper article, which noted that she performed better dives than many members of the "sterner sex."[10]

Adeline Trapp provides a fascinating example of how girls and women could access opportunities to learn to swim and compete alongside men, if they were interested in pushing at the boundaries of societal norms. Adeline's father had a boathouse, and he was naturally concerned about his young children playing near the water. He taught her and her siblings to swim by tying a rope around their waists and having them paddle around the dock. This caused some controversy among the neighbors, including one who announced that swimming was for dock rats, and informed Mr. Trapp that it was a "violation of all propriety to have her do exercises that will teach your daughter's legs to become unacquainted with each other."[11]

Adeline was undeterred by the nosy neighbor, and even began to teach other girls how to swim. "I began teaching in the quiet until I had gathered quite a few girl swimmers around me," she remembered for a reporter many years later. "On the beach, I had to wear the regulation bathing suit. This consisted of a pair of bloomers that ended in ruffles below the knee, usually a big sailor collar, and a voluminous skirt — all of this in heavy flannel. Then there were stockings, bathing shoes of some kind, sleeves which came below the elbow, also ending in ruffles, and a bathing cap that looked like a boudoir cap, or else a straw hat tied under the chin. Besides this, most women wore Nemos all tightened-in that prevented them from bending. (Nemos, my boy, were corsets.) It was not only absurd but dangerous. The skirt would rise over your face when a wave passed. It could drown you. It brought forth a terrible rebellion against the fact that I was compelled to carry this yardage of goods around with me in the water."

Corsets were indeed a part of bathing costumes. In 1896, *Harper's Bazaar* described the latest fashions for bathers, and pointed out that "unless a woman is very slender, bathing corsets should be worn. If they are not laced tightly they are a help instead of a hindrance in swimming, and some support is needed for a figure that is accustomed to wearing stays."[12]

In 1904, Adeline was awarded the First Class Medal of Honor by the U.S. Volunteer Life Saving Corps for saving another girl from drowning. She continued to be involved in the organization, and eventually met Commodore Longfellow. In the 18-year-old Adeline, Longfellow saw an extremely talented swimmer and a golden opportunity to educate the public of women's swimming abilities, and he encouraged her to enter the Corps' annual endurance race, which that year passed through Hell Gate. Hell Gate is at the top of the eastern side of the Bronx, where the waters of Long Island Sound and the East River are forced through a narrow channel. It is an extremely dangerous place for swimmers and watercraft, and hundreds of boats were lost in the rough waters there.

For the swim, Adeline wore a long, one-piece suit that draped her like a muu-muu and had to be imported from Europe for the occasion. She and another woman, Priscilla Higgins, and 40 male members of various lifesaving stations attempted the swim on September 5. Commodore Longfellow fired the starting pistol, and the swimmers dove into the water, each followed by a boat holding two attendants and supplies in case of an emergency. They fought their way through Hell Gate's vicious currents before swimmers started to drop out of the race. To make matters worse, a squall arose, and the swimmers had to fight wind and lunging waves as they battled through water with

The start of the 1909 Hell Gate Swim. Adeline Trapp and Priscilla Higgins are standing to the immediate left of the dog (International Swimming Hall of Fame).

lessening visibility. Halfway through, ten of the men and Miss Higgins had given up, flashing a signal to their boatmen to be hauled aboard. Adeline was the last to finish the race, but the thousands of people watching the finish cheered heartily until she disappeared inside her dressing room. All of the finishers received a medal from the Corps for completing the grueling race.[13]

Many years later, when Adeline recalled her reasons for participating in the race, she said, "I was not trying to make a spot for myself but to try to impress the world, to force the world into accepting women's right to swim."

In 1910, Adeline was employed as the manager of a public indoor pool in Brooklyn. Opened in May of 1910, the pool was specifically designed for swimming as exercise and recreation, and not for hygiene, as the earliest public baths had been intended. In fact, all swimmers had to bathe in tubs or showers prior to entering the pool. Local children, boys and girls both, were making such constant and enthusiastic use of the pool that it was kept open for the entire winter.[14]

In 1911, Adeline swam from Yonkers to Manhattan, an 18-mile swim that took seven hours and seven minutes. She described it as "one of the hardest swims I ever had because of the tides of the Hudson. But I don't believe I mind the Hudson's tides as I do the filth of the East River. Ugh! I felt last Sunday, when I was plowing through that filth, as if I'd never be able to wash it off. But when I got down beyond the Battery I forgot all that. There it was glorious!"[15]

The same year, she set another record when she completed a 22-and-a-half-mile swim from North Beach, Queens, to Staten Island in five hours and six minutes. Once again, she swam through Hell Gate, this time north to south, which whirled her around in the current before she broke free. She had started the swim with four male members of the Volunteer Life Saving Corps, and she was the only one of the five who completed the swim.[16]

She discussed her reasons for swimming, her training methods, and the impact of the endurance swims on her body and mind:

> I learn so much about myself while I am training. I learn that eight hours sleep out of the twenty-four are necessary for health. I learn much about exercise, and food, and I learn how much better it is to go without tea and coffee.
>
> It's mostly for the sport that I take these swims however. I love the sport, and I love the feeling of power it gives me to accomplish a long swim. One feels after such a swim as if one could do anything. One has conquered an unfamiliar element — why, there is nothing one wouldn't be equal to. At least, that's the way a long swim affects me. Another thing — I always hope my swims may influence other women to do something in the art. A girl — every girl — ought to know how to swim. At twelve years of age she should be able to swim five miles without stopping, and without fatigue. At sixteen she ought to be able to cover ten miles with no fatigue.

All stimulants are bad for swimmers. Tobacco and liquors are especially bad. Some men swimmers take champagne when in the water, to keep them up. I don't believe in that. I would never take anything in the water, except, perhaps, some chocolate. On the day I am to swim I take nothing but milk, with eggs beaten up into it. I consume quantities of milk and eggs at all times. During my last swim I lost nine of my 128 pounds of weight — lost it in the water. But I got back three pounds in the last three days, and will have it all back by the end of September.[17]

Adeline attracted attention beyond New York City. A reporter from the *Boston Globe* wrote to her, asking for an interview to be part of a series of articles on the success of women in marathon swimming. The reporter wrote, "My chief aim in publishing these stories is to try to explain the apparent superiority of women over man in swimming, and particularly long distance swimming. It is, I think, the only sport in which woman equals, if she does not excel, man."[18]

9. Elaine Golding, Rose Pitonof, and the Rise of the Female Racer

The acknowledged but unofficial champion swimmer of the era was Elaine Golding, the younger sister of Ethel Golding, the famous swimmer of the previous decade who had died at age 23. Ethel had been heavily involved with the Volunteer Life Saving Corps; in 1901 a full-page photograph of her was included in the New York Corps' annual report, which stated that 18-year-old Ethel "has long been considered the most expert swimmer of her sex ever seen in this country." Ethel had entered and won 24 races over the past five years, and the Corps proudly stated, "She has been the leading lady of the U.S. Volunteer Life Saving Corps for five years, and has for pleasure only instructed many of her young lady friends how to swim."[1]

Elaine followed in Ethel's footsteps and was taking part in the Life Saving Corps water carnivals by age six. At seven the *Brooklyn Eagle* described her as having "a degree of skill and endurance which is little short of marvelous." Elaine's family had a cottage at Bath Beach and were known in the neighborhood as being the earliest to arrive at the beach every morning and the last to leave. They were all "enthusiastic surf bathers" and Elaine's mother had taught all the children to swim at very young ages. Neighbors recalled seeing Mrs. Golding swim out to the float with four-year-old Elaine on her back, and then encourage her to leap off the float into her arms, calling, "Now jump, baby, jump, Elaine." At seven, Elaine had mastered the overhand English racing stroke, and was an impressive diver, regularly making the twenty-foot dive from the bathing pavilion on the Captain's Pier at Bath Beach.[2]

At age 11, Elaine swam the Narrows from Staten Island to Brooklyn. The swim took about two and a half hours, and she beat her competitor, 19-year-old May Behr, by half a length. The ebb tide carried the girls three miles off

69

route, turning a swim of less than a mile into something longer and much more treacherous.[3]

May Behr had first swum the Narrows the previous year, when she and her cousin Florence West completed the swim. Not all family members were avid supporters of the girls' attempts at swimming. "Mrs. Behr, mother of May, had strenuously objected to her daughter attempting the swim, as she was afraid something would happen. May's brother was lost in the bay some time ago, it was said, and since that time Mrs. Behr has had a dread of the water. Not so with May, however, who had made up her mind to swim the Narrows, no matter what happened. Several boats followed the swimmers and a good sized crowd collected at the Fort Hamilton pier to see the girls off." The girls made it through a rough current and a school of snappers in one hour and 40 minutes.[4]

At age 12, Elaine and Clara Hurst raced across the Narrows in a Volunteer Life Saving Corps race, dropping the skirts from their suits and swimming only in "tight jerseys and trunks." Several of the eight men accompanying them left the water because it was too cold. The girls' understanding of the tides was also tested, as "Miss Golding's tactics proved the best, for her rival did not get the benefit of the outgoing tide until she was nearly across the Narrows and far north of the finish."[5]

Elaine excelled in both sprint and marathon races. In 1908, she, Clara Hurst, and two other women raced across the Hudson River at Tappan Zee before thousands of spectators gathered on both shores and bobbing on boats in the river. This race was not arranged by the Volunteer Life Saving Corps; instead, it was sponsored by the Port Comfort Inn, which was savvy enough to know the size of crowds this event would be sure to attract.[6] The four women arrived by boat at the public dock at Irvington, wearing bathrobes over their suits. At the starter's signal, they dropped the robes and dove into the water, each followed closely by an accompanying rowboat. It was no mere straight shot across, and the girls fought the currents every inch of the way. Elaine finished first, covering the three-mile stretch in one hour and 28 minutes, beating Clara by two minutes. The race cemented Elaine's champion reputation. Although there were no officially sanctioned championships for women at the time, organizations were aware of record times, and the newspapers were quick to declare, "Miss Elaine Golding of Bath Beach to-day demonstrated to the satisfaction of a large crowd that she is the champion amateur woman swimmer of this country. She not only defeated the best women swimmers in this section, but swam a distance of three miles in excellent time. In fact few men could have duplicated her performance."[7]

Elaine was interviewed by reporters, jovially telling them, "Oh, I had a dandy bath. I could have swum back again without any trouble."[8] They asked

Elaine Golding leaving the water after a swim (Library of Congress Prints and Photographs Division).

if she would be challenging Annette Kellerman, but Elaine refused to entertain the idea, because to race against Annette, a professional, would endanger her amateur standing. The *Brooklyn Daily Eagle* went on to muse that if Elaine and Annette "ever meet in any kind of a race, it will decide the title of the champion swimmer of the world."[9]

In August of 1908, Elaine was viewed as such a paragon of female athleticism that she was asked to take part in a curious series of experiments conducted by Edwin Fairfax Naulty, a "scientific and athletic amateur," on the effect of oxygen administered to athletes. In a series of demonstration races held at the Chateau des Beaux-Arts in Huntington, Long Island, Naulty administered oxygen to Elaine and two male swimmers, comparing the results with their non-oxygenated efforts. Elaine took the oxygen before a quarter-mile swim that she finished in 8:05⅖, swimming "without distressing effort." Naulty determined that Elaine's improved results were attributable to the effects of the oxygen and not the power of suggestion. "Being unimaginative and somewhat skeptical, Miss Golding was probably not affected by suggestion," he concluded.[10]

In 1910, Elaine was affiliated with the Steeplechase Swimming Club of

Coney Island. In August of that year, she won the alleged "women's championship of the world" by winning a 210-yard race over her clubmate, Dora Hyatt, with a winning time of 3:28, beating the previous winner's time by almost 14 seconds.[11] One week later at Coney Island, she defeated New England's female champion, May McDonough, swimming a half-mile out to sea from Steeplechase Pier and back.[12]

In 1911, Elaine took part in a race from Manhattan's Battery to Coney Island's Steeplechase Pier, a distance of 14 miles. She and two other women, Lillian Howard and Clara Hurst, dove into the grimy water at Manhattan's southern tip at 10:36 in the morning before a huge crowd of watchers. Each swimmer was accompanied in the water by boats of family, friends, and coaches, and they were surrounded by boats full of newspaper reporters, photographers, and even moving-picture camera men. Clara was seized with cramps and left the water after five hours. Elaine completed the course in six hours and one minute.

As Elaine finished, she was greeted with a clamorous outburst from the crowd that illustrated how popular swimmers were, and how admired female swimmers were. The waiting crowd erupted with cheers as she swam into sight, fireworks were exploded, the Steeplechase band began to play, and more people rushed to the beach to catch a glimpse of her. She retired to a dressing room to recuperate, which she did by downing some hot beef broth and ice cream. When Lillian Howard swam ashore 34 minutes later, the crowd greeted her with similar ecstasy.[13]

Elaine was a particularly frank individual, and freely admitted that while many women took up swimming for the sake of their figures, that wasn't her concern. "Although I swim probably more than any woman of my age, I am sorry to say it has never kept me slim. But I happen to be a heavy type of person. I was heavy when I was a champion, too, and one of the first things I used to do after winning a race was to sit down and eat four big slices of brick ice cream. Flesh, of course, is not a handicap in swimming. Some of the best swimmers are heavy."[14] Her weight also kept her warm; in December of 1912, while swimming with a group of men and women, she raced Deputy Police Commissioner Dougherty in a one-mile race off Brighton Beach. The race was too close to call.

In 1913, Elaine decided to do something really fantastic. The fabled Panama Canal, which had been under construction for decades, was finally nearing completion. That fall, Alfred Brown, the captain of a lifesaving station and an avid distance swimmer, sailed for Panama and swam the length of the canal over several days. Just a few days after reports of Captain Brown's canal swim hit the papers, Elaine was boarding a steamer for Central America. She was unable to get permission to swim the unstable Culebra Cut through the

Continental Divide, but she swam the rest of the Canal over five days. She was accompanied by her manager, a female attendant, and a motion-picture photographer who followed her in a boat. She used the breast and trudgeon strokes to power through the often stagnant, smelly water in the canal. The local newspaper mistakenly identified her as a professional, but kindly noted that "she was always genial and talking to different members of the party. This trait is unusual in the average professional, who is, as a rule, constantly making complaints."[15]

The water became cleaner as she progressed, but the Panamanian sun burnt her so badly she had to spend two days recuperating during the swim. But finally she completed the journey with a final push, during which she was stung by jellyfish. A crowd gathered for the finish, and she had enough remaining energy to give them a demonstration of the swimming strokes she had used. Elaine said later that after the swim, her manager told her that she had been followed by sharks the entire time, but given the presence of the locks, this seems unlikely.[16]

That Elaine had the resources and the wherewithal to get herself to Panama for this feat is a testament to how swimming was changing women, how women were changing swimming, and how women were using swimming to change the world and the ways they traveled through it.

Just like New York City, Boston had a big swimming scene, and two stars that came out of it were Rose Pitonof and Elsie Ackroyd. Rose was another childhood prodigy when it came to swimming, a natural swimmer who astounded adults with her swimming precocity and her bravery. In 1909, at age 11, Rose swam across Hull Gut, between the town of Hull and Peddocks Island, and back. It only took 17 minutes, but it required swimming through two strong currents, and she was the first person to swim it roundtrip. The *Boston Globe* trumpeted the event with the headline, "Girl Succeeds Where Men Experts Failed."[17] Rose differed from most other famous female swimmers in that she used the breast stroke, almost exclusively. In 1910, she swam from Charlestown to the Boston Light, covering a distance of ten miles in six hours and 50 minutes, consuming only a small glass of eggnog along the way. She was the first female and only the second person to accomplish the swim, although Annette Kellerman had tried it earlier and failed. The swim received lengthy and enthusiastic coverage in the papers; Rose was on her way to becoming a beloved Boston heroine. She was often described as stocky, laughing, and plucky.

When asked if she was proud of her swim, Rose said, "Of course I am proud. What girl wouldn't be to have done something that no one has ever been able to do before?" The 15-year-old wasn't shying away from further feats, either. "I am glad to have finished the swim, and I'll be ready to try any

Rose Pitonof of Boston in 1910 (Library of Congress Prints and Photographs Division).

other stunt they want to give me any time. I shall certainly try to uphold my claim as the champion girl swimmer."[18]

Elsie Ackroyd was one of Rose's local competitors. Elsie had a motto, "Do or Die!" that she shouted out at the beginning of each swim. "My motto is, do or die. I always say that before I start a swim, and I have never failed yet to win a race or make my hard swim when I said my motto at the start."

In 1910, Elsie swam from Revere Beach to Nahant and back. "It was a long way back, and I was pretty tired, but I'm all right now. It was nothing but fun swimming over, but coming back the water was rough. I got three or four waves in my mouth once, and could hardly get my breath, and the power boats running around got in my way."[19]

In 1910, Rose came to New York City, looking for competitors. She attempted to swim from Manhattan to Coney Island, but failed after five hours. In 1911, she succeeded, becoming the first female to finish the swim from East 26th Street, Manhattan, to Coney Island, covering the 17 miles in eight hours and seven minutes.[20] She was accompanied by a boat carrying her male trainers, pace swimmers, and family members. They were guided by Col. William J. Curran of the Volunteer Life Saving Corps, who had volunteered his intimate knowledge of the Manhattan shoreline for the Bostonian's benefit. Curran led the flotilla in a rowboat, and reportedly rowed the entire 17 miles himself. The water was so rough as Rose left Manhattan that Curran was forced to lead her beneath piers for the first two hours as they traversed the eastern side of Manhattan to the Battery, before cutting across New York Harbor towards Brooklyn and Coney Island. For a while, the tides were so strong that she appeared to be making no progress whatsoever. Despite being a non–New Yorker, her swim was an enormous event. Some 50,000 people waited at Coney Island to see the end of the swim, so many that the attendants at Steeplechase Pier were almost unable to control the crowds swarming in to get a glimpse of the last stretch. As she passed the beaches along Brooklyn's shoreline, swimmers and small boats began to follow her, creating a water-borne parade that trailed along behind her. For the last several hundred yards, Rose was almost solidly surrounded in the water by small watercraft and bathers desperate for a close look at her. Once ashore, the crowds surrounded her so quickly and densely that it required a phalanx of men to push through so that she could finally get to a dressing room and eat some food.

The crowds didn't bother Rose too much. She was a consummate professional, quite literally. Besides swimming in races and endurance feats, she worked as a vaudeville performer. She demonstrated various high dives, her famous breast stroke, and other floating and rolling aquatic tricks, usually as part of a larger slate of performers.[21]

In July of 1912, Rose, then 17, traveled to England to make an attempt on the ultimate swimming challenge, the English Channel. While waiting for a combination of favorable tides and good weather, she broke a record for distance swims in the Thames River. Although she took five-and six-mile training swims into the Channel, she never set off on a full-blown attempt. Twice she was convinced that conditions were ideal for the swim, but last minute weather changes dashed her chances. Still, she returned to Boston feeling like she had a chance to make the swim. "But even if I was prevented from having a try at the Channel, I learned enough to feel satisfied that I can make it," she said on her return.[22]

Prominent female swimmers like Elaine Golding and Rose Pitonof were so popular that their matches were treated with equal interest and respect by the public and the newspapers, and some writers frankly stated that women were as good as men, if not better, in this particular sport. These women were accepted as life-savers, swimming teachers, and athletes. In 1908, one newspaper wrote, "The mermaid of today is the champion woman swimmer, and so completely has she mastered natation that nowadays she is as good a swim-

Start of the women's 100-yard race at a Coney Island water carnival, sometime between 1910 and 1915. Note the cloak carriers behind the female swimmers (Library of Congress Prints and Photographs Division).

mer as her brother. For instance, Miss Annette Kellerman, while she cannot swim as fast as Charles M. Daniels in a sprint race, could undoubtedly take the measure of that redoubtable champion in an endurance race. And there are a host of others who are in the same class with the wonderful Australian mermaid."[23]

10. The National Women's Life Saving League

Commodore Longfellow and the Life Saving Corps had done such an excellent job of recruiting New York City's women and girls to swimming that a new organization was formed to accommodate their unique needs. In 1911, some of the active swimmers and teachers from the Corps, including Adeline Trapp, Clara Hurst, Florence West, and Priscilla Higgins, formed their own organization, the National Women's Life Saving League. The League offered free swimming classes for women and children at the municipal baths and provided instruction and demonstrations in the methods of water rescue and first aid. Girls and women learned how to swim, how to survive if capsized in the water, how to rescue others, and methods of resuscitating drowning victims.

Katherine Mehrtens, the League's president, was interviewed in 1912 about the League, its goals, and the benefits of swimming for girls and women. She appealed to women's vanity in extolling the benefits of swimming, saying, "Teach a girl to swim and you place her in position to gain for herself a perfect body, and a perfect body is the natural abiding place of a healthy mind. It makes a girl hold her head high, place her feet firmly on the ground — and it gives her a wonderful complexion."[1]

Katherine's promotion of swimming was necessary as the League attempted to raise money to acquire its own facility.

> Until we reach that happy point in our onward march where we are provided with a home, a great big building where we can have bowling alleys, swimming tanks, drill room, and all gymnasium equipments beneficial to women, including a dance hall, we are utilizing the public swimming tanks in East Twenty-Third street and West Sixtieth Street, Manhattan, and one in Brooklyn. In two years we have grown from a mere handful to 450 rousing candidates for swimming honors. It's the greatest sport in the world. For 1$ any girl can be initiated into the league. Thereafter dues are fifty cents a year. We have established this minimum rate in order that members may feel absolutely independent. It costs eighty cents to buy

Members of the National Women's Life Saving League at a race in August of 1915. Claire Galligan is fifth from the right. Note the many different bathing suit styles (Library of Congress Prints and Photographs Division).

one of the regulation league tank suits and accessories can be made by members according to their own ideas. Instruction is free, the teachers being expert swimmers who volunteer for the work. Besides swimming classes we have informal social affairs, an annual dance, and "middle drills."[2]

By 1913, the organization had one thousand members. League president Katherine Mehrtens spoke at the annual meeting of the American Association for Promoting Hygiene and Public Baths, and described the League's efforts towards making swimming a part of all elementary education. She also made special notice of the fact that swimming was of great value to women who are employed during the day. "It is especially advantageous to those who have long hours in the office, or at the desk or counter, and is a beneficial recreation."[3]

Chief among their goals was "to encourage and advocate simplicity and rationalism in swimming and bathing costumes." When asked about the ideal swimming costume, Katherine Mehrtens replied, "The most practical one, of course. Our girls wear plain one piece suits that cling close to their body. Over this is a loose slip or outer dress of albatross, brilliantine, or whatever they may choose, as long as it is light and does not retain water. A cap and stockings complete the outfit for beach wear. At the tanks we wear simply a one piece suit. With the extra slip it makes a modest and comfortable suit,

Women wait for the starting gun at a National Women's Life Saving League meet at Sheepshead Bay, New York, July 16, 1914 (Library of Congress Prints and Photographs Division).

proper for the beach and easy for the swimmer. Those old bloomer costumes are all wrong. Some of them held as much as thirty pounds of water. Think of a woman carrying all that added weight and trying to swim."

Katherine also distinguished between the practical swimming suits advocated by the League and fashionable suits that were not designed for swimming. She even warned of the personality characteristics of the non-swimming women who engaged in "the silk stocking swimming, the kind who won't go near the water for fear it will spot your bathing suits. They sit under parasols and simper. They are what you might call the bluffs along the beach, of which wise men beware. Only foolish hearts are wrecked upon their siren charms. A real man goes in for a real girl — the girl that goes into the water without fear of getting her nose sunburned and the marcel wave out of her hair."

As an added incentive, she implied that a woman who could swim was more attractive to men, and mentioned that Clara Hurst had even met her husband, Arthur Bouton, while rescuing one of his friends from drowning.

The League also held water carnivals and an annual local championship. The 1912 meet, at Sheepshead Bay, included six events: the 50-yard swim for novices, the 100-yard swim, the canoe tip-over contest, the 25-yard rescue race, a 200-yard relay and a fancy-diving contest. Adeline Trapp was among the winners of the latter."[4]

Charlotte Epstein was one of the most active members of the League. She had joined in 1911, at age 28, and while she was an adequate swimmer, her true strength was an innate and brilliant ability to navigate, manage, and lead within the complicated bureaucratic structure of amateur athletics. She almost immediately began to take a leadership role in the organization. In 1912, she became a member of the important Athletic Committee, which monitored and organized all athletic competition, and the following year served as its chair.

Because there was no governing body for women's swimming, competitive events were limited to those between branches of the same organization and those between different organizations that were arranged one by one. There was no opportunity for true championships. Eventually, the membership began asking for some form of governorship that would allow for participation in national championships, and the first step towards this goal was the establishment of an athletic committee for the League.

The Athletic Committee of the National Women's Life Saving League was created in an attempt to elevate the League and its competitions to a status as close to pure amateur as possible and to "supervise athletics for women by women, in order to raise the dignity of outdoor sports for the sex, so that all may participate in the healthful exercise of competitive pastimes without being subjected to the embarrassing conditions which frequently arise when men only are in charge of arrangements."[5] Even though the AAU had no authority over the League, the goal was to model themselves as closely as possible on the standards created by the Union in the event that the AAU decided to change its stance by deciding to accept female athletics. Because the League members recruited members from all classes, from swimmers at private clubs to the public baths, it seemed to be attracting an undesirable element. The Athletic Committee was established to create and enforce rules that would keep the undesirables out of competition by creating the same clear division between professionals and amateurs practiced by men's amateur organizations.

11. Looking Towards the Olympic Games

The Athletic Committee of the National Women's Life Saving League may have had another goal in mind, that of situating the League so that its members would be ready to compete in the Olympics, should the opportunity arise. As of yet, American women had not had the opportunity to compete in an Olympiad. Opposition to women's participation in the Olympics came from two separate sources. The first was Pierre de Coubertin, the father and ceremonial head of the modern international Olympic movement, who was steadfastly opposed to the idea of women participating in the Olympic Games. The second source of opposition came from within the United States and was centered in the Amateur Athletic Union and the American Olympic Committee.

Coubertin had revived ancient Greece's Olympic Games in the 1890s, and the modern debut took place in Athens, Greece, in 1896. The Games were exclusively for men. Coubertin was wildly opposed to the idea of women competing in his Games. For one thing, no women had participated in the ancient Olympics, and he did not want his revival to be tarnished by the presence of unauthentic participants. He saw female participation not only as an affront to principles of historical reenactment, but also a violation of the laws of nature. He believed that no one wanted to witness the horrific expressions on the faces of female athletes as they physically strained themselves, and once declared that women's tobogganing was "the most unaesthetic sight human eyes could contemplate." Even in the 1930s, he was still tirelessly insisting that women had no place at the Olympics beyond that of crowning the brows of the male victors with laurels.[1]

Despite Coubertin's official stance, women were gradually able to appear at the Games, mainly as a result of the complicated and decentralized way that the Games were organized. Because the local organizing committees of the host cities had more control over the events and participants than Coubertin's International Olympic Committee (IOC), a very small number of women's events were staged at the early Olympic Games. Separately, each country's Olympic Committee determined which athletes it would send to compete in the events.

Women first appeared at the games in demonstrations or exhibitions. A few women competed in 1900 in lawn tennis and golf. At the 1904 St. Louis games, women competed in lawn tennis and participated in the unofficial demonstration category of archery. The 1908 Games in London were attended by 2,022 competitors from 21 countries, of which 44 were women who competed in archery, figure skating, motorboating, lawn tennis, and yachting, but none of these competitors were from the United States. Two women, Valborg Florström of Finland and Ebba Gisico of Sweden, gave an exhibition in diving that year, the first time that women appeared at the Olympics in an aquatic event.[2]

The 1912 Games were held in Stockholm, Sweden, and this time, out of 2,416 athletes from 27 nations, 53 were women. Coubertin was still opposed to women being present, and the July 1912 issue of *Revue Olympique*, the IOC's journal, reflected his indignation on the matter. He felt strongly that "the Olympic Games must be reserved for men." He was disturbed that women were admitted to some events, but not all events; how did one draw the line between the events that were acceptable for women or not? To be on the safe side, he argued, it was better to exclude them entirely. "In the future, perhaps, will there be women runners or even women football players? Would such sports, played by women, constitute a sight to be recommended before the crowds that gather for an Olympiad? I do not think that any such claim can be made." He did not want women's games to occur alongside those of men: "What is the appeal of that? Organizers are already overworked, deadlines are already too short, the problems posed by housing and ranking are already formidable, costs are already excessive, and all that would have to be doubled! Who would want to take all that on?"

Furthermore, Coubertin stated, "In our view, this feminine semi-Olympiad is impractical, uninteresting, ungainly, and, I do not hesitate to add, improper. It is not in keeping with my concept of the Olympic Games, in which I believe that we have tried, and must continue to try, to put the following expression into practice: the solemn and period exaltation of male athleticism, based on internationalism, by means of fairness, in an artistic setting, with the applause of women as a reward."

Women's swimming was a competitive event at the Olympic Games for the first time in 1912. There were 27 swimmers and 14 divers, representing eight countries. Under the influence of the Amateur Athletic Union, the United States Olympic Committee refused to even consider sending women

The British women's Olympic swim team of 1912, wearing surprisingly revealing bathing suits for the day. They are, in no certain order, Isabella Moore, Jennie Fletcher, Annie Speirs, and Irene Steer (Library of Congress Prints and Photographs Division).

in 1912, but even the countries that allowed their female athletes to participate did not always do so wholeheartedly.

Australia initially did not want to spend money sending its two top female swimmers, Sarah "Fanny" Durack and Wilhelmina Wylie, and when it finally gave permission for them to go, it was under the condition that they raise the money for the trip themselves. It was well worth it for Fanny and Wilhelmina to make the trip from Australia, because they won the 100-meter freestyle gold and silver, respectively. Because there were only two of them, they weren't able to compete in the relay. The relay was won by the British team, a formidable quartet of women who appeared in racing suits that were short, closely cut to their bodies, and, considering the times, quite revealing.[3]

In the United States, decisions about women's participation in the Olympics were made by the American Olympic Committee, which was more or less controlled by the Amateur Athletic Union, an organization that was entirely controlled by one man, James E. Sullivan. Sullivan did not care that other countries were sending women to the Olympic Games and refused to be swayed by international trends. For Sullivan to poke a finger in the eye of international opinion was nothing new. He was the most powerful man in American athletics, and possessed an unwavering confidence in the absolute correctness of his own actions.

Sullivan was a self-made man with an astonishing ability to establish and maintain personal influence over events, organizations, and people. Born in New York City in 1862 to Irish immigrant parents, he began working in publishing at age 16 when he was hired by the Frank Leslie Publishing Company. He went on to write for the *Athletic News*, the *New York City Sporting News*, and the *Morning Journal*. After years as a sportswriter and editor, at age 30 he became the president of the American Sports Publishing Company, the publishing subsidiary of the A. G. Spalding & Brothers Company. Sullivan was a serious competitive boxer and runner from a young age. He was a member of the Pastime Athletic Club, became active in the organization, and eventually became its president and served as Pastime's delegate to the early National Association of Amateur Athletes, the predecessor organization to the AAU.

Sullivan's employer, the Spalding Company, was not opposed to the idea of women participating in athletics at all. By 1895, they offered a complete line of women's athletic supplies, including bicycles, clothing, golf gear, and fencing gear. In recognition of this large and growing market of female athletes, they opened a temporary headquarters just for women, staffed by women, providing private and personal service to the discriminating and stylish athlete. But Sullivan would use his position at the company as a means to prevent women from entering the world of amateur athletics.

Sullivan's rise through the bureaucracy of New York's athletic world occurred at the same time that the AAU became the controlling body of American amateur athletics. After the AAU declared that any athlete who competed in non–AAU sanctioned events would be banned from all future AAU events, most clubs became allied with the AAU. They did the same with collegiate athletes. The AAU, from its start in New York City, developed into a multi-level organization that set its sights on controlling all athletics throughout the country. The regional AAU organizations throughout the country answered to the national AAU governing body. By 1890, the AAU had 30,000 athletes supposedly under their control, but few of them were paying dues. That same year, Sullivan became secretary-treasurer of the AAU, and his borderline obsession with rules became the ultimate impetus to the growth of the AAU. He believed in creating rules, following rules, and punishing those who broke the rules, and he singlehandedly dominated the world of amateur sports.

Sullivan's love of organization and rules was apparent in all of his work and, at times, seems almost manic. In 1909, he wrote a book called *Schoolyard Athletics: Giving Directions for Conducting Organized Athletic Activities in the Schoolyard*, in which he first advised, "Give the boy an example of just what he is to do; then let him play his own game. That is athletics for the schoolboy." He didn't take his own free-wheeling advice, though; quite the opposite: in the very same book he created a labyrinth of rules for boy's athletic events that required a games committee, a director, a referee, a starter, a clerk of the course, inspectors, field judges, judges at the finish, timers, a chief scorer, a marshal, marshal's assistants, an official announcer, and an official reporter.[4]

His rules for the potato race provide an idea of how he left absolutely nothing to chance. "Potato racing is one of the hardest forms of exercises, because it is a steady strain, and under no circumstances should boys be permitted to go in a long potato race. The potatoes should not be more than two feet apart, and there should not be more than four of them. Of course it is out of the question to use potatoes in a race of this kind, therefore small blocks of wood, painted white, about the size of a potato, should be substituted."

Sullivan was obsessed with the registration of athletes. All athletes had to be registered with a club, and all clubs had to be registered with the AAU. All athletes were subject to the rules of the AAU, and could be called before the registration committee of the AAU to answer any charges. Of crucial importance was the issue of pure amateurism, which stipulated that athletes never receive money for competing in an event, nor could they compete against a professional athlete who had ever accepted money for competition. Those that were suspected of doing so were grilled by the registration committee, and those that did not provide satisfactory answers were banned forever from amateur athletics.

In his 1907 annual President's address to the AAU, Sullivan articulated his beliefs about the power of registration and athletic control. "Registration, gentlemen, is the backbone of this organization. It is centralization, it means control. It gives to us what we certainly should have, absolute control over the individual athlete who competes under our protection."[5] He backed it up with numbers, saying that when he became Secretary-Treasurer in 1889, the AAU was bankrupt. By 1907, they had $8,508.59 in the bank, and Sullivan said it was all due to his fierce policing of the ranks and enforcement of registration rules. "As we are situated to-day a great deal of responsibility for the successful carrying on of pure, wholesome, amateur sport rests with our Registration Committees as elected throughout the different districts, and I must impress upon them the importance of being impartial, fearless, and prompt.... When we make laws, they must be lived up to, and the committee, club, or association that does not recognize the AAU had better be careful in the future."[6]

The AAU claimed that this registration of athletes and the policing of the roles was the impetus for almost all positive developments in American society over the last 50 years. In 1910, Everett C. Brown, the president of the Amateur Athletic Union, stated,

> Twenty-five years ago athletics were in chaos. There was no organization worth calling an organization. The small boy and up to the young man then spent most of their time on the street corners, or in the alleys with the big saloon in the immediate vicinity as the headquarters. Boys were taught to become criminals without even knowing that they were assimilating the education which finally graduated them into the penitentiary. At that time a public-spirited body of gentlemen in New York City organized the Amateur Athletic Union of the United States for systematizing control and activities. From this small beginning there has developed not only the Amateur Athletic Union, but the collegiate church athletic leagues, playground organizations, and, in fact, many systematic bodies have been the outgrowth of the primary organization of the Amateur Athletic Union, and now, even on the east side of New York, Bridgeport, and foreign districts on the northwest side of Chicago, the boys, young men, and women in those localities, are patronizing the playgrounds and athletic fields, or playing baseball and training for track and field work daily, bringing the United States into recognition at the present time as a nation of athletes and a leader in athletes among all nations, being conceded the peer of England in all branches of sport.[7]

Sullivan and the AAU also played a very important role in the growing popularity of the Olympic Games in the United States. Although the Olympic Games had been revived by Pierre de Coubertin, Sullivan didn't see any reason why he shouldn't control those as well, and the relationship between Sullivan and Coubertin was a tense one. Coubertin had visited the United States in 1893 to ask for the support of the Amateur Athletic Union for the Games, and met with Sullivan. The two did not take to each other, but Sullivan accepted the invitation to be involved in the Olympic movement, and the American Olympic Committee was formed, essentially by taking the same individuals who were the main players of the AAU and giving them a new title and a new international charge. The men whose organization had almost full control of American amateur sport were more than happy to extend their influence even further. Still, they played almost no role in the 1896 Olympic Games, and athletes from Princeton and the Boston Athletic Club applied directly to the International Olympic Committee rather than through the American Olympic Committee.[8]

American participation in the 1900 Paris games was barely more organized. Universities and athletic clubs again sent teams and individual star athletes, and although the AAU made sure that all athletes were in good standing, there was hardly any centralized control at the national level of who participated. Still, the Americans did everything possible to make sure the French organizers were aware of their presence, beginning with demanding that the opening day of the Games, a Sunday, be changed to Monday, claiming that pious American athletes were offended at being expected to compete on a Sunday.

When it was decided that the 1904 Olympics would take place in the United States, the IOC, headed by Coubertin, and various American interests immediately began battling over the location and other arrangements. In an astonishing display, Sullivan singlehandedly decided that the next Olympic Games would be held in Buffalo, in 1901. The International Committee insisted that the Games stay on their four-year cycle, so while Sullivan did hold a competition in Buffalo, he refrained from calling it the Olympics. The IOC awarded the 1904 Games to Chicago. Unfortunately for Chicago and the IOC, St. Louis was already planning a world's fair for 1904, the Louisiana Purchase Exposition, and Sullivan and the AAU wanted to hold the first American Olympics in conjunction with the fair. Sullivan got his way, and in early 1903 the Games were revoked from Chicago and given to St. Louis.[9]

Coubertin eventually was forced to accept that nothing in American sports happened without Sullivan's approval, and he formally asked the AAU to be responsible for organizing the 1904 events. Then, fed up with the Americans, he had almost nothing further to do with the 1904 Games. Coubertin was so exasperated that he did not even attend.

Sullivan was appointed Director of Physical Culture for the fair, and as such, assumed control of the 1904 Games. He seemed to view them more as an AAU championship between American athletic clubs than as an international gathering of athletes, and athletes were identified by athletic club or hometown rather than by nation. Over the last one hundred years, the 1904 Games have been labeled a failure, and one bizarre event is emblematic of how far the Sullivan's Olympics strayed from Coubertin's glorious ideal. Like many world's fairs of the last century, the St. Louis world's fair featured exhibits of indigenous people from around the world. Sullivan decided to feature an athletic competition of the ethnic people.

Quotes from Sullivan's report of this event reveal his antagonistic attitude. Men from various American and Canadian Indian tribes, "pigmies" from Africa, Patagonians, Ainu from Japan, and Syrians from "Beyrout" were pitted against one another over two days in sprints, the shot put, the javelin throw, a one-mile race, archery, tug-of-war, and more. Sullivan, who referred to the men as "savages" in his report of the Games, was sorely disappointed with the outcome. Despite the fact that most of the men had never before seen or heard of the sports that they were asked to play, Sullivan concluded that "the whole meeting proves conclusively that the savage has been a very much overrated man from an athletic point of view."[10]

He had praise for almost none of the competitors, other than an Igorotte from the Phillipines who gave the "most marvelous performances at pole climbing ever witnessed in this country" and the Ainu who were "without doubt the most polite savages the writer has ever met, extremely so." Otherwise, in "the one hundred yards run the savages proved, of course, that they knew nothing whatever about sprint racing," that "the exhibition of archery shooting by the savage tribes was very disappointing," and that "it can probably be said, without fear of contradiction, that never before in the history of sport in the world were such poor performances recorded for weight throwing."[11]

Sullivan concluded with a directive to all researchers. "Lecturers and authors will in the future please omit all reference to the natural athletic ability of the savage, unless they can substantiate their alleged feat."[12]

Sullivan's obsession with rules led to the exclusion of many athletes from the amateur ranks. In 1912, Sullivan was responsible for the exclusion of one athlete in particular, and the story illustrates both how rigidly he expected his rules to be followed and the kind of power he exerted. The athlete he banished from the amateur ranks was Jim Thorpe, one of the greatest athletes in American history, known for being versatile, strong, and fast. A Sac and Fox Indian from Oklahoma, Thorpe became a football star while attending the Carlisle Indian School of Pennsylvania. His prowess drew national attention when he and his team, coached by the famous Glen Scobey "Pop" Warner, began trouncing Ivy League colleges. In 1912, Thorpe qualified for the Olympics, and brought home gold medals in both the pentathlon and the decathlon. After returning to the United States, he resumed his football career at Carlisle. In 1913, a newspaper reported that Thorpe had played baseball professionally in the summers of 1909 and 1910.

Thorpe's coaches at Carlisle immediately wrote to Sullivan, claiming ignorance of Thorpe's professional activities. Sullivan made the decision to strip Thorpe of his amateur status, and went on to convince the International Olympic Committee to do the same retroactively and thereby revoke his Olympic medals. Sullivan was so obsessed with the need to have his rules followed that he insisted that medals won by an American team member in an international contest should be revoked. Curiously, according to the 1912 Olympic rulebook, challenges to an athlete's amateur status had to be filed within 30 days. In Thorpe's case, Sullivan's challenge was made much later than 30 days. Sullivan insisted that the IOC break their own rules so that he could establish his own rules as inviolate.[13]

12. Sullivan's Last Stand

By 1914, the AAU was feeling the pressure to include women in athletics, but Sullivan was determined to prevent this, and pushed back hard at any group that dared to test his rules on the matter. Curiously, women and men had raced at the same events during the period that Ethel Golding was racing, prior to about 1900. Women's races were held at the same events as men's races, although races between men and women were unusual, with the exception of some of the long-distance exhibition races. But by the time Sullivan gained power, women's races and men's races could not occur at the same event.

When the National Women's Life Saving League and the Public Schools Athletics League dared to hold girls' and boys' races in the same pool on the same day, they received this astonishing letter from Sullivan.

> Dear Sir: I notice in the papers of this morning that you are conducting school-boy races in connection with women's events. I understand your excuse is and you are hiding behind the fact that these are schoolboys. Of course you know the Amateur Athletic Union of the United States does not permit women or girls to be registered in any of its associations, and does not sanction open races for women in connection with AAU events. You have gone a bit further and you have done what you should not have done as a member of the AAU. You have given schoolboy races with open races for women in the same tank on the same day — absolutely something that should not have been done. The Board of Education and the Public Schools Athletic League are very pronounced in relation to open competition for girls in athletics. They have no desire to make the girls public characters. If you desire to keep your membership in the AAU, you had better play the amateur game straight and true day in and day out. I can assure you any of the boys that represent the P.S.A.L. in any mixed meeting you have announced for the future will be prohibited thereafter from taking part in scholastic events by the P.S.A.L.[1]

Sullivan's objections to women entering the world of sports were well known. Ida Schnall, a diver, stage performer, and captain of the New York Female Giants, a women's professional baseball team, criticized him and his antiquated ideas in a letter to the *New York Times*, writing, "This is not from a suffragette standpoint, but a feeling which I had for a long time wished to express. I read in the newspapers wherein James E. Sullivan is again objecting to girls competing with the boys in a swimming contest. He is always objecting, and never doing anything to help the cause along for a girls' AAU. He has objected to my competing in diving at the Olympic Games in Sweden, because I am a girl. He objects to a mild game of ball or any kind of athletics for girls. He objects to girls wearing a comfortable bathing suit. He objects to so many things that it gives me cause to think he must be very narrow minded and that we are in the last century. It's the athletic girl that takes the front seat to-day, and nobody can deny it."[2]

Ida's letter must have both enraged Sullivan and left him feeling vindicated. Ida was a professional athlete, the exact kind of individual he wanted to keep banned from his amateur world. She was an excellent diver who performed in theatre (including the "harem scene" of one stage show) yet also appeared at Life Saving Corps events and carnivals.

In January of 1914, Sullivan reinforced the men-only rule by having the national members of the AAU vote on this resolution: "Resolved: That the AAU does not and will not recognize the registration of women athletes and it is the sense of the Committee that the rules were designedly formed to include none but the male sex."[3] Only one member voted against the resolution. This not only reinforced the barring of women from competing at AAU events, but went even further by banning them from giving exhibitions or holding their own races during AAU events. Previously popular water carnivals that featured races for men and women would no longer be sanctioned by the AAU. Women's swimming clubs began to talk amongst themselves of forming an organization of their own that would organize, promote, and monitor competition for women.

The American Olympic Committee held a straw vote in the spring of 1914 to see how its members felt about women participating in the Games. There was a general agreement that women should not appear in anything other than gymnastic exhibitions. In the words of the *New York Times*, "The Committee was opposed to women taking part in any event in which they would not wear long skirts."[4]

But the majority of the world looked favorably on women swimmers. In June, Sullivan and ten members of the American Olympic Committee traveled to Paris to attend the International Olympic Congress, held for the purposes of planning the 1916 Berlin games. The growing international acceptance of women at the Games was apparent. When Germany proposed that women be formally eligible to compete, 28 countries voted in favor of it. The United States voted against it, with only Turkey, Japan, and France in agreement. Sullivan, speaking for the American delegation, announced that he had been sent to Paris with a mandate to vote against the participation of women.[5]

The delegates also considered how to weight the medals earned by women in the total points tables that ranked each country's overall standing. The British proposed that women's points be included in the tables, and the proposal was adopted. The impending inclusion of women's medals in the points table may have led to many countries finally admitting their female athletes to the Games. If a country's overall standing was impacted by the fact that other countries could count the points earned by its female winners, countries like the United States would eventually have to allow women to attend, or find themselves sinking lower and lower on the points table.

Several days later, when the Olympic Congress voted on which events would be held for women, the United States voted against the inclusion of women's swimming. Italy and France were also opposed to swimming for women, but all the other countries were in favor of it.[6] In the long run, it wouldn't matter, because the 1916 Games were canceled due to the growing threat of war in Europe. For the National Women's Life Saving League, there would be no opportunity to compete in a 1916 Olympics.

Sullivan returned from Paris just in time to put a stop to a swimming meet in Indianapolis, where he had heard that women would be competing in an event organized by a local club. He sent a telegram to the club, reminding them of the AAU rule that prevented women from competing in the same pool or in the same events as men.[7] The Rye Beach Club of New York, a full member of the AAU, held an AAU–sanctioned race and dared to include an exhibition 50-yard swim for women as part of the day's events. The event caused such an uproar at the AAU that they considered barring the Rye club from holding any future AAU events. There was even talk of stripping the club of its AAU membership entirely. Sullivan tauntingly told the press, "If those desiring to have swimming races for females in connection with a sanctioned AAU swimming meeting will come to the annual meeting of the AAU next November and have the rules changed to allow the girls in, all well and good. But so long as the rules are on our AAU books I will insist that they be lived up to."[8]

He certainly would have, if he hadn't died unexpectedly in September of 1914. His funeral was attended by many high-ranking figures of sport and government, and block after block leading to the church was lined with schoolboy athletes clutching the medals they had earned through Sullivan's athletic programs. Sullivan's death was a loss to many, but it changed the course of women's athletics for the good. He himself was an athletic and bureaucratic marvel, but he had made blocking the recognition of women's abilities and desires to compete a personal goal. It is difficult to understand why. As a sportsman himself who followed athletics, living in a city where some of the world's most talented swimmers lived, he was surely aware that women were breaking barriers with or without his stamp of approval.

Sullivan had been absolutely and vehemently opposed to women's competition, both in American amateur athletics and internationally. The Spalding Company published a version of the minutes of the Olympic meetings in Paris, edited by Sullivan before his death, and they gave very little detail on the votes that Sullivan had lost at the meeting. But despite Sullivan's insistence that he had gone to Paris with a mandate to vote against women's participation in the Games, Everett C. Brown, another member of the American delegation, had a different perspective on the issue, and he said that the United States' vote was based entirely on the personal beliefs of Sullivan. Brown said, "I was one of the delegates attending the International Amateur Athletic Federation and [Olympic] Congress and this was discussed at both conventions, and with the exception of France and the United States, every member of the seventeen countries voted for the competition of women. I think the reason the United States voted against the proposition was due to the personal feeling of our late lamented secretary.... I might say, in all the discussion at these meetings, there was never a hint from any of the foreign delegates of any immodesty or immorality and that in the countries where it was practiced there was absolutely the highest regard for women. I personally saw the competitions at Stockholm and if there was any criticism there, it must have been brought about by the foul minds."[9]

In November of 1914, the AAU voted to sanction the registration of women swimmers in the AAU. Sullivan's reign was over.

13. Women Enter the World of Amateur Athletics

In January 1915, girls and women participated for the first time in an AAU–sanctioned event, the Sportsmen's Show at Madison Square Garden. The extravaganza featured races and exhibitions of every sport imaginable, including swimming races and diving contests for women. There was a daily exhibition by the British diver Mae Eccleston, who dove from 70 feet and enhanced the tension and excitement of her performances by feigning fright in the moments before her dives. There was a fancy diving contest, with the trophy presented by none other than Annette Kellerman, now an established film star, and a 140-yard swim for women that was entered by many of the local swimmers. The National Women's Life Saving League competed against the Mermaid Swimming Club of Bath Beach in water polo. Alfred G. Brown, the Panama Canal swimmer and head of a lifesaving crew from Brooklyn, was arrested outside the event for entering his four-year-old daughter, Ethel, in the fancy-diving exhibition. Someone had reported him for breaking the law that disallowed performances by children.[1]

In February 1915, the Metropolitan AAU appointed Katherine Mehrtens to be the official handicapper of the girl swimmers registering with the AAU. Mehrtens and her husband, Colonel George A. Thormann, were influential members of the Board of Directors of the United States Volunteer Life Saving Corps and the decision wasn't without controversy. Mehrtens was chosen over a dozen applicants, and it came as a surprise to many that a woman with such close ties to many of the swimmers was chosen.[2] She herself had no competitive swimming experience; she was a water-safety advocate, but not someone with extensive experience in competitions, a desirable skill for a handicapper. In addition to serving as handicapper, Mehrtens would serve as commissioner and work with the AAU registration committee to weed out accused professionals from the ranks.

Commodore Charles E. Rainard of the United States Life Saving Society criticized the choice, saying, "Mrs. Mehrtens is a splendid woman and able to serve as the head of the National Women's Life Saving Society, but she is not competent enough to act as a handicapper. She has never been a swimmer and has had very little experience in the game.... I thought that Miss Adeline Trapp would be the choice of the AAU officials. She has done more to foster swimming among women than any other person interested in the pastime. She has been a swimmer for nearly a score of years, and has been one of the best long-distance swimmers in the country. She knows the game from every angle, and is deserving of the honor."[3]

Almost immediately, the purging of alleged professionals from the women's ranks began. The AAU was as severe on this issue as they had been with men, and many female swimmers were serious about keeping professional women out of the amateur ranks, filing their own complaints against other women. A number of women were accused of having performed on vaudeville stages for money. The accusations came about after the chair of the AAU's registration committee, Jacob Stumpf, took the extraordinary step of visiting theatrical booking agencies across town, where he procured the names of all women who had been paid to appear in diving or swimming exhibitions. He then cross-checked the list against that of the female athletes hoping for registration with the AAU.[4]

The resulting witch hunt hurt many excellent female swimmers. Elaine Golding, long considered one of the best female swimmers in the country, was challenged because she had taught swimming for four days, and acted in a motion picture, playing the part of a drowning woman.[5] She readily admitted to accepting pay for the motion picture work but denied that she had been paid for the teaching. The uproar at Elaine's being declared professional and barred from further competition was so great that a month later, Stumpf felt the need to clarify her expelling from the sport — she was not barred because of the motion picture work, but because of the four unpaid days of teaching. Forced to give up competing in the sport she loved, Elaine almost immediately began her new career as a swim teacher in the public schools.

Marion Collins was accused of challenging Mae Eccleston, the British fancy diver who was then performing at Madison Square Garden, to a diving contest. Mae Loughlin, a successful competitor prior to AAU control, didn't even bother to deny the charges of professionalism, frankly defending her need for money by telling Stumpf, "You can't eat cups," referring to the silver trophies given to winners. She was correct; you can't eat trophies, but as a woman with both athletic talent and a very real need for an income, Mae was the exact kind of person that the amateur movement sought to exclude from sports.[6]

Bessie O'Neill was accused of having performed in vaudeville, and caused a scandal when she refused to return the trophies she had won at the Sportsmen's Show before her sordid past was discovered.[7] Three other swimmers were accused of having performed in aquatic entertainment shows on the stage. In the end, seven of the 24 female swimmers at the Sportsmen Show were challenged as professionals. Many of the women made the logical complaint that their allegedly professional activities had occurred before the AAU took control of women's swimming, but the AAU maintained their right to retroactively apply the rules and control the women's right to participate in amateur swimming.[8]

Some of the challenges were made by Charlotte Epstein. Charlotte had made it her business to learn the rules of the AAU, and "showed knowledge of the AAU rules that almost staggered the committee. In fact, it appeared that the committee did not know that some of the rules she quoted were in the book." Charlotte was competent, armed with an intimate knowledge of the rules of the governing bodies, and she knew how and when to best argue in the bureaucratic decision-making process.[9]

The AAU also began to dictate rules about what women were allowed to wear while competing. The Metropolitan AAU declared in February of 1915 that women would be required to wear suits of black material that covered them from neck to toe. Katherine Mehrtens was appointed to be the official modiste, responsible for making sure that women met those swimsuit restrictions.[10] By that summer, Charlotte, representing the National Women's Lifesaving League, and Katherine, representing the AAU, agreed that the decision to wear stockings during a race could be left to the discretion of the swimmers themselves. They specifically noted the way that wet stockings led to tiring of the legs and interfered with free movement. One newspaper dryly reported, "Convinced that the freedom of action of a swimmer's limbs in competition is of paramount importance, members of the National Women's Lifesaving League have frowned upon the suggestion that stockings should be worn by all girls in swimming races."[11]

Although women's swimming was now a nationally accepted sport and new clubs for women were organizing throughout the country, the National Women's Life Saving League (which despite its name was not national, but a New York City entity) continued to be a major player in the sport, with its own bureaucracy. In the summer of 1915, the League's president was Ms. Katherine Mehrtens. Florence West was vice-president, Adeline Trapp was secretary, Sarah L. Marrin was treasurer, Teresa Daily was financial secretary, and Charlotte Epstein was chairman of the athletic committee.[12]

The League held its first big outdoor meet since becoming legitimate in the eyes of the AAU at Long Beach, Long Island, on August 14, 1915. In high waves and before large crowds of resort visitors, two dozen women competed in fancy diving, the land and water steeplechase, a 50-yard swim, a 100-yard swim, a rescue race, and a duck race, which involved chasing and capturing actual ducks. The girls were rowed out to an anchored boat 300 yards from shore to begin their races in water so rough that it capsized the boat containing the starter and his starting pistol. Claire Galligan of New Rochelle emerged as a star swimmer, finishing first in two events and third in another. The *New York Times* noted, "It was an interesting sight to see a frail girl swimmer combating the waves successfully, and it was still more interesting to note that they were not even fatigued by their efforts after reaching shore."[13]

Later that month, the League held its own championship meet, which was determined by the outcome of the 220-yard race. Six women entered the race. Claire Galligan and two others immediate left the other three behind, and the three-person race was a tight one, with Claire winning in a burst of speed with a time of 3:28.[14]

The League's events were also public announcements of their politics, which were decidedly in favor of women acquiring the right to vote. A July 1915 exhibition featured an event in which League members saved a dummy that had been made up to look like an anti-suffragette. Wearing a red sash with the words "Anti-suffrage" displayed, the dummy was rowed out to sea and tossed overboard while the League girls raced to its aid. "Fully clothed and hampered alike by her garments and by her principles, being an old-fashioned woman who does not believe it is ladylike to swim, she would certainly have been lost in the waves but for the gallant women who hurried to her rescue," the *New York Times* noted with good humor.[15]

In early August, the AAU sanctioned the first-ever official championship for women in Philadelphia, which largely came down to a contest between the New York–based League and the Philadelphia Turngemeide, home of Olga Dorfner. Olga was the star swimmer of the Turngemeide, and beat Claire Galligan by a nose and set a new record in the 220-yard race, 3:15 ⅖. An intense rivalry developed between the League and the Philadelphia Turnegemeide, and in December of 1915 Claire Galligan again raced Olga Dorfner for the 220-yard championship. Olga had beaten Claire earlier, but this time Claire won in a time of 3:04 ⅖.[16] Claire held the title for two years before Olga took it back in 1917, having lowered the record time to 2:59 ⅗.

The relationship between the AAU and the female athletes was an uneasy one, and it would remain that way for years. In the fall of 1915, the AAU members passed a resolution to continue the registration of female swimmers, to allow them to submit records, and to allow title events, but they were torn about admitting the women's clubs into the AAU. The Registration Committee of the AAU noted, "A situation has arisen in this Association which should be handled with a great deal of care. We are confronted with the ques-

Start of a National Women's Life Saving Race, August of 1915 (Library of Congress Prints and Photographs Division).

tion [of] whether female swimming clubs should be admitted to membership. There are, at the present time, some female swimmers who have registered. Among other applicants for membership is that of the National Women's Life Saving League. Considerable diversity of opinion exists as to the advisability of admitting such club." The consensus of opinion at the AAU seemed to be that a national association of female swimming clubs should be organized, which would have female officers, would follow AAU rules, and be a member of the National AAU. The AAU feared that if they admitted women's clubs to membership, women would want to compete in mixed events against men, and went so far as to specifically ban any kind of mixed meet. "Legislation should be passed forbidding mixed championships or mixed competitive swimming contests."[17]

Individual female swimmers continued to be allowed to register with the Metropolitan AAU. A debate arose as to which events would be considered for title events. The AAU only wanted a few title events, and not the same number or same length events that the men had. They feared that women's title events would be exploited by unscrupulous swimming promoters, and, conversely, they worried that because women's swimming was so new, that it wasn't sure to be a success. The latter concern was clearly ungrounded, given the past acceptance and enthusiasm for women's races.

As yet, there was no way for swimmers in the northeast to compete in true championships, because the Metropolitan Association of the AAU had not made provisions for it, although swimmers in the Middle Atlantic and Pacific Coast associations were able to. In January 1916, Charlotte Epstein filed a complaint with the AAU, alleging prudery as the reason behind the Metropolitan AAU's refusal to sanction championships. "They hold championship events for women in the Middle Atlantic and Pacific Coast Associations, and I don't see why the A. A. U. officials in the Metropolitan Association refuse to sanction championship events for us. If they can do it in other associations it can be done here. The trouble is that the local officials are against women competing in public like men do. I was told by one of the members of the committee that the committee does not like to see women compete in public, and that they should hold their meets behind locked doors, with only woman spectators present."

Finally the Metropolitan AAU relented, and Fred Rubien, president of the Metropolitan AAU and secretary-treasurer of the National AAU, announced, "In view of the fact that the women have taken such interest in swimming in a competitive form throughout the country, I have decided to recommend that sanction be given to hold national championship races for them."[18] After that, individuals could compete locally for the Metropolitan AAU championships, then for the national events.

In April, Claire Galligan was named the first female national swimming champion by the AAU by winning the 100-yard championship. In May she won the 220-yard championship. With the newly sanctioned national championships came the need for travel, as the national events were distributed throughout the country. In July, Olga Dorfner of Philadelphia and Claire Galligan traveled to San Francisco for the 100-yard national championship, with Olga taking home the prize. With this exposure came national attention, and women who had previously been locally well known were suddenly receiving coverage in newspapers all over the country.

The change was welcomed. In the summer of 1916, the *New York Times* expressed what many sports observers must have been thinking: that women's swimming was an unabashed success, even though the AAU had expected it to be a chaotic failure. Contrary to expectations, the stamp of approval from the AAU had enabled women's swimming to be considered no longer "a curiosity or a sensation, as it once was, but a firmly established and recognized athletic activity, which both contestants and public take seriously. This was conclusively proved by the first set of national A. A. U. championships just concluded. Most of the title events brought out representative fields, keen competition was witnessed, brilliant record performances were chronicled, and popular interest manifested itself in the large and enthusiastic crowds which attended the various title meets in New York, Philadelphia, Los Angeles, and San Francisco. The 100-yard championship, in particular, resulted in one of the most stirring races ever seen in this country."[20]

That summer women were able to take part in five national events: the 440-yard race and the high dive, both held in Chicago, the 2-mile and 880-yard swims, both held in St. Louis, and the mile swim, held in New York.

During the AAU annual meeting of 1916, heated discussions occurred during the sessions regarding women's swimming. Some questioned whether the AAU really was the best place for the female swimmers. Some argued that the women would be better served by registering with and competing under the sanctions of an all-female organization. Jacob Stumpf of the registration committee was particularly interested in dropping the women, arguing that an entirely separate organization would best meet their unique needs. The resolution was voted down after long debate that included the suggestion that the regional associations have the right to bar women. While the national AAU was willing to vote on keeping women in amateur athletics, they were not willing to vote on bathing suit regulations. This issue they were turned over to the regional associations.[21]

It was suggested that the National Women's Life Saving League take over the registration and organization of women's swimming, but Charlotte Epstein and the League believed that they should remain a competitive organization rather than a governing one. For one thing, the women in the organizations that the Life Saving League regularly competed with (and often trounced) would not be happy about coming under the League's control. Instead, she suggested that the AAU retain control for now, but invite enough women to take leadership or governing roles so that eventually there would be enough competent women to head an all-women organization for the governance of women's swimming. Charlotte was worried that the sport would lose momentum if energy had to be put into creating a women's athletic governing body that mirrored the AAU.[22]

By 1917, Claire Galligan was being described as "America's foremost swimmer." She held numerous records for both pool and straightaway courses, from 220-yards to the one-mile.[23] Besides Claire and Olga, other great swimmers emerging during this period were Charlotte Boyle and Ethelda Bleibtrey. Charlotte Boyle earned praise for becoming almost as well known as Claire with only a year of experience.

In October of 1917, Charlotte Epstein and some other competition-minded women founded the New York Women's Swimming Association, an organization that would almost single-handedly bring women's competitive swimming in New York City to international attention. First, though, there was one roadblock. Late that year, the war-gripped country experienced a coal shortage. Citizens and industry were encouraged to reduce use of coal, and schools and businesses were asked to reduce hours. The heating of swimming pools was, of course, not a priority, so many of the girls went without indoor pool training that winter.[24]

14. The New York Women's Swimming Association

What differentiated the Women's Swimming Association of New York from the National Women's Life Saving League was its wholehearted embrace of competition. The Life Saving League served to educate swimmers, advocate for swimming education and support lifesaving efforts, in addition to providing a home club for competitive swimmers. The WSA supported those goals as well, but was formed specifically so that women would have the same opportunities as men to compete in amateur swimming on a national level. It would also open the doors to women competing internationally at the Olympics. The WSA moved away from the lifesaving events, such as buoy-throwing and canoe-tipping, and focused on those events sanctioned by the AAU that would allow women to compete for championships. Competition, however, didn't trump sportsmanship; the WSA's team motto was "Good Sportsmanship is Greater than Victory."

The Association stated that its mission was to

> promote interest in swimming among girls and women and provide for them competent, up-to-date instruction, at rates which will enable all to take advantage. We believe every girl and woman should learn to swim, then practice swimming for health, physical development and recreation. We look upon swimming as an essential item in the education of every member of our sex, because proficiency means self-protection and the ability to save others from drowning.[1]
>
> We favor competitive water sports because they offer interesting and healthful pastime; because they serve as an incentive to practice regularly and keep in tiptop condition; because they engender confidence and self-reliance; because the training involved teaches the value of clean living and encourages abstinence from many things which are inadvisable, if not actually harmful; because under proper guidance, they sponsor sportsmanship and the spirit of fair play, important factors in the molding of character.

The WSA also emphasized the unique health and beauty benefits of swimming that might be of particular interest to women. "It develops every part of the body thoroughly and symmetrically; produces supple, graceful, well-rounded muscles; makes for ease of deportment and movement; activates functional organs; clarifies the blood and clears the complexion; strengthens and benefits the entire system so generally that its constant use ensures buoyant good health and marked improvement in appearance. It is also an effective normalizer. Its natural tendency is to establish standard body proportions by eliminating superfluous flesh in the stout and building muscle and tissue in the unduly lean. Lastly, it will correct many physical defects and it has often proved a complete cure for nervous and other complaints."

From the very beginning, the association was designed by Charlotte Epstein and the other founders to be a powerful and self-sustaining organization. It had a 15-member board of governors that made decisions that were then carried out by a number of committees. There was a pool committee that handled the physical plant and operations of the pool, a membership committee that recruited members, a finance committee, a publication committee that handled the newsletter, and an entertainment committee for taking care of visitors, be they competitors or other guests. Last, but not least, there was a sports committee that arranged training and competitions. There were a few paid employees, but all committee work was done by elected volunteers.

L. de B. Handley, a long-time amateur athlete who had been a member of the gold-medal-winning water polo team at the 1904 Olympic Games, was recruited as a volunteer coach. Handley was a formidable coach who was known for promoting the use of the American crawl stroke. One member recalled of him, "He was a real gentleman of the first order. He'd come to the pool, the hot pool and always had on a suit, shirt, and tie. Of course, he would take his jacket off, but he always had a tie on. He was a real gentleman and a wonderful person. He was very fair — the same with each person. He didn't show any preferences."[2]

The WSA was open to all. For a yearly fee, members were entitled to attend one session at the pool per week. For swimmers interested in coming more than once per week, the annual rate could be increased to allow for additional session attendance. All members were required to sign up ahead of time for a session that matched their swimming ability, during which they received instruction in stroke technique. Once beginners were able to swim the length of the pool, they were allowed to move up to the advanced sessions. If a member was capable enough, after six months she could request to try out for the competitive team. According to Coach L. de B. Handley, the six-month waiting period was enabled officials to "ascertain whether or not she is desirable in every way as a representative of the organization."[3]

Members came to the WSA for different reasons and from different backgrounds. Many were originally involved in the National Women's Life Saving

League and joined the WSA when it was formed. Some were business women looking for healthy activity, and others came looking to build strength. Claire Galligan, already a star, had come to the WSA from the Life Saving League, but left soon after to move to California with her husband. Aileen Riggin joined at age 11. A tiny child of delicate health, she first learned to swim in the warm waters of the Philippines, where her father was stationed. After the family returned to New York, Aileen was recovering from Spanish Influenza, and the family doctor suggested she try swimming to rebuild her strength. Just by chance, she encountered the newly formed Women's Swimming Association. Helen Wainwright, of Flushing, New York, was 12, and she and Aileen became close friends as the team traveled to meets. Helen was also a daredevil, and swam Hell Gate at age 13. Ethelda Bleibtrey had come to the Life Saving League to recover from a curvature of the spine caused by polio, and became one of the WSA's best swimmers. Charlotte Boyle, who was the daughter of Captain Joseph Whiteside Boyle, a legendary Canadian adventurer and mining entrepreneur, had grown up living in Coney Island with her mother, where the close proximity of the ocean encouraged her to become a swimmer. Doris O'Mara of Yonkers, New York, was recruited as a young teenager when someone saw her swimming at a race in Connecticut near her family's summer cottage. Gertrude Ederle, the daughter of German immigrants who owned a butcher shop, joined after seeing some WSA girls perform in an exhibition near her family's beach cottage in Highlands, New Jersey. Many of the other members were working women seeking a place to exercise and socialize at the end of a work day.

The group rented a pool in the basement of an apartment building at 145 West 55th Street. It was equipped with "all modern conveniences, including fine dressing rooms, hot and cold showers, hair dryers, etc., as well as an up-to-date filtering plant. Members would be able to buy swimming gear at the pro shop and rent towels. Special team swim suits with the WSA logo were available."[4]

The WSA published a newsletter, the *W.S.A. News*, which became a primary publication of interest to female swimmers, not just in the New York Area but throughout the United States and even beyond. The *News* published information on WSA events and the records that were regularly being broken, but it also became an informative and educational lifeline to women swimmers everywhere. Columnists often described in great detail new swim strokes, and advice on how to correct or improve technique became a regular feature. For example:

> *Question*: An instructor who teaches the breast stroke tells me she does this because the crawl makes people round-shouldered. Is that a fact?
>
> *Answer*: Common sense should tell you it is not. How can the crawl make one

Charlotte Boyle, left, and Ethelda Bleibtrey, right, of the WSA (Library of Congress Prints and Photographs Division).

round-shouldered when the head is held erect and the body gently arched from the head to feet? In matter of fact, correct crawl swimming is one of the most helpful exercises in straightening round shoulders.

Question: I am naturally inclined to turn the feet outward and I experience great difficulty in keeping the pigeon-toes position advocated for the crawl thrash. Does it make much difference whether the feet are turned in or out?

Answer: Yes, it means the difference between an effective and ineffective leg drive. Unless the feet are twisted slightly inward the effort largely is wasted, as they do not afford adequate propelling power when turned outward. Concentrate for a while on holding the prescribed position and you soon will find it quite easy to retain. It is merely a question of practice.

On a regular basis, the *W.S.A. News* published this announcement, which asked the swimmers for quiet: "Out of consideration for our volunteer teachers, who offer their services so freely in the interest of fellow members and the club, we request that less noise be made during periods of instruction. Often the shouting and the laughing is so loud that the teachers are forced to yell at the tops of their lungs in order to be heard at all. This is totally unnecessary and most unfair to those who devote so much time and trouble to your instruction. It is an exhausting task to teach continuously for three hours, at best, and it should not be made harder for the volunteer workers. Have a little thought for those who are helping you. Keep as quiet as possible."

For annual dues of three dollars per year, the members of the competitive team met a few times per week for swimming under the guidance of Coach Handley. Aileen Riggin recalled, "This was a hot, steamy little pool where we would meet once or twice a week and do laps. There was no diving board, of course. It was a shallow pool. It couldn't have been more than 30-feet long. It was tiny. It was like a sauna, it was so hot and steamy. But that was good because in the wintertime in New York it's cold. That was one thing I liked."[5]

The youngest girls at the WSA pool wore boys' swimsuits, which in those days were one piece and covered the chest. In racing competition, the girls wore silk one-piece suits with a skirt that covered the upper legs. They were required to remain cloaked in a robe until the race began. Aileen said,

> We usually showed ourselves only at the start. We would then take off our robes, go to the starting block, and start, because those suits were rather revealing. We did not like to expose ourselves too much. For diving we wore woolen suits. They were warmer, and we felt more comfortable in them. They also had skirts. Once in a while the skirt would fly out and spoil the line of the dive. The older girls who were in high school wore long bathing suits, also made of wool and very flattering, They gave clear, straight lines, no bulges or bumps, and they were very attractive. The girls looked something like seals when they entered the water with those pretty suits.[6]

There weren't any bathing suits for little girls so we wore boys' bathing suits.

In those days the boys had a one piece suit. They didn't go topless. So we had either cotton or wool suits. And the wool suits were more modest, so we used those. And we all had a little skirt over the front of our suit. The men also had a one-piece suit with a little skirt. And I must say, it looked very neat, very tidy. I am sure we would have looked a lot better if we had the bathing suits that the girls have nowadays. Maybe not cut up too high on the thigh because I think that is a bad line, it's not aesthetic. That's my opinion. But just a more form-fitting suit would have been more attractive. Especially for diving, yes, because the line is important.[7]

The older girls and women were still under some pressure to cover their legs and wear cloaks at all times when out of the water. But the younger girls, age 11 or 12, were not pressured to do so. The suits were designed for modesty, not function.

Modesty was important, as Doris O'Mara explained: "We had photographers, reporters or newspapermen there and we had won a race or a relay race, we had to go get our capes on or get another suit to put over our silk suits. They weren't that revealing, but in that day and age the chaperones thought they were. So that's what we had to do."[8]

Aileen Riggin and the girls who wanted to focus on diving faced a particular problem—finding a pool for swimming practice was a chore, but diving boards were almost impossible to find. "When the summer came, we wanted to dive, but we didn't have a diving coach. There wasn't any board anyway. The boards in those days were like nothing that you see now. They were planks, they were just a piece of board, and sometimes they were covered, and sometimes they weren't, and it's very dangerous when it's wet, because it's slippery. We found later that some of the men divers always carried with them coconut matting, tacks, saws, and hammers. They really had to travel to be ready for any emergency when they found a board that didn't work."[9]

Coach Handley did not coach the divers, but occasionally would call in one of his friends for some special diving training. During the winters the divers would visit a pool reserved especially for the session; the diving board was just a plank with almost no spring, placed only a foot above the water. Because there were so few indoor diving boards in New York City, the divers sometimes traveled three hours to a pool in New Jersey that had one. Aileen recalled, "The water was only six feet deep under the board. This was exceedingly dangerous, and all we could think of as we dove was not about our diving and our form, but about quickly putting out our hands and cutting short our dives so we would not hit the bottom with too much force. Of course we hit bottom every time, but the trick was to have your hands ahead and break with your elbows to protect your head. It is hard to concentrate on your diving form when all you can think of is trying to avoid getting injured or killed."[10]

Aileen Riggin executing a dive, 1922 (Library of Congress Prints and Photographs Division).

In warmer weather they would use the diving board at Manhattan Beach's tidal pool, which had its own unique inconvenience that required timing the training sessions with the high tide. Aileen Riggin recalled, "In the summer we started going to the beach, and there it was a tidal pool, Manhattan Beach, New York, which is on Long Island. It was about an hour's commute on the subway, and past Coney Island. And there, as I said, there was a tidal pool, so we'd try to hit the tide. It was a three-meter board, which was about ten feet, and also there was a diving tower." Depending on the tides, the water depth ranged from ten feet to 16 feet, making the plunge part of the dive tricky at times. But as soon as the ice broke in the spring, the girls would be there practicing. "Of course, some time it was high tide at 6 A.M. or 6 P.M. and we were usually in between somewhere. There wasn't a very accurate way of practicing. The board was terrible, but it was there. It was a plank. It was rigid, quite rigid. It didn't give one inch — inflexible. But the lagoon had a muddy bottom too, so the water was murky. None of this leads to interest in going off and practicing."[11]

Diving was dangerous, and Aileen at various times bit through her lip, punctured an eyelid, or hit her face on the bottom of pools. Despite these hardships, the team continued to grow and improve.

15. Championships and the Beginnings of International Competition

The WSA frequently competed at AAU swim meets in Massachusetts, Connecticut, New York, New Jersey, and Philadelphia, against the many other women's swimming clubs and leagues that were springing up. The entire team could not afford to travel long distance, but Charlotte Boyle and Ethelda Bleibtrey (considered the stars of the team) were often sent to compete in distant cities. Back in New York, Coach Handley continued to find and groom talented younger swimmers who could continue to set records while Ethelda and Charlotte were traveling. While Charlotte and Ethelda were touring the west coast and Hawaii in the spring of 1920, the younger girls went to a meet in Detroit. Aileen Riggin remembered, "They sent the second team in, which was Helen Wainwright, Gertrude Ederle, and myself, and Helen Meany. Helen Meany was the oldest, she was 15. Gertrude Ederle was only 12 because she was a year behind me.... Helen Wainwright and I were 13.... This was a national championship, a relay. We competed and nobody could believe this, these little girls, we were really children, getting up on the mark and we won by about a lap. We won by a fantastic amount. We won the national championship. We beat the adult girls and we set a record. This was quite a sensation at that time and people were cheering, and standing up and applauding."[1]

Training was rigorous. Aileen Riggin recalled, "We decided that about a mile was a good training distance. And we'd swim, when we had the opportunity to find a pool, about a mile, 50 or 60 laps in the pool. Even our coach didn't know because it was new to him. We'd just do what we thought was right. We never got tired. We'd just build up. We'd feel exhilarated as we swam, once you got past the first few laps. You'd get your second wind. We didn't sprint. We just tried to maintain a steady pace, and mainly, always have

The young champs of the WSA. From left to right: Aileen Riggin, Helen Wainwright, Helen Meany, and Gertrude Ederle, around 1919 (International Swimming Hall of Fame).

something left for a sprint at the end. We were taught always to have a sprint left, and not to spend all our strength on the beginning."[2]

They also traveled great distances, performing at exhibitions where they would teach strokes, race one another, and demonstrate various dives. For exhibitions, a swimmer would begin by showing just the kick, then just the arm stroke, then both, while Charlotte Epstein announced to the audience exactly what they were seeing. Charlotte became the team manager and usually traveled with the team when they went to competitions or exhibitions. Doris O'Mara remembered Epstein as "brilliant. She always picked the best places. I can't remember where it was — and I think even if I could I probably shouldn't mention the name — but we weren't being taken care of after we swam, as far as sitting down for dinner. Everyone else was being taken care of — the people who had come to see it and everyone else. And Charlotte said, 'That's enough!' She took all of us and said, 'We're leaving.' So we left and went to another restaurant. As far as she was concerned, they weren't treating us right. Of course, we didn't notice it or complain. But that was it. She always got the best for us and took us all over."[3]

One exhibition took them to Asheville, North Carolina. "We gave an exhibition at the Vanderbilt Estate in North Carolina. We swam in their pool. They had friends there too. And when we came in to the mansion they had lackeys standing outside with their hands out. We had our bathing suits and caps and a towel wrapped around us and as each one of us came by we just dropped our towels. We thought that's what they were there for. Evidently it was all right because no one complained. Anyway, we put on an exhibition there for the Vanderbilt family and their friends. That was one of the highlights of traveling around."

The WSA members were the premier swimmers in the country, and they were attractive in a healthy, wholesome way. They received coverage in newspapers around the country. In 1919, Helen Wainwright received a letter from the Associated News Bureau requesting an interview. They promised to write an accurate and authentic account of whatever Helen wanted them to write, but they had one special request of Helen. "Would you be so good as to furnish us with some facts in reference to the matter and as all our articles are illustrated, we should like to have your photograph in swimming costume, if possible for this purpose. This latter request is very important."[4]

Although the 1916 Olympics had been canceled, there was still an interest in international competition. In the summer of 1916, plans were made to invite two Australian swimming champs, Fanny Durack and Mina Wylie, to the United States for competition and touring. Women's swimming was well established in Australia, and American women organizers may have been hoping to learn from the Australians their secrets to public success. The AAU, working with Charlotte Epstein, mapped out a tour of the United States and Canada for the Australians, who were to be accompanied by the president of the New South Wales Ladies' Amateur Swimming Association, Mrs. Hugh McIntosh. Mrs. McIntosh, was eager to share with the Americans information on the growth of swimming in Australia, said: "Organized swimming should be even a greater success in the United States. I think you need a separate body to govern the sport. For the present the Amateur Athletic Union can handle it very well indeed, but in a few years the women should branch out and govern themselves. The National Women's Life Saving League is doing the proper kind of work, and if its influences were extended across the country it would not be long before a separate governing institution could materialize."

Charlotte may have seen the Australian organization as a likely model, one that organized swimming and focused entirely on matters that were unique to female athletes. First, they had a rule that barred female athletes from traveling without a chaperone, known as a manageress. Second, they had strict rules about bathing attire. "We have so thoroughly secured control of the sport that we never have the slightest trouble with our girls anymore. Their costumes are regulated, and cannot be immodest under our rules. Every swimmer must wear a cloak from the time she leaves her dressing room virtually until the moment she hears the starting gun. She has what is called a cloak-maid, who stands behind her at the starting line, ready to receive her cloak as she doffs it preparatory to leaping into the pool. You know, we have only pool swimming in our country, because of the severe surf, which practically prohibits outdoor competition. In swimming competition the women must wear neck and knee costumes, similar to those used in this country, and in diving they wear the Canadian or two-piece costumes."[5] Australians had originally thought that the competitions should only be viewed by other women, but had since changed the rules, and the competitions attracted many male spectators.

Unfortunately, the 1916 trip was canceled because they could not afford to pay for a manageress to accompany them. In 1918, the women got as far as San Francisco before the tour was canceled due to the AAU and its Australian equivalent being unable to agree on terms for the tour. When they finally made it to the United States in 1919, they came to New York City for a championship meet at the Manhattan Beach lagoon. There was a crowd of three thousand people waiting, mostly women, to see Fanny — widely believed to be the best swimmer in the world — compete against the young Americans. Fanny was trounced in the quarter-mile race by Ethelda Bleibtrey, who not only won the race but beat Claire Galligan's two-year-old record by nine seconds. Charlotte Boyle came in a close second after fighting Fanny for the position. The crowd was ecstatic at seeing an American win, reported the *New York Times.* "Spectators slapped one another on the back, jumped in the air with glee; women fondled and hugged one another, and sometimes — in mistake or out of pure, unexalted joy — the man nearest them. Women officials of the meet forgot everything in the excitement of their unleashed joy while they showered hugs and kisses unstintedly on Miss Bleibtrey. Pandemonium reigned without hindrance."[6]

Fanny said that she was unused to swimming in open water, which was indeed true. But for the Americans, victory was sweet. They had been waiting for much longer than three years to engage in international competition, and they had finally been able to prove themselves. They were ready for more. Fanny Durack's American tour ended with a bizarre race in Philadelphia, in which she first refused to race, then forfeited the race when she simply jumped in the pool ahead of her competitors, then climbed out of the pool and left for good. Multiple newspapers reported on the incident in different ways, but the last straw for Fanny seemed to be that she was offered a handicap in a 300-yard race against Ethelda Bleibtrey and Charlotte Boyle, based on all of their performances in the previous Manhattan Beach meet. Fanny had always seen the handicap, essentially a head-start start given to less-skilled competitors, given to her competitors, not to her, and the insult was perhaps more than she could bear. The Australian women's tour of the United States ended after a few performances, and unhappy ones at that.[7]

16. The 1920 Olympic Games

The Olympic Games returned in 1920 after having been canceled because of the war. They were held in Antwerp, Belgium, which had been devastated by the war. Although the events would be determined by the local organizing committee, American participation in the Olympics was governed entirely by the American Olympic Committee, from whether the United States would take part in the games at all, to control of the try-outs, and whether or not to send female athletes.

The girls at the WSA were thrilled when they heard that women's swimming had been accepted as an event by the Antwerp organizers. Aileen Riggin recalled, "We heard about the Olympics and were elated. We heard that girls, or women, were going to be admitted to the Olympics in swimming for the first time, and we heard the rumor, and then we pursued it."[1] It wasn't easy to find out what they needed to know about tryouts and the actual rules and requirements for each event. "There was nowhere we could find out anything about the Olympics and no one seemed to know anything about it. So we wrote to the French Olympic Committee and asked for information on what the rules were going to be. They took forever to arrive. But when they did come they were all in French and we had to have them translated."

Aileen and Helen Wainwright were especially interested in the diving events. As Aileen recalled: "When we finally saw the rules we thought they were silly dives. I really can't remember many of them, but they had running and standing, which was silly to begin with. And standing on a springboard is ridiculous when it has any resiliency. But they were dives."[2]

The United States Olympic Committee initially continued its opposition to women taking part in the Olympic Games. From Aileen Riggin's perspective, the opposition "wasn't from the general public. It was from the ruling body. They didn't want women to compete in any sport in the Olympic Games. They wanted it to remain as it had been in ancient Greece. They wanted it to remain like that. I guess they thought that women would be a nuisance. I don't know what they thought." Charlotte Epstein, as usual, stepped in to fight for her team's right to compete. "Our manager was very much for it. She went down and told them that this was silly, that other countries were going to compete. That sort of turned the tide."[3]

The public's attitude toward the swimmers was not as strict as the Olympic Committee's. As Aileen recalled, "there wasn't a lot of encouragement, but there wasn't a lot of discouragement either. We were considered sort of weird, I guess, unique, doing what we were doing because we did it well and nobody else did, really."[4]

By December 1919, the only events on the program for women were ice skating, lawn tennis, golf, and swimming. Women would be exhibiting in gymnastics, but not competing. The women's swimming events planned for the games were the 100-meter freestyle, three-meter springboard diving, ten-meter high diving, and the 400-meter relay.[5] Male swimmers would be competing in the 100-meter freestyle, 100-meter backstroke, 200-meter breaststroke, 400-meter freestyle, 400-meter breaststroke, the 1500-meter freestyle, the 800-meter relay, and water polo. Women's swimming associations in the U.S. began to request that more swimming events for women be included in the program once they realized that there were so many more events for male than for female swimmers, and so a 300-meter freestyle race was added.[6] Aileen Riggin remembered, "For some reason they had a 300, which is ridiculous. Three hundred meters is a nothing distance: it's not one-eighth of a mile; it's not a quarter of a mile; it's just nothing. But they thought that men did the 400, and that was just about enough, and women couldn't do that, so the 300 would be adequate."[7]

The makeup of the team was determined partly by the results of the AAU national championships with the final decision made by the American Olympic Committee. The roster created controversy because Aileen Riggin and Helen Wainwright, although among the top three finishers nationally, were each only 14 years old. The Committee did not feel that children belonged on the team, and it was again only through Charlotte's extensive campaigning that Helen and Aileen were allowed on the team. During a very tense meeting of the American Olympic Committee, six members of the WSA were named to the Olympic swim team. Ethelda Bleibtrey, Charlotte Boyle, Helen Meany, Helen Wainwright, Alice Lord, and Aileen Riggin joined seven other women from swimming clubs all over the country — from Detroit to Honolulu — to make up the team.[8]

The group departed for Europe on a Navy transport ship, the *Princess Matoika*, with the rest of the American athletes, a group of about 200 men, 15 female swimmers, and the girls' five chaperones. The Olympic Committee had decided not to send any women golfers after all, and the only other female athlete was a figure skater who had left for Belgium earlier. The ceremonies of the departure were slightly marred when the male athletes discovered where they would sleep. The *Princess Matoika* was no luxury ocean liner, and had most recently been transporting the coffins of American servicemen home from the battlefields of Europe. The men were disturbed to discover that they would be sleeping below the waterline in uncomfortable quarters. The better quarters were reserved for Olympic officials, trainers, coaches, and the women's swimming team. The indignant president of the Committee was forced to interrupt the departure ceremonies to explain from the stage of the Manhattan Opera House that it would have been impossible from a financial standpoint to send the team across in first-class passage.[9]

Helen Meany recalled, "I was just 15 years old when I was on the boat going to Antwerp for the 1920 Olympics. A lot of the people on the Olympic team complained about the food, the training facilities, and the smell. I didn't really notice a smell, but some of the others said they could smell formaldehyde because the boat was used to carry bodies back from Europe after the war. I remember that Norman Ross, the famous swimmer, was a leader, and he insisted that we would not come home on that boat. There was almost a mutiny, a strike on the beach so to speak, and we didn't take that boat home. But being a kid, I thought everything was wonderful, just great." [10]

The deck of the ship was turned into a temporary gymnasium. Javelin throwers tossed javelins overboard and reeled them back in on ropes. Athletes practiced calisthenics and tried to jog about the decks without slipping and sliding. In a time where the fastest ships could cross the Atlantic in four days, the *Princess Matoika* took 13. By the time they arrived in Europe, the team was desperate for some proper exercise. Aileen remembered,

> They put up a pool for us, which was a little canvas tank. It was just long enough for a tall man to stretch out with his arms outstretched. We had some tall swimmers, so it must have been about 7 or 8 feet long, and not quite as wide. It was held together with struts on each side of wood that were hammered together. There was a little hose from the Gulf Stream that came up and was running water, it changed the water, and also went out. It changed the water constantly. We wore a belt that was attached to each side of the little pool, tank, whatever you want to call it. Tank, I guess, is better. And we'd swim by the clock. The real swimmers who were competing in real swimming events got more time than we did. We got what was left over. It was usually five minutes at the very end. The divers didn't get as good a workout as the swimmers. And we were frantic for any exercise, because being on a ship is sort of restraining.[11]

All of Europe had been hard hit by the war, and the Olympic facilities were nothing like those seen today. The war, in fact, was so recent and the landscape still so raw that the nearby battlefields were littered with bullet, helmets, and clothing. Aileen remembered that they had stopped on the way to visit the battlefield to buy some Dutch wooden shoes. "They warned us the battlefield was a mess. We were allowed to wander around at will. My feet hurt like crazy because they told us to buy the shoes big. The peasants in the fields stuffed them with straw and woolen socks. We didn't know about that. We limped around, peeking in pill boxes and trenches, picking up things, souvenirs we shouldn't have had — German helmets and cartridge cases, shells." Aileen, exploring a pill-box bunker at Ypres, picked up a German boot and was shocked to see that it still contained a withered foot.[12]

The swimming events were held in a ditch-like canal that Aileen thought may have at one time been the city's moat. The water in the canal was so cold that it was almost impossible to practice. The frigid water became such a problem that it was necessary to change the rules for water polo and shorten the periods because the men were almost losing consciousness in the cold. There was a tower for the diving events at the same canal, and divers had to check before diving to make certain that they weren't about to dive directly onto an unsuspecting swimmer below. The water was deep black, not clear at all, and Aileen developed a minor phobia that she would get stuck in the mud headfirst on a dive.

The entire American team was issued team uniforms, which for the women was a long white skirt and a navy blue blazer, topped off with a straw hat. The girls were issued team bathing suits, made of one piece, with no skirt, that reached to the knee. Aileen recalled, "We just died when we saw them. They were made of mercerized cotton, which is transparent of course. You can see right through that, and when it's wet, it clings. And it had sleeves. They had sleeves to the elbow." Aileen and the other divers decided to compete in their own wool suits instead. "We wore our own because we looked so terrible in these suits. We laughed when we tried them on. We just went into hysterics, it was so ridiculous."[13]

There were other problems with the suits. Thelma Payne Sanborn recalled, "I couldn't wear it because when I tucked in my diving, I split the back end out. It was real thin and when it was wet it looked like you didn't have anything on. It was black, but it was very transparent. So, when I started doing the tuck dives, why, I ripped the rear end out, so I wore my own Jantzen suit."[14]

The team did extraordinarily well at the Games. They took home all of the medals in the 100-and 300-meter freestyle, with Ethelda Bleibtrey capturing both gold medals, and finished first in the relay, finishing 29 seconds ahead of the second-place team, Great Britain. They also took home every medal in the springboard-diving competition, with Aileen taking the gold and Helen Wainwright the silver, but none in the ten-meter high dive. The medals were distributed during the closing ceremonies, given to each of the winners by King Albert of Belgium and his sons.

Following the end of the Games, the team went to Paris. They went sightseeing, competed in races on the Seine River, and demonstrated diving from a 40-foot-tall derrick. Aileen was too frightened to dive from it, but said, "Helen Meany and Alice Lord Landon went up there, and they dove off. They didn't care how high anything was. They didn't have any fear at all."[15]

Helen Meany recalled, "No one would dive, so my coach Charlotte 'Eppie' Epstein, asked if I would do it, and I agreed. They rigged up a derrick next to the Seine, and they had to put two ladders together so that I could climb up. It was at least 40 feet high, higher than I had ever dived before, at least on ladders like that. I nearly froze, but I made it up three times and made three dives."[16]

The Olympic Games had been a complete success for the swimmers. America was now aware that women could compete successfully in intense competition.

17. Famous Athletes

The Olympic team was greeted by adoring crowds upon their return to New York. They were met with a huge parade, had dinner at the Waldorf-Astoria, and were presented with medals by the mayor in a ceremony at City Hall. The crowds at City Hall Plaza pressed so hard to catch sight of the team that a police guard was called in to rescue them from the crush. As the parade of Olympians passed through the streets, the girl swimmers received the loudest cheers, rivaled only by those for the Navy shell crew team, and the youngest, Aileen Riggin and Helen Wainwright, received especially adoring cheers.[1]

The girls and women of the WSA had attracted so much attention that they became minor celebrities, illustrated by the incidents surrounding Charlotte Boyle's courtship and wedding. Charlotte's husband-to-be, Henry Clune, a sportswriter, first spotted her in the newspaper. Attracted to her looks, he and a friend attended a swimming meet at Brighton Beach, and Henry later wrote, "They seemed more impressive in the flesh than in their attractive newspaper photograph that had been the catalyst of this sweltering exhibition. I left Marks and walked by their bench, ogling them surreptitiously."[2]

After Henry convinced a friend to arrange for a swimming event to bring the women to Rochester, and after only meeting a few more times, Henry and Charlotte decided to marry. Charlotte announced her engagement, with the wedding to occur only a week later, and the WSA girls discussed ways of giving her a wedding shower. Feeling there was too little notice, Elsie Viets arranged one at her home, inviting some, but not all, of the WSA members and some friends not affiliated with the club.

Ethelda Bleibtrey was not invited, and apparently felt so socially stung that she publicly announced her resignation from the club. The papers covered the event as if it were a scandal, digging out gossip about the club that many members surely would have preferred to stay private. Anonymous sources alleged that the WSA fostered "a spirit of social divisiveness instead of encouraging social goodwill and unity among all its members." Charlotte Boyle and Ethelda were competitors, despite swimming for the same team, and during the summer Ethelda had closely beaten Charlotte in two races, which some insinuated had triggered bad feelings between the two.

When Ethelda went public with her resignation, Charlotte Epstein reacted angrily, saying, "It's the most stupid thing I ever heard of. The Women's Swimming Association has no control over the social activities of its various members and is certainly in no position to say whom they shall invite over [to] their homes. Miss Viets was a close friend of Miss Boyle's and she took this opportunity to pay her this courtesy. The Swimming Association has nothing to do with it. I am amazed that Miss Bleibtrey would come out in the papers and confess to being angry that she was snubbed socially." At the time, Ethelda was widely considered to be one of the best, if not *the* best, swimmers in the world, and the WSA's loss was a big one. Under AAU rules Ethelda would have to compete with no affiliation for the period of one year. She must have taken the social slight extremely hard for her to leave the club with which she had been swimming for three years and go unaffiliated for a year.

Elsie Viets shrugged the whole thing off, saying, "I scarcely know Miss Bleibtrey. There was no reason on earth why I should have invited her."[3] Charlotte Boyle's wedding went off smashingly; her maid of honor was Charlotte Epstein, and many of the WSA team members were present at the ceremony.[4] Although the couple was to settle in Rochester, where Henry lived, the new Mrs. Clune continued to swim for the WSA.

In terms of publicity, it was not a good year for Ethelda. When she was ordered off the beach in Atlantic City while playing a game of beach baseball for wearing a bathing suit without stockings, the story made the papers, too. Inexplicably, this occurred in December. Ethelda argued that she was not aware of any laws that she was breaking, and that there was nothing indecent about her suit, but she was still ordered off the beach.[5] The following spring, she made up her mind to leave amateur swimming behind to join the professional ranks.[6]

One of the younger members of the WSA, Gertrude "Trudy" Ederle, was to benefit from Ethelda's departure from the team. Gertrude had been a member of the WSA for a while, but in 1922 she captured the attention of the swimming world when she won the Joseph P. Day Cup, a three-and-a-half mile race from Manhattan Beach to Brighton Beach. She was only 15 years old and had not been expected to place. She was competing against Hilda James, widely believed to be Europe's best female swimmer, and 50 of the best swimmers in the United States. Gertrude finished first, 60 yards ahead of Helen Wainwright. Behind Helen was Hilda James, followed by Aileen Riggin. Gertrude, also known as Trudy, became a star in competition, but unlike some of the other girls, she was not flamboyant and did not enjoy the spotlight. She was a quiet, workmanlike swimmer who was hearing impaired and did not enjoy being the center of attention.[7]

In September of 1922, Gertrude broke five records in a single day. The event was a special invitational 500-meter swim held at the Brighton Beach pool, with times taken at 300 yards, 400 yards, 400 meters, 440 yards, and 500 yards. She set new records for all six intervals, beating Helen Wainwright and the other closest competitor, Hilda James of Liverpool, England. As was the procedure, Charlotte Epstein immediately sent documenting times and witness statements to the Amateur Athletic Union and the International Records Committee. The *New York Times* described Trudy's performance as "one of the most remarkable exhibitions of aquatic ability in the history of women's swimming competition in this country."[8]

In the fall of 1922, some of the team was invited to Bermuda to take part in a swimming meet. Helen Wainwright, Aileen Riggin, Gertrude Ederle, Doris O'Mara and some girls from other clubs, including Sybil Bauer of Chicago, were invited to Bermuda by some prominent business men hoping to

The girls of the New York Women's Swimming Association, on their way to Bermuda. Helen Wainwright is shown on the far left playing the ukulele. Gertrude Ederle is seated in the center of the first row and Aileen Riggin is on the far right in the first row (International Swimming Hall of Fame).

increase interest in their own swimming scene. The girls traveled by boat, entertaining other passengers by demonstrating their swimming strokes. The event was a major happening for the Bermudians, and turnout was enormous to see the American swimming stars. The crowd watched as Sybil Bauer became the first woman to break an existing men's record in the 440-yard backstroke, lowering it by four seconds to 6:24 ⅘. As an added bonus, Gertrude Ederle broke the existing record for the 150-yard freestyle, previously held by Charlotte Boyle. The rest of the trip was spent giving exhibitions at hotels, shopping, and generally being the toast of the island.[9]

A 1923 attempt at team travel did not come off so well. In the fall of 1922, the British Amateur Swimming Association invited Gertrude Ederle, Aileen Riggin, and Helen Wainwright (at that time considered the best amateur swimmers in the United States) to come to England to take part in a competitive swimming tour. The WSA board was heartily enthusiastic in approving the trip, but the AAU was not. The WSA applied to the Metropolitan AAU for permits for the athletes to travel, which were approved and forwarded to the registration committee of the National AAU. Instead of giving its approval, however, the registration committee turned the process over to a brand new committee, the foreign relations committee, which ruled in April of 1923 that no American athlete would be allowed to compete abroad that summer. They did, however, make an exception for the Yale and Harvard track teams, who were going to England to compete against the Oxford and Cambridge teams.

Charlotte Epstein was furious. She quoted the AAU rule book, which made no mention of this new committee or their right to prevent athletes from competing abroad. The WSA had heard nothing from the AAU since submitting the applications, and had continued to work with the British colleagues overseas organizing the tour. In fact, Charlotte said, the BASA had organized their entire women's competitive swimming season around the American visit. The WSA hired a lawyer to press the case and appealed to the Board of Governors of the AAU.

The WSA issued a statement, declaring, "The Women's Swimming Association proposes to carry its fight to the end, and will leave nothing undone to ensure the presence of the girls in the scheduled races, bookings having been obtained some time ago for May 18. One of the stormiest battles in the history of the AAU is assured."[10]

One of the reasons given for the refusal was that the tour would be too grueling on the girl's health, an idea that the WSA soundly rejected by saying the real fear of the AAU was that having three of its greatest stars absent for the summer racing season would deprive them of ticket sales. The WSA's lawyer pointed to the group's proven ability to protect the health of its members, and threatened to sue the AAU if he even suspected that the Board's vote was not fair and impartial. The Board was asked to vote, not on the WSA's case, but on whether any athletes should be allowed to compete overseas, and they voted no.

On May 12, the WSA announced that the three swimmers would be going to England with or without the approval of the AAU. The AAU, in turn, pointed out that under the rules of the International Amateur Federation, athletes could not compete abroad without the approval of their home association, and that legally, the British were not permitted to allow them to compete. Further, they threatened, if the girls competed overseas, they would effectively suspend themselves from any further amateur competition.

The WSA, in full rebellion, countered with this statement: "The girl swimmers will sail on Tuesday convinced that their action will be upheld by the general athletic public and by the fair-minded, unbiased, and independent element in the AAU. The WSA will carry on its fight and interesting developments may be looked for very shortly to continue to the floor of the AAU convention next November."[11]

They set sail on the *Berengaria* and, by all accounts, immensely enjoyed the trip. Also on board was the American boxing team, headed to a championship in England, and some professional golfers. There were concerts and a costume ball, for which Gertrude dressed up as a Dutch boy, Helen as a gypsy, and Aileen as Peter Pan. On the 23rd they arrived in London, where they met with the Secretary of the International Swimming Federation, who gave them clearance to compete. But Charlotte Epstein rethought her position on the trip and finally decided that the girls would not compete, specifically because she did not want the controversy to continue to spiral into an international incident. Instead, the girls spent the next five days touring London and visiting the swimming pools of the clubs, which were far larger and better equipped than the ones they used at home.[12]

The girls continued to travel extensively for exhibitions and championships, usually as a team but sometimes individual swimmers were sent to competitions as well. In October 1923, Gertrude traveled to Hawaii for a match with the Outrigger Canoe Club, and was accompanied by Elsie Viets as chaperone. The constant meets required that the girls train almost daily. "There are so many girls holding championships whose all around swimming ability is just about the same as mine that if I stop long enough to do anything else I will lose my place on the team," said Aileen. "I believe that excelling at watersports is altogether a matter of training. Anyway, I know that I, like Theodore Roosevelt, was born without any of the special aptitude or heroic qualities that champions are supposed to have. I like the water and wanted to be a diver, that was all."

Aileen described the rigors of training and spoke about the team's attitudes towards training and the desire to be taken seriously as an athlete.

> I always feel nervous about going into contests, but I think all of the girls do, a little bit. But you never get that really scared feeling if you are in good physical condition. That is why such regular hours are necessary, and why so much rest is needed. I suppose it is why our director always warns us against taking sodas, sundaes, and things like that. A girl who has made good on the stage can 'soldier' if she isn't feeling top notch, but there isn't a bit of fake about holding championships in sports. You have to keep proving all of the time that it is still yours, or it isn't. And there are certainly plenty of people around ready to take it from you.
>
> I have lots of fun. Training to keep in form is fun. I love traveling around to meets and exhibition with the other women's swimming association title holders and members of the Olympic teams in all sorts of water sports.
>
> [On the topic of competing interests facing women in the 1920s:] Being a flapper doesn't appeal to me. I'm not interested in flapper ideas, but lots of the girls are. Some of them are very good swimmers, too. Their attitude is the same as that toward everything- they do it just for fun. And that is not a bad idea. We don't any of us take our championships very seriously, except girls whose parents would take it hard if they were defeated. We're pretty keen to keep them, and mostly do all we can to keep in form, but we don't worry about losing out.[13]

In fact, the WSA was taking things so seriously that, in 1923, they scored 141 points in the national senior aquatic championships while all other competing clubs scored an average of 116. Gertrude Ederle and Aileen Riggin had each contributed 38 of those points, and Ethel McGary, Helen Meany, Virginia Whitenack, and Agnes Geraghty were all standout performers as well.[14]

18. The 1924 Olympic Games

During the war, Pierre de Coubertin had relocated the IOC from Paris to Switzerland. He dreamed of returning the Games to Paris in 1924 and giving the postwar world an enormous, triumphant Olympiad. It was to be the birth of a new era, with the world united in a glorious, peaceful celebration of sport. He convinced the government of France to contribute 20 million francs for staging the games, in exchange for allowing the French Olympic Organizing Committee to be directed by the French Ministry of Foreign Affairs. The entire country was seized with Olympic excitement, and the event included a parallel literary and art competition that offered medals in artistic categories. A massive new stadium and a beautiful new aquatics facility were constructed.

The 1924 games were to be entirely different from the 1920 Antwerp Games. The Amateur Athletic Union began planning American participation a full year in advance. They planned to send over 300 athletes, and needed to raise approximately $1,500 for each one's travel expenses. An official was sent to investigate where the American athletes could be housed. He reserved the beautiful grand Chateau Rocquencourt, about an hour outside of Paris, for the cost of approximately $27,000. The committee was particularly excited about the chateau. [1]

Colonel Robert M. Thompson, president of the American Olympic Committee, announced with great pleasure, "We selected Rocquencourt not with the idea of using the chateau as a residence for athletes, but for control of the park, with its grand old trees, its beautiful gardens, its fine air and for its historical association with the Murat family and through them with the great Napoleon. Our men will be comfortably housed in rooms with only two beds, which are readily accessible to the lavatories and shower supplied with hot and cold water. They will dine under the trees, or in rainy weather in a roomy pavilion.... Men who have finished their competitions or who are waiting their turn can go on excursions to Versailles, Fontainebleu, Paris with its great historical monuments, the battlefields of the late war, etc. In fact, our boys will come home having received not only the plaudits of the spectators in the stadium for the intelligent use of their fine bodies, but with all the educational benefits of a short European tour." An ocean liner was chartered for the price of $186,000. The committee attempted to raise the money to fund the excursion by selling additional tickets on the chartered liner, by charging for attendance at the Olympic tryouts, and by private subscription.[2]

To encourage public support, an effort was made to stir powerful American patriotism by subtly chiding physically unfit Americans and reminding non-athletes how they could support the national heroes who would present American physicality to the world. Major General Henry T. Allen, vice-president of the American Olympic Committee, announced, "Behind all of this sport is the question of national physical culture, in which the entire country is interested. Statistics of the selective draft in showing such a great percentage of our youth who were incapable of carrying a knapsack and rifle under war conditions were an amazing surprise. The question of sport and participation in national and international contests is, therefore, a patriotic one. The games will be the most hotly contested of any ever held in these historic competitions. The prowess of American athletes will be tested as never before. It, therefore, becomes a matter of American pride to leave nothing undone to encourage the best selection of contestants, and to provide transportation and conditions for them."[3]

The local chapters of the AAU were asked to raise the money, and assigned target amounts; New York's target was $100,000 of the approximately $350,000 needed. John D. Rockefeller gave $5,000, with the provision that four other Americans match his donation. Other prominent New Yorkers and companies gave smaller amounts. For those with smaller bank accounts, the AAU sold stamp booklets for one dollar.[4] By March the New York AAU was still $70,000 away from its goal, and was reduced to accepting money from the door counts at a professional boxing meet held at a Madison Square Garden fundraiser, and asking racetracks and baseball stadiums to hold special fundraising days for the Olympic fund. The national fund was $225,000 away from its goal of $350,000. As a result of the funding crisis, the AOC was forced to consider reducing the number of athletes selected to go to Paris. It was even suggested that the water polo team stay home and be replaced by swimmers from other events who were also reasonably skilled at water polo, but this idea was quickly rejected.

In late May, a fundraising rally was held on the steps of the Treasury Building on Wall Street. Governor Al Smith declared the day "Olympics Day," and Gertrude Ederle and Aileen Riggin were among the prominent athletes introduced before a cheering crowd.[5]

The swimming teams were selected in early June. The men's tryouts were held in Chicago and the women's were held in Briarcliff Manor, New York. Trudy, current holder of the record, placed first in the 400-meter freestyle, with Helen Wainwright five seconds behind her, guaranteeing both a place on the team. On the second day of tryouts, Trudy established a new world record of 1:53⅗ for the 150-meter swim and qualified to compete in the 400-meter freestyle, the 100-meter freestyle, and the relay. In all, 24 women were selected, although six of them were alternates who would be sent to the Games only if the funding was available.

Once again, the WSA was heavily represented on the team, with Helen Wainwright and Martha Norelius qualifying for the 400-meter, Agnes Geraghty and Mathilda Shurich for the 200-meter breaststroke, Doris O'Mara for the 100-meter backstroke, and Aileen Riggin and Helen Meany for diving.[6] Aileen also qualified for the 100-meter. Women from Chicago's Illinois Athletic Club, the Philadelphia Turngemeinde, the Outrigger Canoe Club of Honolulu, and the Panama Canal Zone also made the team.

Coach Handley was selected to coach the American women's swimming team. Charlotte Epstein went as well and was appointed a timing judge in the swimming events, marking the first time that a woman had been named as an official at the Olympic Games.[7]

The team gave an exhibition at a fundraiser water carnival in Long Beach, New York. Trudy swam the 100-meter freestyle in 1:07⅖, while Johnny Weissmuller, the future Tarzan of movie fame, swam it in a separate exhibition in 56 seconds ⅕. It was noted that all times were slower than usual because of the unusually cold water.[8] Trudy and Johnny were unequivocally the stars of the Olympic team — in the weeks leading up to the games, their names were household words and the two were expected to be the American swim team's most powerful weapons.

This time, the team traveled to Europe on the S.S. *America*, a much nicer ship than the *Princess Matoika*. A great effort had been made to equip the ocean liner with training facilities for the athletes. A track was laid out on the promenade deck. A boxing ring was erected and a place on deck reserved for wrestling matches. Another canvas tank was set up, with the belt and rope that attached swimmers to the side of the pool for swimming in place. L. de B. Handley timed them, telling them to swim as fast as they could until they had swum what he estimated to be 400 meters. There was almost no way for the divers to train onboard, but a rope and pulley system was set up so that they could at least practice somersaulting in the air.[9]

The team settled in at Chateau Rocquencourt. The girls were lodged in the gatehouses, the officials in the chateau, and the men in temporary barracks built for the occasion. The chateau and its grounds were beautiful, full of gardens and winding paths.

A traumatic event occurred their first night at the chateau. As the athletes were settling in and exploring the nearby village, they were startled to hear a woman's hysterical screams. Running toward the sounds, they saw that the woman's husband had attempted to put out a fire on the electric wires outside of their home. The man was instantly electrocuted, and dangled dead before them, his hands smoking and tangled in the wires, while a rescue crew attempted to remove him without electrocuting themselves. Tragically, the electrical fire may have been related to the athletes themselves. Aileen thought that it had been caused by the overloading of the wires for the extra electricity required by the Americans in their makeshift barracks and the Chateau.[10] Doris O'Mara Murphy, then 16, noticed that when the athletes arrived and turned on the lights in their lodging, the lights in the little village began to flicker and flash. One of the athletes helping to put out the fire was Jack Kelly, of the sculling team, who later became the father of Grace Kelly.[11]

The athletes were deeply upset by the tragedy, and a collection was taken for the dead man's family. It was a horribly upsetting experience to happen on their first night in France. Fears of fire lingered, and Aileen insisted on keeping the door to the gatehouse open because the windows were barred and she did not want to be trapped in the gatehouse in case of a fire.[12]

The Opening Day ceremonies were held on July 5, 1924, a dazzlingly sunny day. Over 3,000 athletes from 44 countries marched into Columbes Stadium: 135 of them were women. The American women wore white flannel skirts and jackets while the men wore blue blazers over white pants and flat-brimmed hats. After the Olympic oath was administered, celebratory fireworks were shot into the air and passenger pigeons were released from baskets, winging back to their home countries to carry the news that the Olympic Games had begun.

For diver Clarita Hunsberger, the experience was stunning, and one that she remembered vividly for the rest of her life. "We were all lined up there underneath the stadium ready to come out of the tunnel, and I recall that they passed the word along, 'Let's all walk in with our heads high.' They also passed the word that we were to come in at the signal that the French announcer gave, which was the United States in French, *les Etats-Unis.* So we were primed and it happened. We stood up so tall. I see people now come in so casual; but not in 1924 or '28. We stood very tall when we marched in. We came out of that darkness, that tunnel, into the light of day. Well, the whole place, I couldn't believe it, it just came alive. I couldn't have anticipated what it was going to be. Coming out into the bright light and having everybody stand up, and people were standing and cheering and shouting and waving flags, and the tears rolled down our faces. I turned and looked behind me, and men had the tears, too."[13]

Aileen Riggin, Gertrude Ederle, and Helen Wainwright, left to right, in their official Olympic uniforms, 1924 (Library of Congress Prints and Photographs Division).

Other than the distressing experience of the first night, life in Paris was astonishing and fun for most of the American athletes. They were fed in a giant dining hall, all of them at once. They had bonded on the trip over and, of course, many of the young and attractive athletes had eyes for each other. They took trips into Paris, dining out and going shopping. The team chaperones kept a strict eye on the women. One day Aileen and two other girls went on a daytime date with three team members from Yale, Harvard, and Princeton to a dance hall called the Chateau Madrid, where they were so swept up in tango dancing they missed the team bus back to the chateau. Digging deep for taxi money, they returned late in the afternoon. "When we arrived, the chaperones were all seated in chairs in front of our rooms, ready to reprimand us and give us hell. They were going to put us off the team. They were going to send us home.... They really gave us a bad time over that."[14]

Paris was wonderful, and they all reveled in its European sophistication. "Being 18 and being in Paris was wonderful. The sun was shining, we read Hemingway, and we were just carried away," Aileen remembered.[15]

Although they were athletes and representing the United States on an international stage, teenage goofiness and its accompanying hilarity could not be suppressed. Aileen recalled, "We all played a game called Beaver that was very popular that summer. I think it started in England, but I am not sure. If you saw a man with a beard you'd yell 'beaver.' The first one would win so many points. And you'd get points if it was a gray beard, or a black beard, or a white beard, or a red beard. Oh boy, that was the jackpot. And we were playing that much to the French people's disgust. We'd say, 'Beaver, beaver, beaver! I saw him first, I saw him first!' But at the Folies Bergère there was a scene where a little man was in bed for some reason, and he had a beard, and he had it under the covers. He didn't know whether to put it under the covers or over the covers. But anyway, when the lights went up on the stage, one of the girls said, 'Beaver!' And the whole theater erupted because it was unexpected."[16]

The French had built a wonderful pool complex for the swimming events. Clarita Hunsberger recalled, "We arrived there and we were thrilled to death. It was almost a brand-new pool. It was beautiful. Not only that, it was up on a hill, and from that hillside you had the most marvelous view out to the city of Paris; and from the top platform it was simply stupendous. So we couldn't wait to get in." It wasn't perfect for the divers, however. "We got up onto the low platforms first and finally got up to the upper platform, and at some point there it dawned on us what was wrong: the architects had constructed the diving apparatus so you dived the width of the pool. Now every pool you knew, you dived the length. When you were on the top platform particularly — it's bad enough on the low platform — and you were going to do a running dive, you are standing at the back and the platform extends out in front of you so you see no water, absolutely none. And you run the length of that platform and fling yourself out into the cement seats of the spectators on the other side. It was psychological ... but really, it was not good."[17]

Unfortunately, the pool was so far from the chateau that getting to it required riding a bus over an hour each way on bumpy roads. Some of the girls were moved temporarily to a hotel closer to the pool so that they could fit in enough training time. They would rise at five in the morning and take a taxi to the stadium, arriving in the chilly hour just before dawn.

Trudy Ederle was particularly troubled by this; the time spent on the crowded bus in stop-and-start traffic left her legs cramped and in terrible shape for the competitions. The Hawaiians on the team had brought a masseuse, and she made daily use of the service, but it wasn't enough. Her muscles turned tight, hard as walnuts, the masseuse said.

Her performances in the trials were far behind her usual record-breaking ones. The *New York Times* blared "Miss Ederle is Defeated" when her teammates Mariechen Wehselau and Ethel Lackie outpaced her in the trial for the 100-meter freestyle, especially embarrassing for Trudy because she held the world record. But expectations were high for a reason — the country had come to know her as an athlete who quietly won races and steadily broke records. The *Times* said that she was "generally conceded to be the world's greatest woman performer, and the ace of the American feminine contingent."[18]

The French were proud to be hosting the world's Olympics, but not all was peaceful between the nations. Coubertin's vision of the Olympic Games bringing together the nations of the world to bask in the glory of pure athletic competition was marred by overt nationalism. Instead of reveling in the pure sportsmanship of the games regardless of the victor's nationality, spectators were supporting their own country's athletes, sometimes in quite unsportsmanlike fashion.

The United States rugby team was at the center of some of the controversy. The team won the rugby championship, but during the game, one French star player was accidentally kicked in the face by an American player he was tackling, drawing blood. When a second French player was injured, American and French spectators began brawling. One young spectator, an art student from Illinois, was knocked unconscious by a cane-wielding rugby fan. When the Americans, several of whom had little-to-no experience playing rugby, trounced the French veterans 17–3, the crowd of 30,000 expressed their anger loudly. The hooliganism was roundly denounced by officials.[19]

In other clashes, a controversial scoring of a fencing bout between France and Italy ended with the Italian team marching out of the building singing a fascist hymn before their angry and noisy supporters.[20] Another Italian fencer was barred permanently from Olympic competition for challenging a Hungarian fencing judge to a duel.[21]

Aileen Riggin recalled the French public's displeasure as the United States continued to win event after event. "At the swimming stadium, the American flag was going up, and 'The Star-Spangled Banner' was playing after practically every event. There were a lot of French men in the audience, and they all wore straw hats with colored bands on them. The Frenchmen didn't stand up and didn't take their hats off at any time. We became kind of indignant about it when they didn't stand and hold their hats when 'The Star Spangled Banner' was played. So the swimmers got together, and the next day they brought some track men to the pool who were finished with their races. When the American anthem played and the flag went up for the first time, these men rushed the Frenchmen, grabbed all their hats, and sailed them into the pool. It was beautiful! There could have been an international incident over that, and I don't know how it was avoided. It's funny how indignant you can get about something some other country is doing."[22]

By the middle of the Games, it was clear that the women were an essential part of America's athletic powerhouse when it was determined that swimming victories placed the Americans so far ahead on the swimming scoreboard. So much so that even if Sweden, the closest competitor, won every single event from then on, they would not be able to catch up with the U.S. There was no distinction in the news coverage of women's events as opposed to men's; the women were clearly recognized as being equal contributors to the medals count.

The Americans were dominating the competition in diving as well, although this wasn't well received by all spectators. When the American women swept the fancy-diving competition, spectators roundly booed and threatened to throw the judges into the pool.[23]

By the time the team trials wrapped up, Trudy's condition and performance seemed to be improving. The U.S. women swept the first three heats of the 400-meter. Trudy was first with a time of 6:12 ⅕, well ahead of her other successful teammates in the other heats, Helen Wainwright's 6:45 ⅗ and Martha Norelius's 6:27 ⅕.[24] In the semi-final heats, Trudy finished far ahead of Vera Tanner of Great Britain. Trudy, Helen, and Martha advanced to the final. But in the final competition, Martha took the gold, Helen the silver, and Trudy the bronze medal.[25] For her final event, the 100-meter freestyle, Trudy qualified with a time of 1:12 ⅗, but was again disappointed when she finished third in the final against Mariechen Wehselau and Ethel Lackie. Trudy was shocked at not winning the events that she had expected to easily dominate, but was part of the relay team that won a gold medal.[26]

The American women had swept the aquatics events. Of the six diving

Members of the United States Olympic team returning from the Olympic Games in
Paris. All of the women are swimmers. The six women in white are, from left to right,
an unidentified swimmer, Helen Wainwright, Marichay Wehselau (standing slightly
behind), Helen Meany, Ethel Lackie, and Aileen Riggin (Library of Congress Prints
and Photographs Division).

medals given, five went to the American women, and of the 18 swimming
medals, 13 to the American women. With only 15 female athletes, the women
had won 18 out of all 99 American medals, and nine of 45 American gold
medals. They had proven, without a doubt, that Americans were the best
swimmers in the world, and they had proven that women were an essential
part of the American athletic success story.

19. Gertrude Ederle

Most of the women from the WSA had returned from the Olympics feeling good about their performances, but not Trudy Ederle. She had sailed for France assuming that she would bring home gold, and instead she felt like a failure. Although she had contributed to the gold medal relay win, her two bronze medals didn't seem like trophies to her; instead, they were reminders of races that she should have won easily. The poor performance would haunt her for her entire life. Over 50 years later she would still describe the Olympic loss as the "greatest disappointment of my swimming career."[1]

In August of 1924 she set a new record for the half-mile in Boston's Charles River Basin, breaking her own previously held record. Through the fall of that year she continued to swim in competitions for the WSA.

The WSA had been seeking to send a swimmer to attempt the ultimate long-distance swimming challenge, the English Channel. The WSA had been positioning Helen Wainwright as the most likely challenger. When Charlotte Epstein, as chairman of the WSA's Sports Committee, received approval from the Board of Governors of the WSA to begin formalizing plans to send Helen to England in the summer of 1925, the news made the front page of the *New York Times*.[2] Along with the approval of the Board came a promise of financial support to pay for the trip, which could easily cost $2,000.

Trudy approached Charlotte Epstein and told her that she, too, wanted to try the Channel. At the April 1925 meeting of the WSA, Charlotte went before the Board of Governors again, this time asking for additional money to send Trudy to England along with Helen. The Board granted its approval. The *New York Times* was prompt to point out that Trudy was faster than Helen. In fact, they reminded readers (perhaps trying to create a rivalry by intentionally opening old wounds) it was Helen who had been expected to win the Day Cup race in 1923. But it had been Trudy, the "virtually unknown youngster of fifteen," who astonished the international swimming scene by winning the race with a display of "totally unsuspected speed and endurance."[3]

In early June, only nine days before their scheduled departure for

England, Helen Wainwright surprised the press when she announced that she would not be attempting the Channel swim that summer after all. That spring, she had injured herself getting off a trolley, something her friends at the WSA certainly knew. She had wanted to make the swim, but didn't want to try it with an injured leg. But even more surprising, Helen announced her intention to go professional, and her intent to accept paid employment as a swim coach. To do this she would have to leave the WSA, and with that departure, she could no longer accept the funding offered by the WSA to try the Channel that summer.

"It will be a wrench to break away from amateur competition, of course," Helen declared. "Most of my friends are in it and I have derived no end of pleasure from it, but for one thing, I want to earn a living; for another, I plan to swim the English Channel next year. By taking up a career as a teacher and coach I will be doing the work I like most and for which I feel I am best fitted. And though I would have preferred to make the swim as an amateur, representing the WSA, which was kind enough to offer to finance my proposed trial of this summer, I could not think of asking the organization to again incur the great expense next season, now that it has arranged for Gertrude Ederle to make the attempt next month. While I have recovered from the injury which caused me to give up the Channel venture for the time being, so that I am about to resume training, it is too late for me to get in condition for so great a test this year, and I believe that as a professional I will have greater opportunities to get ready for it in 1926 and find it easier to make the financial arrangements also."[4]

Charlotte Epstein and Coach Handley took the announcement in stride, seeing Helen's departure as a loss for the team but a win for the future of the sport. Charlotte, always focusing on the big picture, magnanimously announced, "We all regret to see a champion of Helen's ability and versatility lost to the sport. But competition is not the main object of our association. Our chief purpose is to encourage girls and women to swim and provide them with the best of instruction. Helen will further our aims, for she will prove far more valuable as a teacher than a contestant."

Coach Handley stated, "It seems a great pity that Helen should be lost to amateur sports for she is one of the finest and gamest competitors I ever knew and I am sure she has her best swimming before her. But I think she is wise in taking advantage of the unusually good opportunities open to her and, after all, there is no doubt that she can be of greater service to swimming in the new capacity than in the old. I know she will make good."[5]

Despite these public statements of appreciation and support, it seems possible that Helen was asked to not come to England, given that her injury had prevented her from training. The WSA could not afford to send a competitor to England who was unprepared for fierce battle. Trudy was left as the WSA's sole hope for swimming the Channel that year. Helen, however, was not to be pitied. She accepted a summer swim instructor position at the exclusive Wentworth Pool at the summer colony of Portsmouth, New Hampshire, that paid an astounding $5,000 for three months' work.[6]

Three days before departing for England, Trudy attempted a 21-mile swim from the southern tip of Manhattan to New Jersey's Sandy Hook. Although approximately the same distance as the Channel swim, this water was mostly protected bay and did not possess the fierce tides and unpredictable weather of the English Channel.

Trudy was accompanied by two boats, one a rowboat and the other a powerboat. The powerboat, the Helys, carried members of the board of governors of the Women's Swimming Association, including Charlotte Epstein and Elsie Viets, Trudy's father Henry Ederle, several reporters, and, for some reason, the fire commissioner of Hoboken. Coach Handley stayed close to Trudy in the rowboat, where he could call to her with encouragement and directions.

They hadn't timed the departure well and the tide initially worked against her as she headed southeast towards Brooklyn, with the Statue of Liberty rising behind her in the darkness. As the sun rose, the tides turned and the swim became easier about the time she was stroking past Governor's Island. The new light coming up in the sky made it easier for the party to see oncoming ships and floating objects.

The course hugged the Brooklyn coast as far as Bay Ridge before turning south and heading past Hoffman and Swinburne Islands into lower New York Bay, then headed into the open ocean towards Sandy Hook, New Jersey. By 10:30, Trudy's only complaint was that the salt water was irritating her eyes, but later she would have other aches. In those pre-sunscreen days, long swims resulted in severe sunburn. Seven hours and 11 minutes after plunging off Manhattan, she cruised into shore at Sandy Hook, where she was greeted by a small crowd. She stretched out on the sand and had her eyes rinsed out. Her first request was for food. She hadn't eaten since her breakfast on shore.

Reporters noted with astonishment that Trudy needed almost no rest after the swim, and chatted and continued to eat on the boat ride home. They asked if she was tired, and she responded, "Not much. I could have kept on going if I had to." She added, "I usually feel a little tired during the first mile, but after that I am all right."[7]

She had broken the record for the swim, held by a man, by seven minutes and 30 seconds. The sports pages of the *New York Times* noted with respectful awe that Trudy had not only broken the previously held men's record, but that she had done it in far harsher conditions. The men's record had been set in 1914 by an AAU swimming champ from Boston, George R. Meehan, who had beaten 30 of his best competitors. In other words, 18-year-old Trudy had beaten the best of the best men. The paper also pointed out that the men's record had been set in mid–July when the water was significantly warmer than the water Trudy had been swimming in.

The swim to Sandy Hook served a more important purpose than training; in fact, it was fairly useless for training purposes beyond that of providing Trudy with mental assurances of her own abilities to swim long distances through open water. Instead, the success bolstered the confidence of the WSA and its financial supporters. The Channel endeavor was expensive, and they likely could not have justified sending her to England without a proven record for performing in long-distance swims. The New York Harbor swim was last-minute, and the WSA needed this reassurance that they were sending their very best competitor to England.

Two days later, Trudy was sailing for England on the *Berengaria* with Elsie Viets, her chaperone from the WSA.[8] She was ready to face the ultimate swimming challenge.

20. The English Channel

Following Captain Webb's 1875 conquest of the English Channel with a time of 21 hours and 50 minutes, many more swimmers attempted the feat. Not one succeeded until 1911, when Thomas Burgess finally repeated Webb's achievement, completing the swim with a time 40 minutes longer than Webb's.[1] Burgess, a Paris-based blacksmith originally from Yorkshire, England, had made 15 attempts before finally succeeding. He had started his swim on a "good old English breakfast" of eggs and ham. In the water, he had consumed chicken, chocolate and tea. Using the over-arm sidestroke and later the back-stroke, he powered through rough seas for 22½ hours, eventually covering a distance that was estimated to be close to 60 miles.

Burgess was frank about the physical and emotional stress of the endeavor. He was stung by "thousands" of jellyfish, particularly big purple ones, and spoke of wanting to quit the swim many times. "I was never uncon-scious on the way, though I sometimes go to sleep in the water, but I had hal-lucinations and saw all sorts of horrible things — too horrible to describe to you.

"The first thing I did when I got to land at Gris Nez was to have a jolly good cry. It relieved me. I could not stand up at all at first, after being tossed up and down for so many hours, but I quickly recovered and walked up the beach."

He was too sick to eat, but was forced to accept a glass of champagne, which didn't help his upset stomach. He spoke of "several flattering offers for the future," but vowed not to neglect his blacksmithing operation in Paris.[2]

For years after that, hundreds of people attempted unsuccessfully to swim the Channel, including Rose Pitonoff of Boston. In 1923, the London newspaper *The Daily Sketch* offered 1,000 pounds to anyone who could. That year, the streak of failures ended.

The first was Henry Sullivan of Lowell, Massachusetts, who made the swim in 27 hours. He stumbled out of the water in front of the Calais Casino, dead on his feet and barely aware of the cheering crowds pressing about him.

He was carried to a hotel room and fell asleep even as his trainer rubbed his muscles in an attempt to return warmth to his exhausted limbs.[3] Sullivan was 30 years old and had made his first Channel attempt ten years earlier. He collected his thousand pounds from the *Sketch* and returned to Massachusetts.

The next two swimmers dramatically shortened the swim time by conducting the swim in the opposite direction — from France to England, rather than from England to France. A week after Sullivan landed in France, Enrique Tirabocchi of Argentina made the swim in 16 hours and 33 minutes, seizing the record.[4] Because of the direction he was swimming and his speediness, Tirabocchi had only had to contend with three changing tides, whereas Sullivan had encountered five. Tirabocchi also collected a thousand pounds from the *Sketch* and headed to Italy for a tour, where the Argentinian of Italian heritage was praised by Premiere Mussolini for representing Italy so well.[5]

At the end of August, with the *Daily Sketch*'s September 7 deadline for the thousand pounds approaching quickly, many swimmers were making plans for final, desperate attempts. Meanwhile, the water grew colder and wilder.[6] On September 5, Charles Toth of Boston, Omar Perrault of Montreal, Carbis Walker of Cleveland, Frank Perks of Birmingham, England, and Georges Michel of France, all attempted the swim. All failed.

On September 10, Charles Toth finally covered the course in 16 hours and 40 minutes, swimming from France to England. He was piloted by Thomas Burgess, and attributed his successful course to the veteran swimmer's knowledge of the crossing. Having missed *The Daily Sketch*'s deadline, he did not collect 1,000 pounds. Still, he was pleased that he had been able "to prove to the folks back home that I could do it."[7]

Among those making the attempt that year was Mrs. Mille Gade Corson, a swim teacher at the Naval Militia of New York. She gave up the second attempt 14½ hours after starting, having gotten close enough to France to see the twinkling village lights on the shore.[8] She vowed to try again, but not that year.

As the crow flies, the shortest distance between England and France is 21 miles. But as the swimmer swims, it is a different story altogether. For its size, the English Channel is one of the world's most unpredictable and dangerous bodies of water. Various impacts of geology, time, tides, and currents have combined to create this utterly unique place.

Several 18th century geologists noted that the white cliffs of Dover, England, and the cliffs at Cap Blanc-Nez, France, were remarkably similar, and gradually came to conclude that the two masses had once been connected. Geologically, the channel is thought to have origins in the mid–Tertiary period, when sea levels may have been as much as 700 feet higher than today. During the icy Pleistocene Epoch, water levels dropped as glaciers formed elsewhere, trapping water. The drop resulted in sea levels that may have been 300 feet lower than today's, and revealed a land bridge that connected France and England. As the great ice sheets melted, about 10,000 years ago, and the water returned to the Channel, torrents of water wore away at the land bridge, leaving behind sandbars and sunken shoals that threaten ships in the English Channel to this day.

The narrowest part of the Channel is the Strait of Dover, which marks the dividing line between the Atlantic Ocean and the North Sea. Those two bodies of water meeting in the narrow strait create very complicated and highly unpredictable water patterns. The tides and currents, in combination with high winds, can be deadly to sailors and swimmers alike. The weather in the Channel is dangerously unpredictable, and even in summer frightening storms spontaneously arise with such fury that ship crossings must be canceled. Many ships haven't escaped the Channel's terrible storms; there are thought to be hundreds and hundreds of shipwrecks on the floor of the Channel, although, to be accurate, many were sunk in naval battles.

For swimmers, the crossing is even more dangerous. The water rarely gets above 64 degrees, even at the height of summer. The tides make it impossible to cut straight across the Channel in only 21 miles and necessitate a swerving path that can result in a final swim distance of well over 30 hard-fought miles. Often the swimmer is either swimming directly against the tide or at a right angle to it. The swimmer must also calculate carefully and time the swim to avoid being caught on outgoing tidal currents that lengthen the swim or waste hours of effort to simply remain in place and not be pulled backwards. It is also crucial to watch the moon because the tides vary greatly during the different lunar phases. Spring tides occur during full moons and new moons (when the moon is invisible) and produce higher than usual high tides, and lower than usual low tides. Neap tides occur during quarter moons, and produce weak tides. Because of all these factors, swimming the English Channel requires far more than perseverance and strength.

21. Training

Once in England, Trudy Ederle and Elsie Viets headed first to Brighton to meet the coach who had been hired by the WSA, Jabez Wolffe. Wolffe was a noted channel swimming expert who had attempted to swim the Channel over 20 times, once even failing within a mile of the opposite shore. Trudy spent two weeks in Brighton simply trying to acclimate herself to the temperature of the water, which she believed was colder than any she had encountered on the Atlantic coast of the United States.[1] Once she had become accustomed to the water temperature, she took daily swims, swimming out into the ocean against the tides, which were not as strong as those she would encounter in the Channel. Her swims were watched by crowds leaning on the rails of the Brighton Pier, the city's epicenter for entertainment and leisure.[2] Her training consisted of a four-day cycle, with one hour of swimming on the first day, two hours on the second, three on the third, then a day to recover.[3]

In July, the group relocated to Cap Gris-Nez, a tiny French village located on a point of land that juts into the channel, making it France's closest point to England and the jumping-off point for most Channel attempts. The small town was crowded with fellow aspiring Channel swimmers, men and women alike. Male competitors included Ishak Helmy, a wealthy Egyptian, and Setou Nishimira, a Japanese long-distance swimmer. But all eyes were really on the women. Many believed that this was the year a woman would complete the swim.

Trudy's main competitors for the prize were Lillian Harrison of Argentina and Jane Sion of France. Argentina, apparently, wanted to be the holder of both the male and female records. Both women had tried to swim the channel the previous summer and failed.[4]

The three women had notably different patterns of training. Trudy's consisted of swims not more than three hours or so, always accompanied by a motorboat so that she would become accustomed to following a boat in the water. She also took long walks. Lillian Harrison, on the other hand, took part in aggressive feats of strength all summer long. She was being coached by

Thomas Burgess, the second man to complete the channel swim. On July 3, Lillian swam 17 miles in the ocean from Cap Gris-Nez past Boulogne-sur-Mer in just over five hours.[5] She made an attempt on the Channel on July 16, while Trudy was still in Brighton, covering about 15 miles in just under eight hours and 57 minutes.[6] On August 2, she participated in a grueling 26-mile race down the Seine River to Paris. The temperature of the water was below 60 degrees and a driving rain chilled the air. An enthusiastic crowd of 50,000 cheered her when she finally climbed out of the water near the Eiffel Tower. She placed fourth, the only woman in a field of 24 men.

The three women also used different swim strokes. Trudy continued to use the American crawl taught to her by Coach Handley, Lillian Harrison used the breast stroke, and Jane Sion utilized the "over-arm" stroke, a variation of a side stroke.[7]

The swimmers' diets were of great interest to the public. As the daughter of a butcher, Trudy's meaty diet was hyped as the key to her success. Actually, she ate anything she wanted, from mutton to cake and chocolates. Lillian, on the other hand, was a vegetarian. Another swimmer, Setsu Nishimura of Japan, was limiting himself to vegetables and eggs.

On August 2, Jabez Wolffe announced his confidence in Trudy. "I firmly believe that Miss Ederle will succeed, and if she does, she will lower the record." He hypothesized that if the weather was ideal, the swim could be completed in 14 hours, close to two-and-a-half hours shorter than the current record of 16 hours and 25 minutes. He had only one complaint about Trudy. "If there is any fault to be found with Miss Ederle's swimming, it is that her pace is too fast. She swims approximately 28 strokes to the minute, and we want to reduce this pace to 24. There is no doubt that she can maintain 28 for eight or nine hours, but I would prefer a slightly slower stroke for a swim which may require 16 to 20 hours."[8]

All of the activities at the Channel were eagerly reported on a daily basis by papers in the United States. Even news of a shopping trip Trudy took to Boulogne-sur-Mer was relayed back to the Americans watching this international battle.[9] They also read about her fantastic chest expansion, which, when measured by an astonished physician, was determined to be nearly eight inches. "This is the most wonderful lung development I have ever seen in my career," the unidentified doctor was quoted as saying. "She must have wonderful endurance and vitality. If I were a betting man I would wager that she can swim the Channel."[10]

Plenty of people took the helpful doctor's unsolicited advice. Lloyd's of London, while making it clear that they were "underwriters" and not some sort of gambling agency, received so many orders for "policies" in support of Trudy's attempt that odds dropped from 20 to one to 7 to one.[11]

It was difficult for the swimmers and their coaches to plan for an exact date for the swim. Coaches and pilots did their best to select a good range of days within the lunar cycle, but the limitations of predicting the weather meant that swimmers might not know until the night before whether or not an attempt would actually take place.

On August 5, Jane Sion made her attempt, getting within a mile and a half of the Dover shore in just 13 hours. A few days later, she eloquently explained the terrible fears that confront the swimmer, alone in the dark water, miles from land with nothing but shipwrecks and seamonsters in the darkness below. It was neither the cold nor the fatigue that broke her, she said, but a "stroke of 'cafard.'" *Cafard* is a French term that refers to a crushing sense of discouragement. It is often felt by exhausted and demoralized soldiers in the trenches of war.

As Jane recalled: "I swam courageously against the tide as long as daylight lasted, but when night began to envelop me a feeling of weary dejection came upon me and the thought that those lights on the English coast, which it seemed I could reach out and touch, would actually take three or four more hours to reach, froze me more than the water and I had no will to continue. The water was all right; it was not too cold. I still believe that I am capable of swimming the Channel, but night made me afraid, and darkness alone was responsible for my defeat."[12]

Each swimmer watched gingerly as the others made their attempts, publicly putting on a face of support for the others. The newspapers were eager to create nationalistic rivalries between the women while simultaneously maintaining the fiction that the women were not truly competing against one another. Interpersonal competition seemed to be either too vulgar for women to concern themselves with, or a luxury or a vanity perhaps reserved for men. The *New York Times* maintained that Trudy and Lillian were the "best of friends," while presenting no evidence whatsoever to back up the claim.[13]

For a time the idea was floated that all three women would race simultaneously, but Jane had exhausted her finances and was unable to do so.[14] Then it was announced that Lillian and Trudy would both swim across on the evening of August 7. It was not to be a race, technically, as the women would leave at slightly staggered times, not simultaneously. Of course, the newspapers continued to treat the event as a race.[15] Coach Wolffe announced that Trudy would be the likely winner, while Lillian's coach, Thomas Burgess, had the same confidence in Lillian. The plan was for Lillian and Trudy to spend the afternoon in Boulogne-sur-Mer before boarding separate tugboats to take them to Cap Gris-Nez, where they would enter the water sometime after 9 P.M. Boulogne-sur-Mer was crammed with photographers, newspaper men, and movie-camera operators, all vying for a spot on either tug. Thousands of spectators roamed through the town, hoping to catch a glimpse of Lillian and Trudy.

But that night, Trudy became ill and decided not to try the swim until August 17. The unstoppable Lillian was ready to try the swim on her own the very next day, when her irate father arrived and put an end to the media circus. "Weather conditions no doubt are good, but they are not good enough," announced Mr. Harrison. "We are not going to be pushed into the water by anybody. We are here to swim the Channel and not to provide copy for the newspapers and pictures for the movies."[16]

Lillian made her next attempt, her second of that summer, on August 10 in very difficult weather conditions. She left Gris-Nez around noon. Ishak Helmy and Jane Sion occasionally joined her in the water, swimming alongside her to keep her company and provide encouragement. By all reports, Lillian was making excellent time and had covered 13 miles when she fainted in midstroke. Helmy caught her and hoisted her out of the water and into the boat. As she regained her senses on the tug, reporters heard her say that she would never again attempt to swim the English Channel.[17]

A doctor who examined her announced that she had not been properly greased and that she hadn't eaten enough beforehand. By the next day, Lillian had forgotten her vow to leave the Channel alone, and she was ready to try again.[18] Trudy's coach, Jabez Wolffe, announced his opinion that it was Lillian's vegetarian diet that was ruining her chances. Trudy, the butcher's daughter, didn't have to worry about this. She had been eating well all summer, and had gained 14 pounds since leaving New York.[19] She was also getting itchy for some action. "It can't come too quick. I am rather tired of this suspense."[20]

As August 17 approached, it became clear that something had changed drastically in Trudy's relationship with Coach Wolffe. On August 8, Wolffe announced to the press that he did not think Trudy would be able to swim the channel. "I think Miss Ederle is the fastest swimmer alive, but I do not expect her to succeed in swimming the channel this time. First, she refuses to train and plays the ukulele all day. She made her records without training and does not see why she should train now. Second, she is too fast a swimmer for such a great distance. If she swims fast, she will collapse, and she cannot swim slowly because her feet have a trick of hanging down when she is swimming slowly."[21]

Wolffe and Elsie Viets had begun to disagree on the best methods for Trudy's training even earlier in the summer. Miss Viets apparently thought a combination of swimming about two hours per day combined with walking was ideal, while Wolffe began complaining that Trudy wasn't spending enough time in the water. When Wolffe took his complaints to the press, Ms. Viets retorted that, while Wolffe may have been an expert on the Channel, he knew very little about the "temperament and feelings of an 18-year-old girl swimmer."[22]

On the 17th, Trudy announced that her training had ended and that she would not enter the water again before her Channel swim the following day. Somehow, Trudy remained confident, but Wolffe continued to make statements that must have unnerved her. He complained to the press that he had been allowed very little to do with her training. He announced the day before the swim that he wanted to quit his responsibility as her trainer, and had only been persuaded to see the endeavor through by some friends who prevented him from catching the boat back to England.

"Miss Ederle doubtless is the finest exponent of swimming who was ever tried the channel," he announced petulantly. "She can swim the channel, and I would have felt confident of her success had she followed my training instructions. She may be one of those athletic marvels who don't require any special training for tremendous tasks."[23]

The weather was finally fair, and the water appeared settled at 63 degrees. The final preparations for the swim were set. The tugboat *La Morinie* was loaded with supplies, and would be accompanied by a rowboat. *La Morinie* would carry Thomas Burgess, Ishak Helmy, the British swimmer Vera Tanner, Lillian Harrison, Jane Sion, many reporters, and a four-piece jazz band. As Jane Sion could say from experience, "Music is just as essential to a Channel swimmer as food." Trudy added, "We want real American jazz — hard-boiled music. Nothing in the minor chord for me."[24] In addition to the band, the rowboat would carry a gramophone, a special gift from the WSA.

Trudy radiated nonchalance in the days before the swim. She took little interest in the last-minute deliberations of her team as they struggled to decide on the best time and place of departure. They couldn't predict the weather, but daily they measured the temperatures of the water and the air and studied wind speeds and weather reports from other regions. The team hired Joe Costa, a boat pilot and Channel navigation expert, to make the final determination of departure time and place. Costa decided that the best place from which to depart was from the very tip of the promontory of Cap Gris-Nez, a jagged point stabbing into the English Channel. The slope from the heights of the headland down to the water are covered with huge sharp boulders that tumble down the steep cliffs into the water, forming a fan of rocks that poke from the water and make approaching the shore by boat almost impossible. The alternative starting point was from a beach closer to Trudy's training camp, but the swim out past the cape into open water was thought to be even more dangerous than the swim that started directly from the cape.[25] Joe Costa would be on board the *La Morinie*, directing the tug's captain with charts of the Channel's depths and tides.

Trudy took little interest in the machinations of the team, telling Elsie, "Just look after all those details. My job is to swim the Channel."[26] She showed the press her bright pink swimming cap, and joked that she had chosen the bright colors so that she would be visible when she swam into Dover. Even reports that two six-foot sharks had been caught off of Boulogne-sur-Mer the night before didn't chill her enthusiasm. She joked that the presence of sharks could only improve her speed.[27]

Wolffe continued to make disparaging remarks right up until the last possible moment. At midnight the night of the swim, he made a final inspection of the tugboat and its supplies and rations. "Miss Ederle has every qualification for success. She is the finest swimmer who ever made the attempt. I am sorry she has not followed stricter training but her ideas have frequently been opposed to mine. I have told her that this marathon swim is different from anything she has tried. But what man can argue successfully with a woman?"[28]

Trudy woke that morning in Boulogne-sur-Mer at 4 A.M. She ate a breakfast of beef stew, then rose from the table and announced, "I'm all ready for it. Bring on your old Channel."[29] Trudy and Elsie were on their way to board La Morinie when Trudy noticed that her skirt was inside-out. Elsie asked if she wanted to go back to change, but Trudy declined, joking that it would bring her good luck. Crowds of spectators lined the docks to see her off, cheering heartily as she strode up the gangplank. As the tug headed out of the harbor, Trudy went below, where she applied a heavy coating of sticky lard and lanolin grease to protect her from the cold water.[30]

22. Gone to Neptune

The tug was packed with Trudy's team, reporters, and supporters. Ishak Helmy, Jane Sion, and Lillian Harrision were there to join her in the water for short periods, both to serve as pacers and to keep her mind occupied and off the grueling task of swimming for 15 hours.

The newsmen had set up a mobile office on deck, complete with typewriters. There were photographers and even movie-camera operators. Some were using the wireless to report home, the messages first being sent to a station on the coast of England, and then relayed on to North America. Others were sending their updates back to shore, using a steady fleet of quick motor boats, and some were even relying on carrier pigeons.[1]

Shortly after seven in the morning, Trudy was rowed to the headland so that she could touch the shore for the official start. She slapped the rock, and then entered the 64-degree water. The morning was dawning with a beautiful light, with no visible swells on the Channel and nothing but a soft breeze coming from the southeast. The weather appeared almost perfect for the attempt.[2]

She followed the rowboat back out through the rocks. A mere 15 minutes later, as she caught up with *La Morinie* about 500 yards off the cape, the jazz band began to play "March of the Allies," which didn't fit Trudy's mood. "Give me 'Yes! We Have No Bananas,'" she called back.

Wolffe and Helmy were in the rowboat, staying within a few yards of Trudy at all times. She started off with exceptional speed, spurting away from the shore so forcefully, at 27 strokes a minute, that Wolffe tried to slow her down. "This is not a 1,500-meter race, Miss Ederle," he yelled from the rowboat.[3]

Thomas Burgess thought that in all his years of Channel swimming and coaching, he had never seen any swimmer leave France behind so quickly. Trudy alternated between the trudgeon, the crawl, and the breast stroke. In an hour she was three miles from the coast of France. Three hours into the swim, she called, "Send someone in with me! I'm getting lonesome."[4]

Trudy receiving some nourishment from Wolffe (Library of Congress Prints and Photographs Collection).

Vera Tanner jumped in to help with pacing. Vera and Trudy knew each other from the Olympics in Paris; they had both competed in the 100-meter freestyle. Trudy had won the bronze, and Vera had come in fifth.

Wolffe directed them not to talk, or turn the swim into a race, advice that Trudy and Vera ignored. A massive liner passed the entourage. Passengers cheered from the deck as Trudy and Vera waved back from their place far below in the waves. Wolffe called to them to get serious. "Cut that talking out, girls."

After an hour, Trudy was already in need of a snack. She paddled in place next to the rowboat as Wolffe passed her some beef tea on the end of a stick. She pulled out the cork with her teeth, but the bottle slipped from her hands and disappeared beneath the waves despite her attempts to retrieve it, much to the amusement of those on the tug. "Five shillings of nourishment gone to Neptune," Wolffe complained as he tied another to the stick and passed it to her. "*A votre sante!*" she called, then tossed the bottle behind her.

The dialogue between Wolffe and Trudy wasn't exactly friendly, and some reporters gleefully focused on their barbed exchanges. As Wolffe continued to tell her to slow down, he called, "Don't waste your energy! The temperature is still at 64 and you need all your reserve!" "All right!" she called back, ignoring his directions completely. Around nine in the morning, Trudy paddled alongside the rowboat for a drink of water, as Wolffe chided her not to lose the bottle this time. "Is it nice and warm in there?" he inquired, to which she snapped, "Yes, it's a real treat." She took some coffee and chocolate.[5]

A bit later, Trudy complained of some stomach discomfort, saying "I can feel that beef stew yet." Not long after, Wolffe handed over to her some liquid beef extract that he tied to the end of a long stick and passed to her in the water. Trudy wasn't allowed solid food, and in deference to her appetite, he required everyone on the tug to eat on the opposite side of the boat. He himself hunched politely behind a book in the rowboat as he ate his own lunch.

At 10:45, they were ten miles from Cap Gris Nez. With the tide in her favor, Trudy had beaten all records, set by men or women, for distance covered in that period of time. Around noon, Vera Tanner left the water and was replaced by Captain Greenier. By now they were mid–Channel, and the water was measured at 63 degrees, one degree cooler than at the start.

Four hours in, Trudy had to swim through a school of jellyfish. Her skin became irritated from the stinging, but worse still was the horrible feeling of gliding over and through them. Six hours into the swim, Lillian Harrison joined Trudy in the water. The weather had begun to change and the sunshine was disappearing behind a solid bank of dark clouds that stretched as far as they could see. The waves began to deepen. "There's too much up and down in this ocean," Trudy said, but then corrected herself, "Oh, I don't mind it. A little can't rattle me."

Eight hours into the swim, she was six-and-a-half miles from Dover, whose white cliffs were just beginning to come into view to those on the tug, when the weather changed dramatically. No storms had been predicted for that day, and the squall that hit took everyone by surprise. The foaming, slamming sea was so rough that reporters and jazz musicians became seasick. The trombonist, the cornetist, and the clarinetist headed for the rails to be sick; only the concertina player held his own.[6] In an attempt to keep the musical encouragement coming, some newspaper men took over for the incapacitated trio.[7]

Helmy jumped in to help with pacing. Trudy found herself fighting high waves and wind as the ocean smashed into her face. For two miles she headed into the wind and fought the waves. She swallowed salt water over and over but gamely struggled on. Her strokes became uneven and she began to take breaks every few hundred yards.[8] Her hands shook as she reached again for the beef tea.

What happened next became difficult to verify. Markedly different accounts were to come from the people in the rowboat, on the tug, Wolffe, Burgess, Helmy, and Trudy. At 3:58, Trudy was swimming alongside Helmy when a wave slapped into her face. She coughed and gasped for air.

"Grab her!" shouted Wolffe. Helmy reached over and grabbed Trudy. The contact instantly disqualified her. The attempt was officially over.

Reporters on the tug gave different interpretations of what had happened in the water. The *Daily News* reporter saw Helmy as a hero for saving the "hardly conscious" Trudy, having "seized the American girl, and with long powerful strokes brought her to the official boat."[9] The *Washington Post* reported, "She sobbed as if her heart would break when she was dragged aboard a row boat after having been kept afloat by Ishak Helmy, the Egyptian swimmer, who at a sign from Jabez Wolffe, the ever watchful trainer, threw his arms about the sinking girl."[10]

Alec Rutherford, from the *Los Angeles Times*, wrote, "Wolfe called on Helmy to stand close by and a few moments later Helmy saw that the American girl was choking and apparently unable to keep afloat. Mme. Sion assisted Helmy in getting a towel around her body and then they dragged her over to the tug and got her onboard."[11]

Once on board, Helmy told Rutherford what he had seen at eye-level. "I kept my eye on her all the time. Presently I noticed her gasp, choke and splutter, the water coming through her mouth and nose. I said, 'Steady, Gertie, steady. Take it easy.' She appeared eased up. Suddenly she threw her head back, and was on the point of collapse. Then Wolffe ordered me to seize her."[12]

Trudy recovered quickly, devouring a chocolate bar and then sleeping soundly until the boat returned to Boulogne-sur-Mer.[13] Trudy avoided answering questions from reporters, but they noted that she seemed dejected. The party had dinner at the Boulogne Hotel, and then headed back to Cap Gris-Nez. She reported feeling fine and experiencing no muscle soreness at all, although the stings of the jellyfish and the memory of the encounter stayed with her. "The feeling of these slimy things against my arms and legs perhaps had as much to do with upsetting my stomach as swallowing the salt water," she shuddered.[14] She slept late the next day, ate a hearty breakfast, and then went for a walk on the dunes before announcing that Jabez Wolffe was no longer her trainer. She announced that she had hired Thomas Burgess to replace Wolffe, and that she would make a second attempt within the next ten days.[15] Burgess, of course, had actually swum the Channel, unlike Wolffe, a fact the American papers were happy to point out. One slyly noted, "Why Wolffe should be engaged as a trainer for ambitious young Channel swimmers merely because of the frequency of his failures isn't particularly clear."[16] Wolffe left immediately for home in England.[17]

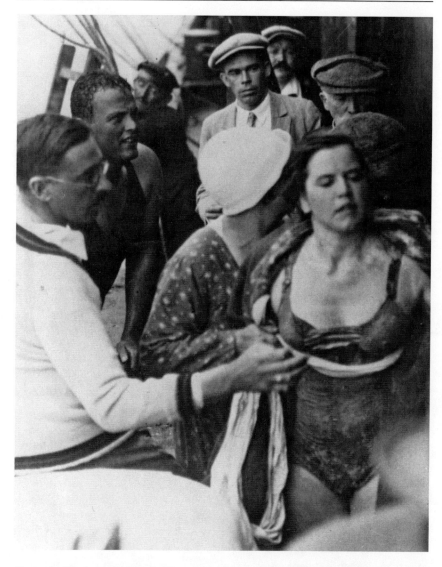

Gertrude Ederle immediately after the end of her first attempt to swim the English Channel. Elsie Viets is behind her; Ishak Helmy is the man in the bathing suit (International Swimming Hall of Fame).

One newspaper raised the possibility that Trudy and Lillian would attempt the swim together. Two days later, the same paper reported that Jane Sion might join them, although all three would have separate tugs and entourages, and it was by no means to be considered a race between their three respective nations.[18] Jane, though, was suffering from a lack of funding and other support. She was paying for the swim with her own savings, and noted, "I wish I could afford expert trainers, special food and good masseurs. I feel sure I could swim the Channel. I stinted myself of every luxury of life for four years to get sufficient funds to pay the expenses of my Channel swim. I even refrained from buying a new hat this summer. Look at this one — it has been remodeled twice since 1923."[19]

The swimmers returned to training and waited for the weather to improve, but it did not. Normally, late August offered the most helpful tides, but after September 10, the waters would become so rough that even crossing by boat becomes unpleasant. Other attempts were made, including a failed one by Setsu Nishimura of Japan, which lasted less than two hours. He may have been hampered by his outfit, an "ordinary swimming suit and a dress reaching to his knees."[20] Dr. G. B. Brewster embarked while ten-foot-tall, gale-driven waves were pounding the shores at Cap Gris Nez, and somehow managed to swim 13 miles before giving up.[21] One day Trudy, Ishak Helmy, and Vera Tanner planned on a three-hour swim, but were forced back to shore after only 20 minutes.[22]

Trudy continued to train and kept *La Morinie* on retainer in case a day broke with good weather, but even as she waited for the rough seas to subside, the water temperature became colder by the day. Nights were cold and fog enveloped the shoreline. The stress of waiting for the weather to improve was immense. When a reporter presented Trudy with a copy of a newspaper article about her parents and how supportive they were of her, Trudy burst into tears upon reading it. "I must do it for them. I must try it again, I must. I must."[23]

The jazz band, however, was not kept on retainer in case of a second attempt. They had been so traumatized by the storm and the seasickness they had suffered on board that they returned to their hometown of Lille without stopping first to get paid. When Joe Costa wrote to ask them to keep their schedules open, they refused, replying, "Send us the thousand francs due us by mail. We are sorry we cannot undertake to play again on the tug, even for three times that amount."[24]

By the third of September, there was no way to avoid facing the painful fact that the channel was becoming more dangerous by the hour, and another attempt wasn't going to happen that year. They had missed the window of opportunity. Trudy sighed, "This is tougher than swimming from the Battery to Coney Island. I am very much afraid the folks at home will be disappointed."[25]

Trudy and Elsie headed for Paris to catch the *Mauretania* for the trip home. Back at the Channel, Ishak Helmy made a final attempt. He spent 14 hours and 32 minutes in the 59-degree water, getting within three and a half miles of Dover before giving up.[26]

23. Suspicions and Facts

Trudy and Elsie arrived back in New York on the 18th. They were greeted by crowds of friends and reporters, but Elsie kept Trudy under tight control. The two stayed onboard and refused to speak to reporters until the WSA contingent arrived. Aileen Riggin, Coach Handley, Charlotte Epstein, and Margaret Johnson, president of the WSA, met Trudy at the pier and sequestered her from reporters. Elsie announced that Trudy would not be making any statements "until after certain matters have been cleared up," but Trudy insisted on speaking to the press. Charlotte finally allowed it. "I could have gone on. But whether I would have finished, no one could tell. I stopped because Helmy touched me and that was disqualification." A reporter asked why Helmy had done that, and Trudy bitterly answered, "Ask Wolffe."[1]

"I could have kept going," she added. "There was no truth in the story that I collapsed."[2]

Coach Handley also made a statement to the press. "The suspicion is indicated that Miss Ederle was taken out of the water prematurely. Motion pictures of the incident show that she sat up in the boat. If she had been exhausted she would have collapsed."[3]

Eventually Trudy escaped the reporters and was taken home to the Ederle family's beach house in Highlands, New Jersey. The next day she indignantly began to respond to the things Wolffe had said about her during her training, beginning with his assertions that she spent more time playing the ukulele than training. "That is all a lie. Of course I played my uke, but I played it only evenings after my training had been concluded. It was my only relaxation. I did everything Wolffe told me to do. He cannot name an instance where I disobeyed an order."[4]

Wolffe responded quickly to Trudy's statements, reiterating the same ukulele charge. "Her statements are quite untrue. I take it her story was meant to cover her noncompliance with my repeated efforts to get her to train. It was evident to observers that her training consisted mainly of playing the ukulele." He also denied that he gave the order for Ishak Helmy to grab Trudy.

"At the sixth hour of the swim, Miss Ederle complained of a cramp and I begged her to carry on a little longer. At the eighth hour she was suffering intense agony, purely owing to lack of condition. After eight hours and fifteen minutes she collapsed. I gave no instructions for Helmy to touch her, but as there was a risk of being drowned, Helmy went to her aid. I was standing by on a small boat and immediately got to her and put the lifesaving apparatus on her, as she was unconscious." Furthermore, he stated, "One only has to observe the pictures of her collapse in the water to see that she was incapable of making any further effort. I am of the opinion that had Miss Ederle followed instructions she would have succeeded in swimming the Channel. I still think she is capable of doing so, if properly trained."[5]

Others chimed in. Thomas Burgess, back in Boulogne, tended to agree with Wolffe's determination that Trudy had been in real difficulty. On the other hand, Joe Costa, the pilot, thought she could have gone farther.

The following day, Elsie Viets declared that Wolffe had indeed given Helmy the order to grab Trudy. "I distinctly heard Wolffe cry out, 'Grab her, Helmy!' The ever-important ukulele accusations she dismissed as well. "She did everything Wolffe asked her to do, and if she played the ukulele she did so in the same manner that another person would play the piano or any other musical instrument. It did not affect her training and was done during her spare moments."

Elsie also disagreed with Wolffe's description of Trudy's condition as she left the water. She stated that after Trudy was grabbed by Helmy, she swam under her own power to the stern of the rowboat and pulled herself in with just a small push from Helmy. Once the boat came alongside the tug, Trudy was able to climb up the side herself and walk to her dressing room unaided. Trudy did not need any lifesaving apparatus, and according to Elsie, there was nothing resembling a lifesaving apparatus on the rowboat other than an ordinary towel. Wolffe had wrapped this around Trudy's waist, apparently so tight that Trudy snapped, "Loosen that, you're hurting me."[6]

The following day, September 21, 1925, Trudy returned from New Jersey and gave another statement to reporters.

> I want to say again that I was pulled out of the water at the orders of Trainer Wolffe, and his statements that he did not make such an order are not true. I distinctly heard him give the order to Helmy. Helmy towed me to the rowboat and Wolffe pulled me on board using the towel. I wasn't exhausted at all. I was having a bad spell, however, but every Channel swimmer has bad spells. It is a great strain and I have been told by many who have tried to swim the Channel and by Burgess, who did swim it, that every swimmer had bad spells. I blame Wolffe for his judgement in ordering me out when he did. He should have had me take a rest. He was experienced in Channel swimming while I was not.[7]
>
> I will try again next year if I possibly can. I think I will have Burgess as a trainer.

He seemed to think I had a wonderful chance. Of course, luck plays a big part in a Channel swim. Tides, winds, temperature of water all make a big difference, and I guess the trainer and coach have a lot to do with it too. If I try again I will give my best, and I certainly would like to succeed, but it is no disgrace not to succeed, for look at all those who have tried and failed.[8]

Elsie Viets also issued another statement, asserting that Trudy was being "placed in a false light before the American public by statements of her English trainer."[9] She accused Wolffe of wanting Trudy to fail, saying,

> Jabez Wolffe is quoted as saying that Miss Ederle failed to follow his instructions in training; that L. deB. Handley, amateur coach of the WSA, interfered with his plans; that Miss Ederle became unconscious during her attempt and had to be rescued by the Egyptian swimmer, Helmy, though he [Wolffe] issued no order for her to be taken from the water. These statements are absolutely untrue and I have a number of letters from reliable resources to prove every one false. Miss Ederle followed Wolffe's instructions to the letter. Mr. Handley not only did not interfere but told both Miss Ederle and myself to be guided entirely by Wolffe; the motion pictures of the swim afford the best evidence that Miss Ederle did not collapse; but I have the written testimony of eye witnesses for collaboration; Mr. Helmy himself, and others present, vouch over their signatures that Wolffe ordered Miss Ederle out of the water before she was exhausted. For the rest, though Wolffe was paid to help Miss Ederle in her great undertaking, his actions before and during the swim conveyed to myself and others the very strong impression that he was not anxious to see her succeed. That Miss Ederle collapsed is entirely untrue. She was tired, as anyone must be after nine hours of swimming, but she was making progress when Wolffe ordered Helmy, then with her, to bring her in. She never was unconscious and the motion pictures of the swim show that she was able to sit up unassisted in the rowboat and to climb from the rowboat on the tug, though rough water made this no easy matter.[10]

In a formal statement issued by the WSA, Elsie made more specific allegations.

> Shortly after our arrival in Brighton, Wolffe endeavored to make Miss Ederle discard the crawl stroke, which enabled her to swim to Sandy Hook in the record time of seven hours eleven minutes in June, and tried to make her adopt the side stroke, which she had never used. Fortunately, W. J. Howcroft, the noted British expert, was in Brighton at the time and spoke so forcefully against the absurd step that Wolffe abandoned it. Wolffe, consciously or otherwise, did everything imaginable to break Miss Ederle's morale. He was the one to tell her there were sharks in the Channel, although he must have known the fish seen were porpoises. He never allowed her to practice with other swimmers and kept her always in the shallow water, despite her request to be sent out where she could get used to conditions; usually he did not permit her to swim more than fifteen minutes to half an hour per day. He told everyone, myself included, that she had no chance. He spoke to her everlastingly of the difficulties of the feat and of all the unpleasant things which might happen to her. He gave her absolutely no encouragement and

found fault with everything she did. Then, during the attempt, he did not even have a compass with him in the boat from which he piloted her so that the course he steered was snake-like from start to finish.[11]

The WSA's statement included an affidavit from Alec Rutherford, the *Los Angeles Times* reporter, who not only confirmed the accounts of how Wolffe had treated Trudy, but elaborated on Wolffe's behavior.

> I have heard criticism of the so-called lack of co-operation between Miss Ederle and Wolffe. The lack was not on the part of Miss Ederle. It seemed to me that Wolffe on every occasion jammed down her throat the difficulties she would meet, the struggles she would have, the possible illnesses she would experience. He appeared to take an antagonistic attitude toward all connected with Miss Ederle. He was not backward in seeing that every press representative was well informed that he thought Miss Ederle would prove a dismal failure, and even when she was climbing into the tug he was holding forth with his inevitable, "I told you so." I feel very strongly on the matter of the disgraceful attitude adopted toward Miss Viets and Miss Ederle.

In Paris, Ishak Helmy provided his side of the story. He confirmed that Wolffe had indeed given the order to grab Trudy, but also said that, "Miss Ederle was completely finished and unconscious when I gathered her in. She never objected to my touching her or to my assisting her to keep afloat. I believe she was too far gone to know what was going on. She soon recuperated, however, and was in fine physical shape after she had been on the tug a few minutes."[12]

The same night that the WSA issued their formal statement condemning Wolffe's actions, they held a celebration for Trudy at New York's Hippodrome. It was quite a fantastic evening, with addresses given by the president of the Amateur Athletic Union, Mr. Murray Hulbert, and, far more exciting to the female swimmers gathered there, Annette Kellerman. Mr. Hulburt cracked a joke about Trudy having been warned of sharks in the Channel, but not of a "Wolffe." The WSA's motto hung over the stage in banner form, the words "Sportsmanship is greater than victory," likely both irritating and silencing many in the crowd who would have preferred that Trudy possess both. Annette Kellerman entertained the crowd with one of her signature diving extravaganzas and then presented the WSA with two trophy cups to be awarded to the best long-distance swimmer of the year and the swimmer with the best and most graceful strokes. The WSA presented Trudy with a diamond bracelet. For at least the second time in a week, she surprised them with her uncooperative behavior. She refused to come to the stage to accept the bracelet, and WSA President Margaret W. Johnson made the presentation in the box where Trudy was seated.[13]

The next morning, Trudy was interviewed on the radio station WOR, and she informed New York City that she had "many suspicions and facts" yet to reveal about Jabez Wolffe. She provocatively announced that if the Women's Swimming Association did not make those suspicions public within the next 30 days, she would do it herself.[14] She added that she would be ready to face the Channel again the next summer. "My motto is, 'If at first you don't succeed, try, try again.' And I want the public to know that I am going to attempt to swim the English Channel again next July."

Trudy didn't make good on her threats to reveal more about Wolffe, but over a year later there were clues to what suspicions she may have been referring. In the fall of 1926, reporter Julia Harpman wrote a two-part article for *Liberty* magazine in which she stated that Wolffe had doped Trudy with a "foreign mixture" containing cocaine the morning of the swim. The article noted that Trudy was absolutely unaccustomed to narcotics and intoxicants, and had never before ingested a stimulant. Trudy attributed her headache and a sense of heaviness that day to the drug. "I felt like a heavy band was being pressed against my head," she recalled. "My main trouble last year was the absence of encouragement and that queer feeling in my head." The article stated that Wolffe had admitted to doping Trudy, thinking the cocaine would stimulate her, and quoted Thomas Burgess saying, "Gertie was doped."[15]

Later in October of 1926, Trudy was interviewed for the Harvard University student paper, the *Crimson*, and made the same claim. "The first attempt I made, I nearly went to sleep in the water. Someone had put drugs in the beef tea I drank before starting. My trainer proved this beyond any doubt."[16]

Somehow, there was no reaction whatsoever to this in the papers.

Was it possible that Wolffe had slipped Trudy cocaine? One has to assume that the intended effect of cocaine would have been to make her swim faster or for a longer period of time. If his previous statements to the press indicated that he did not really think she could finish the swim on her own, did he think the cocaine would help her finish? Why would he want to help her finish under false means if he himself had never finished?

Wolffe wasn't opposed to using performance enhancers in Channel swims. On one of his own attempts in 1908, he used oxygen to regain his strength. Wolffe was accompanied by Dr. Martin Flack of the London Medical College who conducted on Wolffe the same sort of experiment of which Elaine Golding had been a part. When Wolffe became exhausted, Flack and his oxygen tank and a large apparatus were transferred to the rowboat, and Flack administered oxygen via a tube every 15 minutes. Wolffe revived temporarily, but not for long.[17] At the time scientists were actively looking for ways to improve the strength and endurance of athletes and soldiers, and there were no rules barring such things in 1908. But whether Wolffe secretly slipped such a substance to Trudy in 1925 will remain forever unknown.

24. Turning Professional

The WSA preferred to let the controversy disappear. In the fall of 1925, the WSA announced that Trudy was giving up her amateur standing and going professional. Trudy would be heading for Miami with Aileen Riggin, who was also turning pro, where teaching jobs awaited them at the glamorous Deauville Hotel. Charlotte Epstein expressed regret that the two would no longer represent the WSA in competition, but tried to focus on the positive contribution the two would bring to the world of swimming as professionals. "Naturally we regret to see Gertrude and Aileen lost to our team. But in the new capacity they will be better able to carry out the constructive work to which our organization is devoted, to more effectively promote our aims and ideals. Girl teachers thoroughly trained in all branches of watermanship and imbued with high principles of sportsmanship can be of invaluable help. In so far as any temporary setback which the double defection may cause in our competitive activities, we are not worried. We hope to develop worthy successors to Gertrude and Aileen before long. Meanwhile they have our heartiest good wishes."[1]

Trudy may have wanted to leave the WSA for reasons relating to her swim and the Wolffe charges, but she also simply needed to start earning her own money. Aileen and Trudy started their jobs in Miami on January 1, 1926. Aileen later recalled that their primary responsibility was to be seen and mingle. "We were around the pool. We'd greet people. We'd swim. We'd put on little exhibitions and diving. There was a diving board. There was a pool deep enough for diving, and it was right on the beach. So it was in a lovely location. We'd go in the ocean and swim. Our duty was to be seen and give lessons, if anybody cared about it. People on vacation don't usually rush out and take swimming lessons. But we had an awfully good time there."[2]

The girls lived at the hotel and ate their meals in the elegant dining room along with the guests. The Deauville had just been built and the managers wanted some attractive and friendly celebrity swimmers on site to attract a clientele to their giant oval shaped salt-water pool. "It was enormous," Aileen remembered. "This pool was large enough to have a canoe in it. There was a full band that would play every day."

Trudy and Aileen weren't the only swimmers from New York spending the winter in Florida; Helen Wainwright was there, too. On New Year's Eve, when football star Red Grange was stopped by the police for speeding, Helen was in the car with him, along with golf stars Jim Barnes and Johnny Farrell.[3] She was hounded by reporters and grew tired of photographers asking her to pose again and again. One paper noted, "She only recently turned professional and has not entirely forgotten when she could pose or decline to pose at her own pleasure."[4]

On March 23, Helen swam around Tampa Bay's Davis Island, covering 11 miles in four hours and 50 minutes in choppy seas brought on by a storm. That evening she was feted at a party thrown for her by D. P. Davis, the wealthy developer whose dredging project had created the island. He announced that he would pay Helen $2,500 if she swam the English Channel that summer.[5] Helen didn't take him up on the offer and Davis was unable to follow through even if she had. He died seven months later after falling off the ocean liner *Majestic* en route to Paris.

While working at the Deauville, Trudy happened to meet Dudley Field Malone, a lawyer from New York City. Malone had worked as the collector of the Port of New York, had been an active opponent of Tammany Hall politics, and was a highly visible supporter of women's rights and the Irish independence movement. He had served as Woodrow Wilson's third assistant secretary of state, with William Jennings Bryan as his superior in the position of secretary of state. The year before Trudy met him, Malone had served as Clarence Darrow's assistant defense counsel in the famous Tennessee Scopes trial, where Malone argued against the prosecutor, who happened to be his old boss, William Jennings Bryan. Prior to his role in the Scopes trial, which made him infamous throughout the country, Malone had been living in Paris, where he had developed a successful practice representing wealthy Americans seeking divorce.[6]

Malone spent part of the winter in Palm Beach, recuperating from the Scopes trial.[7] Malone was not one to shy away from a high-stakes, high-profile opportunity, and offered to advance Trudy the money for another attack on the English Channel. Later, he said that Trudy had asked him to advance the money when they met in Miami, but this sort of bold fundraising seems out of character for Trudy.[8] He then began looking for someone to cover his own bet. He contacted some newspapers looking for money in exchange for exclusive access to Trudy's story. On May 29, 1926, she signed a contract with the *New York Daily News* and its distribution arm, the Chicago Tribune Press Service. The *News* agreed to provide $5,000 to Trudy to pay for the expedition. Should she complete the swim successfully, she would receive another $2,500. In addition, Trudy would write stories for the paper and be trailed by a writer and photographer for the entire trip.

Trudy's father, Henry "Pop" Ederle, and Malone hovered above her as she signed the contract.[9] Both were undoubtedly excited about the potential income that Trudy could generate. Despite having gone professional, Trudy was essentially still under the control of her father. He deposited all of her earnings from her Deauville job and other appearances into a bank account and only allowed her a small allowance. At one point she asked to buy a car, but he wouldn't allow it.[10] She had her heart set on a red roadster.

After the season at the Deauville pool ended, Aileen, Helen, and Trudy returned to New York to appear at the Hippodrome Theater. They were part of a cast of many athletes that included Helen's golfer friend from Florida, Johnny Farrell. The theater had purchased a glass tank that had previously belonged to Annette Kellerman, and the three performed two shows a day for weeks in front of crowds of 6,000 people. Years later, Aileen recalled the shows at the Hippodrome. "So there we were, and it was held over, and held over for weeks. They had sports representatives from all sports: golf and tennis, not only swimming and others. I guess ours was probably the hit of the show, along with ice skating. They had a little ice skating rink there with, not ice, but it was a kind of was substance that they used to skate on. We were there for quite a while. I loved that because it was in New York City, where I lived. And I was home and my friends would all come, and they would come back-stage and everything. We weren't really professionals. We were sports who happened to be on the stage. You know there is a difference. We weren't really old pros yet."[11]

25. Try, Try Again

Trudy left for France on June 2, 1926. She had already hired Thomas Burgess to be her trainer, and declined to discuss the previous year's problems with Jabez Wolffe during the dockside departure celebrations. An excited crowd of supportive family and friends, including Aileen Riggin and Helen Wainwright, came to the docks that morning to see her off. Aileen told reporters that Trudy had never been in better condition and was sure to succeed this time.[1]

This time, Trudy made sure that she was accompanied by an entourage of supporters. Her father, Henry "Pop" Ederle, came along and so did her sister Meg. The *Daily News* sent its own people: photographer Arthur Sorenson and writer Julia Harpman, who were there to cover Trudy's training and, they hoped, her successful conquest of the channel.

The *Daily News* had only been established six years before when the idea of the tabloid newspaper was birthed as a way for publishers to compete for New Yorkers' dimes with more established papers like the more restrained *New York Times*. The *Times* may have printed all the news that was fit to print, but the tabloids printed what average people actually wanted to read. The *Daily News'* main competitor was William Randolph Hearst's *New York Daily Mirror*, and both went to enormous lengths to keep their papers in demand by providing readers with steady coverage of murders, crimes, abductions, the private lives of film stars, charming tales of heroic family pets, gangsters, scandalous age-discrepant marriages, and much more. Julia Harpman had spent six years covering crime for the *Daily News*, providing readers with compelling, detailed, and often shocking stories. Over and over, she was first at the scene of the crime. She tracked down potential witnesses, was there when bodies were unearthed, and even convinced gangsters to tell her their stories. This was a new kind of journalism, and Julia was committed, tenacious, and smart enough to be one of the best of the era.[2]

The assignment to cover Trudy's channel attempt must have felt like a vacation compared to her regular strenuous beat, and probably came as a reward for her stellar record of guaranteeing delivery of stories that were detailed and well written, scandalous yet accurate.

Julia was married to Westbrook Pegler, a sportswriter, who also came along for part of the trip. He didn't stay in France for the entire summer, but he embarked on the *Berengaria* with the rest of the group. He became a great supporter of Trudy and continued to write about her long after the events of that summer.

Dudley Field Malone was coming to France later in the summer, but not for the purposes of joining Trudy's party. Malone's wife, Doris Stevens, a prominent activist for women's rights, was presiding over a delegation of 25 activists from the National Women's Suffrage Party who were attending the convention of the International Women's Suffrage Party in Paris. Dudley spoke at the dinner party given on board the ocean liner *Tuscania* just before the ship sailed for France. "Go over and shake Europe up," he exhorted the gathering of feminists. "Teach them that there can be no progress until men and women play an equal part in the world."[3] Trudy wasn't there, but his words applied to her as much as to his feminist audience.

Trudy went directly to France to meet her new coach, Thomas Burgess. On June 9, the party arrived at the coast where they were welcomed happily by locals in Boulogne-sur-Mer and Cap Gris-Nez. Although Trudy didn't speak French, she had a friendly and unpretentious demeanor, and was fondly remembered by the locals for her attempt the previous year. The group checked in at Hotel du Phare in Cap Gris-Nez and met up with Thomas Burgess, who had thrown a wrench into the works. Burgess, it was determined, had reneged on the deal that Trudy had set up with him earlier in the year. She had hired Burgess to train her exclusively and pilot her across the channel. Instead, he was simultaneously training Lillian Cannon, a swimmer from Baltimore who had arrived in France with her two Chesapeake Bay retrievers, Chesacroft Drake and Chesacroft Mary Montauk, who were intended to accompany her in the water during the channel swim.[4] Lillian had been engaged by the *Baltimore Post* and the Scripps-Howard newspaper syndicate for sponsorship and exclusive articles, similar to Trudy's deal with the *Daily News*. In mid–May, Lillian drew attention to her Channel attempt when she and Chesacroft Drake jumped off the 96th Street Pier into the Hudson River. She swam only a quarter of a mile before heading back to shore.[5] Trudy certainly knew of Lillian's plans, but she was shocked to discover that Burgess had agreed to coach the other woman.

Within a few days, the matter had been settled, and Lillian was out of luck. A very precise and serious column published under Trudy's byline, but most likely written by Julia, made it clear that Trudy and the *Daily News* were not to be trifled with. "Months ago, I made an agreement with William

Burgess ... that he was to train me and no other woman.... When I arrived at Gris-Nez last Thursday I discovered Miss Lillian Cannon of Baltimore unhappily situated because Burgess had agreed to train her only if I gave my consent. I felt it necessary for the protection of my own interest to reject such an arrangement and thus Miss Cannon is temporarily without a trainer. I am sorry this situation has arisen, but it is through no fault of mine."[6]

She also pointed out, quite logically, "Suppose one man coached two women, both desirous of making the attempt on the first good day. One is a slow swimmer and the other a sprinter. Obviously, it would be impossible for this trainer to accompany both in the water."

For her part, Lillian wrote in her newspaper column that there were no problems between herself and Trudy, but only "complete friendliness."[7]

Although Trudy had sent Burgess a retainer on the agreed upon coaching fee of 20,000 francs during the winter, he insisted on rewriting the arrangement. Trudy, her father Henry, her sister Meg, Julia Harpman, and Westbrook Pegler frantically tried to keep the original arrangement in place. Dudley Field Malone, Trudy's lawyer, didn't offer to come to the Channel outpost to assist in writing a better contract, despite being in Paris. Westbrook Pegler and Julia sent telegrams to the *Daily News* for assistance, and Pegler took note of Malone's less-than-helpful actions and held a grudge for years over Malone's abandoning of Trudy when she was in a tight spot.

This was not the ideal way to begin a summer that would be spent in close quarters under a tense spell of competitive anxiety. The rocky start to the summer spawned tensions that flared into conflict several times during the coming months. Trudy's party never fully trusted Burgess after that initial problem, and Henry Ederle especially resented how the trainer had treated his daughter. One of the amenities of the Hotel du Phare was an open beer tap for guests, and on a few occasions unlimited ale led to some taut moments between Henry Ederle and Burgess. One night, as Burgess was speaking French to the tugboat pilot, Joe Costa, Henry loudly and angrily interrupted them, demanding that everyone involved in his daughter's Channel attempt speak English.[8]

Training began in the midst of the drama and tension. Trudy ventured into the cold waters of the Channel to begin acclimating herself to its frigid temperatures. She managed to stay in for ten minutes before racing back to the beach. Her training extended to the bathtub where she only took cold baths the entire summer to keep her body accustomed to cold water.

Burgess prescribed walking as an important part of a Channel swimmer's training.[9] On a six-mile trek through the farmlands around Gris-Nez, Trudy, Meg, and Arthur Sorenson were chased by a bull into a brook, then became somewhat lost before finding their way back to the beach. Burgess declared the walk enough training for one day. He was a big believer in the power of massage as well. Trudy had been reluctant to allow Wolffe to get his hands on her the previous year, but stated in one of this year's articles that she viewed Burgess "much as another woman would look upon her physician. I am advised that the best massages for me are those by a man, especially a qualified trainer who understands the proper treatment of the muscles, particularly those of the shoulders, those being the most important."[10]

The little outpost's population of swimmers was growing on a weekly basis. Ishak Helmy arrived in mid–June, and there appeared to be no hard feelings resulting from his role in Trudy's failure the previous year. Asked to comment on Trudy's chances, he said, "She is a brave girl. I swam with her the last two hours on the first attempt. I know that she was blinded and only half conscious for the last hour. She was swimming on pure instinct and pure courage. I am sure she hardly knew what she was doing. There is no reason why she should not make the swim this year. It is my opinion that she might have made it last year if she had not set so fast a pace. She wanted to break the records made by the men and she did not save herself. She fought the Channel by direct attack and nobody can fight the Channel that way. The Channel is treacherous and cunning and one must also use the wits to try and outwit the Channel."[11]

A new female contender, Clarabelle Barrett of New Rochelle, New York, arrived in England in early July. She was 32 years old, six feet tall, and, reportedly, two hundred pounds. Clarabelle had been a longtime member of the National Women's Life Saving League and was well known in New York swimming circles. She had turned professional to support herself and her mother almost eight years earlier when her father died. The previous summer she attracted attention anew when she was the only person, male or female, to complete a ten-mile race from New Rochelle. Unlike many of the other swimmers, Clarabelle did not have a financial backer, and was paying her own way with her earnings as a high school swim teacher.

Although Clarabelle's training camp was on the British side of the Channel, Trudy's party was aware of her arrival. In mid–July, Julia Harpman published a facetious column describing Jabez Wolffe waiting in vain at Gris-Nez for Clarabelle, who had tried to contact him earlier. Harpman sassily wrote of Wolffe desperately scanning the horizon for sight of his trainee Clarabelle, afraid that "the woman, who is reported to measure six feet and weigh well over 200 pounds, has been kidnapped or inveigled by the lures of Paris."[12]

Clarabelle had not been kidnapped. She had headed for Brighton and sought out Walter Brickett, the British Olympic swim team's trainer. Clarabelle hadn't done much research prior to sailing for England, and she was quite taken aback when told how much money it would cost to hire a trainer, rent a boat, and find a captain who knew how to navigate the complex tides of the Channel, all while paying for lodging, possibly for months, while waiting for good weather. Brickett was so impressed with Clarabelle's swimming, however, that he agreed to assist her for one week without pay, stating, "I cannot leave such a splendid woman in difficulty. She may surprise all. I consider her good for twenty hours."[13]

And she was. On the morning of August 2, she left Dover and didn't stop swimming for almost 22 hours. Although sunny in the morning, the weather changed and a cold, dense fog left her vulnerable to the traffic of massive ships traversing the channel. Within two miles of Cap Gris-Nez, Clarabelle was forced to give up the fight when she missed the tide that would have sent her towards the French shore.[14] A riveting account of the swim was published in the *New York Times* on August 4, and Clarabelle's financial fortunes rapidly improved. A New York City woman offered to send $500, and the New Rochelle Rotary Club began a fundraising drive in support of her effort.[15]

Jane Sion, who had suffered the previous year from a lack of funds, was back with the support of her hometown of Dunkirk. This allowed her to hire a tug and a pilot.[16] Mercedes Gleitze, a 19-year-old typist from London, had already tried the Channel twice, once in 1923, and once in 1925.[17] Her July 24, 1926, attempt ended after five hours. Other contenders were lining up on the British side of the channel. Mille Gade Corson, who also went by her married name, Mrs. Clemington Corson, was another professional based in New York, where she taught sailors to swim at the New York Naval Militia on the Hudson River. Born in Denmark and an accomplished swimmer, she had moved to New York to pursue the sport. By 1921, she was best known for swimming from Albany to the southern tip of Manhattan. The 153-mile swim had taken five days, with Mille swimming between 19 and 26 miles each day, with overnight breaks for sleep onboard a boat. All told, she spent 63 hours in the water over five days.[18] She had attempted to swim the Channel once before, in 1923, and was within two miles of the French coast before the tides swept her back seven miles, forcing her to give up. She was being coached long-distance by a co-worker at the Naval Militia, the "champion heel to toe walker" Louis Leibgold.[19]

Mrs. Corson attracted special attention from the newspapers because of her unique status as a mother, and upon arrival in England told a newspaper reporter, "You bet I will swim your channel. Why would I come over here otherwise, leaving my husband and two kids at home? This is no pleasure trip."[20]

Trudy and Julia's articles appeared in the various *Daily News* and *Chicago Tribune* syndicate papers. The stories were simple but descriptive in a way that was extremely charming. They described life on the coast of France, and mentioned everything from the appearance of recently shorn sheep to the lingering relics of the World War, the gun battlements on the cliffs and the beached wrecks of ships that had been sunk by mines. Before the Fourth of July, Trudy talked about walking to another village to buy fireworks.[21]

The columns were also used to take sly jabs at others. Trudy wrote of running into Wolffe by surprise in Boulogne-sur-Mer, and mentioned that Wolffe was so chubby that he made Pop look like a chorus girl. She described Joe Costa, the tug pilot, as the "worst weather prophet in the world." She announced that she had given up training with Helmy, as "he swims so slowly that trying to slow down to his pace ruins my own."[22]

She informed readers of what she intended to eat on the day of the swim. Her meaty training diet was already well known, but she discussed some changes to what she would eat while swimming. The previous year she had consumed nothing but beef tea during the swim. This year, she intended to incorporate salad and small pieces of chicken into the menu, a diet that she and Burgess tested out on a five-hour training swim.[23]

The *Daily News* even engaged in a sort of meta-journalism. Perhaps feeling that the articles by Trudy and Julia might not engage the public's attention in the weeks leading up to the swim, they published stories about how they had landed the exclusive and how the photographs were to be radioed home. A photo montage in the *Daily News* featured shots of Trudy in France, engaged in such activities as carrying buckets with a yoke, hugging a cow, and hunching intently over a typewriter. Possibly reacting to natural suspicions that Trudy was, in fact, not the actual author of some of the stories, they captioned the typewriter photo with, "Here we have Miss Ederle in her most profound literary mood — writing one of her signed and absolutely exclusive stories for The News."[24]

26. The Channel Again

Trudy had two pressing equipment problems. The first was her bathing suit. Swimming for hours on end in a one-piece bathing suit led to painful chafing on the shoulders. She and Meg worked to devise a different kind of bathing suit that would maximize her reach while still offering modesty and protection from the scores of camera-toting men that would be following the swim.

First, they tried using a different kind of material. Meg had heard of a new kind of silk, alleged to be lightweight but not transparent, and went to Paris to see if she could find some. She didn't find it, but returned with a dark blue jersey silk. For the design, Trudy and Meg decided to try making a brassiere top to go with short trunks. The previous year, she had worn a regulation swimming suit, which was tight about the arms and chafed, but was also stretchy so that it filled with water and dragged behind her. Changing to trunks and a brassiere would solve the problem of the ballooning suit and the painful shoulders.[1] They sewed a small American flag to the left side of the brassiere top, and the WSA symbol to the right. Trudy remained convinced for the rest of her life that she and Meg had invented the bikini.

Trudy was also desperate to figure out a way to waterproof her goggles. She had been worried since the first swim the year before, when she realized how painful the Channel water was going to be to her eyes. In New York, Trudy had gone to an optical company and had goggles made to order. First of all, she didn't want the kind with two separate eyepieces; she thought they gave her a headache. She ordered a pair with a full eye-view, like ski goggles. The salespeople at the optical company said, "Well, Miss Ederle, we think we can make them up for you, but we cannot guarantee they will be water proof."[2]

They weren't. The goggles failed almost immediately, and Trudy was worried.[3]

For weeks, Trudy and Meg tried to make them waterproof, with no success. Meg tried sewing chamois on them. She tried coating them with paint.

Nothing worked, and Trudy was beginning to dread making the swim with leaky goggles. Then, on the night of August 4, came a brilliant flash, as Trudy told it later. "So, that night, I'm sitting in the hotel having dinner, and we had no electric, just candlelight. I saw the candles flickering and I said, "Gee, Meg, maybe we should melt candle on the inside of the goggles." So the next day we went and melted the candle inside. Margaret went down to the water with me, and I swam down the coast and up the coast and nothing came in. I was just crazy with joy."

"Meg, Meg," she yelled, "I think we got them waterproof!"[4]

They had, and with only a day to spare. The night of August 5, a Thursday, Burgess decided that Trudy would make the swim the very next day. He announced his decision to the group as they gathered in the bar of the hotel. The entire team went into action, but not before some nervous energy was expended in a rousing cheer and a round of drinks.

The tug captain required at least six-hours notice, and as Cap Griz-Nez lost telephone service after dark, someone was immediately dispatched by automobile to Boulogne-sur-Mer to inform Joe Costa, the pilot. Costa informed the tugboat *Alsace*'s Captain Corthes to be ready to leave at 4 A.M. to meet the party at the base of Cap Gris-Nez the next morning.

Trudy was sent to bed, but Meg, Julia, Burgess, and the others stayed awake making last-minute preparations. The proprietress of the hotel, Madam Blondiau, and her mother-in-law stayed up throughout the night, cooking the broths and other food that Trudy would need. The hotel had no refrigeration, so it hadn't been possible to prepare it in advance. Then everyone except for Burgess, Meg, Julia and Trudy departed for Boulogne-sur-Mer to be onboard the tug by 4 A.M.

Julia and Meg awakened Trudy at 4 A.M. She gazed at them sleepily and said, "Do we go?" She had slept much better than any of the rest of the team, and consumed a huge breakfast of corn flakes, a peach, milky coffee, and half a chicken. They waited for her to digest her breakfast before beginning the application of the various greases. First, Trudy was rubbed down with olive oil, and then they waited an hour for it to be fully absorbed. Next came a layer of lanolin, a thick, sticky, water-repelling wax produced by sheep and a byproduct of the process used to clean shorn wool. Then came petroleum jelly, and finally, a layer of straight lard. The final layer was applied down at the beach, where villagers and tourists alike crowded around Trudy to watch the start of the swim. A small black and white dog circled them, eating up the blobs of fat and lard dropping to the sand.

At 7:05 A.M., Trudy entered the water. "Cheerio!" she called to the people on the beach. "Cheerio!" they called back. Meg, Julia, and Burgess clambered into the rowboat. They waved an American flag to signal to the tug that Trudy

Lillian Cannon and Gertrude Ederle right before the 1926 swim (Library of Congress Prints and Photographs Collection).

had started. Then the rowboat headed out to open ocean, guiding Trudy through the rocks.[5]

After just 45 minutes, Trudy had gone two miles. By 9 o'clock, she had gone three-and-a-half miles, and Captain Corthes remarked that he had never seen a Channel swimmer make the kind of progress she was making. When Burgess urged her to slow her pace, she hollered up to her father, "Come on in, Pop, I am going slow enough for you to keep up now!"[6] She was averaging 22 strokes of the American crawl per minute, keeping time with the music being played on the phonograph.

Julia sat at her desk on the tug, writing dispatches for the wireless. Arthur Sorenson took off his shoes so that he could scramble up and down the rail of the tug, leaning out over the water and getting as close to Trudy as he could shoot. At 9:45, a motorboat arrived from the English side of the Channel, retrieved the film from the first part of the swim, and headed back to England. The photos were to be cabled from London to newspapers all over the world.

Ominously, the wind was beginning to strengthen, and the members of the party onboard the tug could see the white cliffs on English shore, which wasn't a good sign. That kind of visibility usually meant that the wind was exceptionally strong.

"That doesn't look so good, does it?" said Julia to Burgess.

"No," he replied, "but don't let Gertie know. I told her not to look up toward the English shore until the ninth hour, and I don't want anyone to let her know before then that we can see the cliffs."[7]

The waves were beginning to grow large as well. Ishak Helmy joined her in the 61 degree water for a while to keep her company. Meg joined her for a while as well, and when she got back on board the tug, she told Julia that, on the high crests of the waves, it was possible to see the white cliffs of Dover, although Trudy hadn't said anything about it.

Around ten, the sun came out in full, which cheered everyone. Another tug came into view and chugged next to the *Alsace*. It was *La Morinie*, the tug Trudy had used the previous year. It was packed with reporters, photographers, and movie-camera operators from various papers and agencies. Lillian Cannon was on board as well. Trudy waved, and continued swimming. Around noon, she had her lunch. At this point, she was over an hour ahead of her projected schedule. The tide was still in her favor and she was more than ten-and-a-half miles from the coast of France. But suddenly, the sky darkened and the winds picked up even more in force. At noon, she stopped for a chicken leg, sugar cubes, and pineapple slices. By 1:30, the wind was a punishing gale, and Burgess and Captain Corthes both told Julia that if the weather did not improve, it wouldn't be possible to finish the swim. Trudy soldiered on. Burgess began to think about how to alter the course. The north wind was blowing hard, and they were heading almost east, up towards the North Sea.

Around three in the afternoon, Helmy swam over to the Alsace and asked Lillian Cannon if she was interested in keeping Trudy company in the water. Lillian was, and joined Trudy in the rough water.

"Hello, Lillian, we seem to be fifty miles from nowhere," Trudy affably said to her rival.

"Why, my dear, you are almost there," responded Lillian.[8]

Burgess and Corthes scanned the rough sea for signs of the Varne Buoy, which marked a point six miles off the coast of England. Once Trudy passed the buoy, her chance of finishing would increase, because it meant that she would catch the tide that would help send her towards England.

Trudy kept going, undeterred by the weather. The wind continued to howl and the rain came down in sheets. Some of the people on the tug were seasick, but down in the water Trudy was fine even as the tug rolled from side to side above her. She took a snack of hot cocoa and a chunk of chocolate. The radio operator received a message from her brother and sister, who were in the wireless room at the *Daily News* in New York City, breathlessly waiting on every dispatch that came through. British swimmer Louis Timson joined Trudy in the water for a period before he realized that his preferred stroke, the breast stroke, was too slow to keep up with her relentless crawl stroke.

"Have I got to take you into training, too?" Trudy joked, as Timson climbed back onto the tug.[9] Meg joined Trudy in the water again after Timson left.

At six in the evening, with waves smashing onto the deck of the *Alsace*, Burgess and Corthes began to discuss abandoning the attempt. Corthes wasn't even sure if he would be able to land the tug at Dover in such terrible weather. Burgess took Meg and Pop aside, and suggested it might be time to break the news to Trudy that she should quit. Meg refused, insisting that if Trudy wasn't complaining about the storm, those on the tug had no right to. Just after 7 P.M., Burgess took Julia aside and urgently said, "She must come out, I will not take the responsibility of waiting for a sign from her indicating that she wished to come out!"[10]

Just then someone leaned over the edge of the tug and yelled, "Gertie, you must come out!"

Trudy paused, looking up in genuine amazement. "What for?" she called back, astonished, as she bobbed up and down next to the heaving tug. Everyone cheered, at least those who were not too seasick, and the reporters rushed to the wireless. It was the dismissal heard round the world. Trudy's two-word rejection of failure was flashed around the world, and almost instantaneously became a rallying cry for American tenacity.

At 7:15, they reached the most treacherous part of the Channel crossing, the Goodwin Sands. The Sands are about six miles off the coast of England, a cluster of submerged sandbanks about 15 feet below sea level, running southwest to northeast for approximately ten miles. The Sands shift in height and position constantly and are implicated in over 2,000 shipwrecks, some of whose masts still stick up out of the shallow water of the sands, an ominous warning to other ships. Corthes refused to take the tug between the Sands and the Goodwin Lightship, so Burgess had Corthes steer a course entirely around the Sands. It would take longer, but was safer for all involved.

The other tug, *La Morinie*, crowded with reporters and photographers, began to come too close to Trudy, on several occasions almost close enough that she had to swim out of its way. She would have been disqualified if she touched it.

The storm eventually subsided and Burgess and Corthes regained their courage and their faith that the swim might end in success. But they now had a new concern. It was imperative for Trudy to land in the area between the South Foreland Light and the town of Ramsgate, which juts eastward into the Channel. If she swam too far north and missed Ramsgate, there wouldn't be another landing spot for hours.

The British waiting on shore knew it as well. The reporters on *La Morinie* and the *Alsace* were cabling Trudy's position to England, and the news had gotten out in the small towns along the shore. The coastal residents were accustomed to Channel attempts, but when they heard Trudy was so close to the finish, they reacted. Residents of the small seaside towns headed to the beaches with as much dry wood as they could collect, setting up bonfires that could be seen from the water. From the tug, tiny points of light began appearing in the distance. When the tugs came into sight of those on the beach, lighting up the water with their own searchlights and flares, the people on shore let loose with a roar of excitement. Thousands of men, women, and children lined the beaches, shouting encouragement. About 500 yards offshore, Trudy heard them, raised an arm in greeting, and kept swimming.[11]

Meg, Burgess, Julia, and Henry Ederle leaned over the rails, screaming with excitement. "You are sure to make it, Gertie, if you swim!" cried Burgess.[12]

Trudy swam into shore, not slowing, until finally her feet touched bottom. It was 9:39 P.M. People ran into the water to help her up the beach, but she yelled at them to get back, knowing that any assistance could result in another disqualification. Meg leapt into the water to come ashore behind Trudy. The *Alsace* came in as close as it could; the entourage was leaping into the water to come ashore with Trudy. The crowds went wild, cheering and yelling, while boats along the shore set off their sirens and whistles. They knew that they were witnessing history. A woman had finally swum the English Channel, and she had beaten all existing records.

Reporters from *La Morinie* leapt into the water and dashed up the beach to find telephones. Their wireless had failed about an hour previously, and the correspondents onboard were desperate to get their updates out to the wider world that was waiting for any news. The wireless operator, with nothing to do, dropped overboard and waded towards Trudy to congratulate her.

Trudy stood on the beach, silently taking in the chaos around her and internally registering the fact that her limbs had stopped moving for the first time in 14 hours and 39 minutes. Her face was swollen beyond its normal size, but she had been able to walk up the shore, unaided. She had not only conquered the English Channel, but had broken by almost two hours the previous record.

She turned around and began to swim back to the tug, but was held back. No one was ready to see her swim back to the boat. She was wrapped in blankets. Eventually, the rowboat was brought and she was bundled into it. She finally turned to her father and said, "Well, Pop, I guess I get my roadster."[13]

She was able to climb the ladder onto the tug without assistance. As they departed the beach and headed for Dover, she took shelter on a couch in the cabin and asked for a slice of pineapple to sooth her tongue and mouth, battered and stinging from the salt water. She wanted to be warm, and she wanted to sleep. When they arrived at Dover, and she rose to get off the couch, she could scarcely stand.

One more obstacle greeted them at Dover. They had forgotten their passports, and the agents kept them for an hour before allowing them to proceed to a hotel.

27. Victory

They checked into the Grand Hotel and Trudy headed for bed after a hot bath. It was the first hot bath she had taken in almost two months. She had been forsaking warm water as a way of acclimating herself to the Channel, and the bath was positively heavenly. After that, she ate four ham sandwiches.

Julia stayed up to finish writing the stories that would appear in the next day's papers all over the United States. She wired long, detailed stories home, lauding Trudy as a determined hero, and she didn't hide her irritation at Burgess, Corthes, and the others who had doubted Trudy at the height of the storm. Stories appeared the very next day under Trudy's byline, but in her state she could not possibly have written them herself. The photographer's film from the swim was relayed from England to New York by steamer and plane in a race to be the first newspaper to publish photos of the feat. The *Daily News*'s prints were given to a man who sailed from England on the *Empress of Scotland*, headed for Quebec. As the ship neared the Canadian shore, the waterproof packet was thrown overboard to a waiting seaplane, which took off and flew 250 miles, where it landed. The prints were then divided up and sent in two separate planes to New Jersey, where a messenger whisked them by train to the *Daily News* offices.[1]

New York exploded in a celebration of its hometown girl's victory. Other cities were riveted as well; in Boston, hundreds of people had called the *Boston Post* throughout the night to hear if Trudy had completed the swim. Trudy's brother and sister had waited by the wireless at the *Daily News* throughout the day; Mrs. Ederle and the younger kids got the news at the beach house in Highlands, New Jersey; and the rest of the family got the news by cable at the butcher shop where one of the uncles celebrated by throwing strings of sausages to the crowds gathering in the street outside the Amsterdam Avenue butcher shop. In response to a reporter's question, Mrs. Ederle said, "Strong? Of course she is. I brought her up to do things for herself. She washed the floors, polished the kitchen stove, and has done housework regularly. Those are the things that gave her her endurance."[2]

The next day, after a restless night of nervous exhaustion that left her too frazzled to sleep much, Trudy rose with barely a stiff muscle, which she attributed to her late-night hot bath. She took another hot bath, and Burgess administered a massage. Porters brought armloads of congratulatory flowers to her room, and the cables of congratulations from all over the world began to pile up. At breakfast she told the group, "I'm feeling fine. I'm not a bit lame and none the worse for my workout. But I don't know what was the matter with me last night. I thought I'd sleep soundly, but I couldn't. If it was nerves, or excitement, it was all new to me. I never laid awake at night before — never in my life."[3]

The day gave Trudy her first taste of what it was going to mean to be an international celebrity. After breakfast, she put her suit back on and trotted down to the beach for a short swim. As she passed the hordes of well-wishers filling the streets outside the hotel, she joked to them, "No, I'm not going to swim back to Boulogne, though I feel sure I could make it."[4]

Mid-morning, the mayor of Dover came to congratulate her, and the two posed for photographs in front of the Captain Webb memorial statue. Crowds, happily waving American flags, hefted Trudy about their shoulders and carried her back to the hotel. Trudy greeted the crowds reluctantly from the balcony of the hotel. She met with reporters, telling them, "You bet I am tickled to death to take back the honors for America. What spurred me most were the old-time American songs. They sang 'Rosie O'Grady' and 'After the Ball Was Over,' but my favourite was 'Let Me Call You Sweetheart.'" The roadster, of course, was motivation as well. "One time, when we had five more hours to go, I said to myself, 'Five hours are worthwhile for a roadster.'"

Speaking to the mass of reporters, she said, "The great point in my swimming at all was to show that a girl could do it, that an American girl could do it, and that I was the American girl. I went to sleep last night in my hotel at Boulogne, and I woke up this morning in my hotel in Dover — but what happened in between seems quite unreal.

"I felt that the worst was over when I got within sight of England, but afterward the sight of England became discouraging instead of encouraging. When I was a few miles offshore, it looked as if it got no nearer. That was very bad for me, and I knew it, so I quit looking and swam as if I were right in the middle of the Channel and making fast progress."[5]

Pop was interviewed, too. "I don't know anything about Channel swimming, but I've sure got the greatest little girl in the world." His little girl had also made him a pile of money. Julia Harpman wrote in the *Boston Post* that Pop had wagered $25,000 on seven to one odds, giving him a prize of $175,000, but another paper reported that he had only won $11,000.[6]

Gertrude Ederle in her roadster, a prize for swimming the English Channel (Library of Congress Prints and Photographs Collection).

The entourage headed back to the docks to catch the afternoon boat to return to France, followed all the way by an excited crowd. On the ferry back to France, Trudy told Julia, "It's a lot easier to swim the Channel than to make a speech." She also told Julia that she felt like running and hiding from the crowds that were coming to see her. The fact that Julia divulged this statements in an article the day after the swim, and that she referred to Trudy's speech from the balcony as "faltering," is somewhat curious. Julia may have felt protective towards the shy Trudy, and by mentioning these quirks may have been trying to prepare the United States for a reluctant heroine so that they would not overwhelm Trudy.[7]

Boulogne greeted Trudy as exuberantly as Dover, if not more. After all, she had been training on their ground for two summers. French locals and Americans expats greeted the boat with cheers and tossed hats as it arrived at Boulogne. The entourage was whisked to American Consulate, where "America's wonderful mermaid" was toasted enthusiastically. The convoy then headed to Cap Griz-Nez, but their progress slowed as they passed through the small towns along the way. Pop hosted a party that went on through the night, while the guests consumed 70 bottles of champagne. Burgess was moved by the success, saying, "There never has been and never will be again such a swim. She is the most wonderful girl that ever lived and I'm tremendously proud of being her trainer. My mind is still in a whirl but I find myself wiping the tears away at the memory of Gertie's struggle. No man living would have stood the punishment she took smiling."[8]

Unfortunately, the working relationship between Burgess and Trudy did not end well. She and her party were still angry at the mess he had created when they first arrived. After the swim, she paid him for his services, and nothing more. According to one gossipy newspaper reporter, when Burgess asked her for a bonus, given that he'd helped her succeed, "She gave him a look that fried him to a crackling, and walked out without ever a polite farewell."[9]

Jabez Wolffe was interviewed, and, typically, he found ways to downplay Trudy's achievement. He even minimized the storm that everyone else had found terrifying. "Miss Ederle carried out a marvelous work. She disregarded all expert opinions about tide, wind, and sea. She started from the sands a mile eastward of last year instead of from the rocks. She ran counter to all accepted methods of training, about her only concession being an intensive massage to keep her muscles supple. There was very little ebb tide during the day, all of the flood tide, with a southwest wind backing it up, throwing her on to the English coast. On the ebb tide swimmers usually go to Varne Buoy, but a strong wind stopped the ebb and instead of losing ground she gained ground. It is unique. She was then swimming on the near tide instead of the spring tide. When the flood tide actually came she rushed with the wind behind her down the Channel and got into Downes. It was remarkable that she got rough water in that sheltered position. It was a stupendous effort that she made and I congratulate her heartily."[10]

Offers for Trudy were arriving by the hour. Cables and telegrams continued to pour in by the hundreds from around the world. They were from theaters, broadcasters, motion picture makers, and advertising agencies. Instead of accepting any of them, Trudy decided to make no decisions or personal appearances until she was back in the United States.

On August 10, Trudy, Meg, and Henry Ederle departed Cap Gris-Nez for Germany to visit the German branch of the Ederle family. They headed first to Calais, where they were met by a large crowd and taken for a reception at the home of the United States consul. The two thousand employees of the Foundation Company of America had been given the day off, and most of them filled the streets between the train station and the Consulate. The Foundation Company sponsored a banquet, at which Trudy was presented with a silver lace scarf. Then they went on to an official reception at City Hall where the mayor and city council men honored her as well.[11]

Trudy was hoping for rest, but she wasn't going to get it anytime soon. At the end of the busy day, they departed by train for Bissengen, near Stuttgart, where Trudy's grandmother ran a farm and inn. Henry Ederle had been born there, and 19 of his brothers and sisters and untold numbers of cousins still lived there. The entire town had been heatedly preparing for the visit. Greeting the American Ederles at the train station were a brass band, trumpeters, and 300 school children who lined the thoroughfares of the town holding lanterns.[12] It took an hour for them to even reach the automobile that would take them to Bissingen. Stuttgart's officials formally welcomed Trudy with speeches and honorifics suitable for royalty. Eventually, the police gave assistance in getting through the crowds, and Trudy was hoisted on someone's shoulders to the car.

The convoy traveled through a number of small villages on the way to Bissengen, and in each one, crowds thronged the streets, hoping for glimpse of Trudy. She was welcomed by Bissengen's magistrate, while a fireman's band played German songs and the singing society serenaded her with folk songs. One paper reported that the exhausted Trudy, not understanding much German and overwhelmed by the proceedings, slipped off to a barn during the mayor's address and "was discovered very overwrought, but calmly happy, with her arms around a cow's neck."[13]

When they finally arrived at the Ederle home, Trudy embraced her old grandmother, who announced with tears streaming down her face, "I never dreamed the name of Ederle would achieve world fame."[14]

A grand reunion was held inside the Lamb's Inn for the hundred or so relatives present. Bissengen continued celebrating outside with a torchlight parade, which Trudy watched from the inn's balcony. At some point during the party, a relative slipped up and mentioned the recent death of Trudy's aunt in New York, which had been kept from her so as not to interfere with the Channel swim, and Trudy fell apart. She sobbed brokenheartedly at the news. The next day she still had not recovered, and spent almost the entire day sequestered indoors, emerging only once to wave to a parade of children.

The crowds and their hysterical levels of attention were getting on her nerves. More frighteningly, Julia reported that there were many young men intent on meeting the shy Trudy, including several who had forced their way into the home and gotten as far as Trudy's bedroom.[15] Trudy told Julia, "I thought I was going to get some rest here, but if this keeps up I'll have a nervous breakdown before I get home. It's nice of people to pay me so much attention, but it gets on my nerves to have photographers following my every step. They seem to spring out of the ground by the dozens."[16]

By the next day, she was feeling even worse. "If I had known what was in store for me here I would never have come. I can't get home quickly enough to suit me."[17] American and European writers saw more to the trip than a simple visit to a grandmother. One wrote, "Gertrude Ederle has unconsciously done more to consolidate German-American relationships by her reception in the old home and to convince those of German descent born on American soil that there exists another Germany apart from that of the war years, than all the German books of propaganda ever written."[18]

Business offers for Trudy continued to arrive by the hour, but she refused all of them. Although she had earlier declared that she would make no public appearance before returning to New York, she was besieged by requests from swimming clubs and promoters to make an appearance.

Not all the news arriving was good. Critics in England and France were beginning to accuse Trudy of having received help from the tugboats making her swim easier. Whether it was the fact that Trudy was an American, or a woman, or an American woman, critics were beginning to find ways to claim that her accomplishment was far less than it was.

The *Westminster Gazette* wrote, "Every Channel swimmer is entitled to swim the course in any way he or she chooses, since there are no rules. At the same time the point raised is whether a swim assisted by adventitious aids, such as the shelter of a tugboat, is comparable with the unaided efforts of other swimmers who have succeeded."[19] The paper also quoted an unnamed British pilot, who said, "Ederle swam under the lee of one steamer, while the other navigated so as to keep off the heavy seas. The girl was swimming in calm water and making twice the speed she could have made under ordinary circumstances. By keeping close to one boat she was also drawn along by the suction of the vessel."[20]

The fact was that only one of the tugs was Trudy's and the other, full of reporters and observers, actually got in the way. But now it was being claimed that the two tugs worked in unison to provide a safe passage for her through the storm. Clemington Corson, the husband of Mille Gade Corson, stated that the tugs had helped Trudy, but that that should be acceptable for a woman, while British champ Louis Timson stated that the second tug had actually gotten in the way and almost swamped Trudy at least once.

On August 16, the witnesses from the swim wrote and signed a statement in support of Trudy and her swim. It read, "We, the undersigned witnesses of the Channel swim of Miss Gertrude Ederle, hereby certify in the presence of the American Consul, M. Gaston Smith, that on the morning of Friday, Aug. 6, Miss Ederle walked into the water at Cap Gris Nez and swam to Kingsdown, England, where she arrived 14½ hours later and that she received no aid in her swimming and that she abided faithfully by all the rules of Channel swimming and international sportsmanship."[21] The statement was signed by Frederick K. Abbott of the International News Service, Minnott

Saunders, who was Lillian Cannon's manager, Alec Rutherford of the *Los Angeles Times*, Arthur Sorenson, Henry Ederle, Amedee Blondiau, Meg Ederle, and Julia Harpman.

Thomas Burgess issued a public statement saying, "Reports about Miss Ederle's swim are so silly that there is nothing to reply to. Miss Ederle swam the channel in a perfectly proper manner under the same conditions in which others have failed or succeeded. Her swim was witnessed by more people than any other successful swim since Captain Webb's, and one of those witnesses was Miss Cannon, who was aboard the tug and would have had something to say if unfair aid had been given Miss Ederle in any manner."[22]

Back in New York, Charlotte Epstein said, "The persons who have criticized Gertrude for being accompanied by a tug are apparently not familiar with the methods used by previous swimmers of the channel. All of them, without exception, were accompanied by a boat and in some cases by the same tug, *Alsace*, under Captain Costa."

L. de B. Handley followed up by stating, "It is ridiculous to assume that any tug can stem the drift of the Channel tide."[23]

After the initial argument had been refuted, the *Gazette* issued another statement, this time saying that the tides and winds had coincided so perfectly that the swim had been easy.[24] Trudy had just been lucky.

The trip to Germany had been exhausting and overwhelming for Trudy, but it was nothing compared to how New York would greet her. The entourage returned to France after a week in Germany. Dudley Field Malone had sent Trudy a cable asking her to come home earlier because Mayor Walker of New York was clamoring to hold a large celebration for her, but it was too late to make any changes to their travel plans. They spent two more days in Paris, before heading back to the *Berengaria* for the return home. Even at Cherbourg, where the boat departed, there was one last celebration honoring Trudy. She received a partial reprieve from the onslaught of attention onboard the ship, but was convinced to give a talk as part of a benefit performance for the support of British and American war veterans, although she did state that she would rather swim the Channel again than engage in public speaking, so great was her discomfort with public appearances.

Trudy let Julia Harpman do some of her talking for her through the newspaper columns, conveying some information that she may have been too shy or overwhelmed to say at the time. "My greatest satisfaction in having made the swim was in proving that a woman could do it. It always gave me such a pain in the neck to hear people say a woman couldn't do as much as a man in the water. For that matter, any woman with determination can do anything she sets out to do." Her philosophy was one of self-reliance; she stated that she had turned professional to be able to make a way for herself in the world, and to take care of her children, should she ever get married and have any. But she wasn't looking for a beau, and she made that clear as well, saying, "I have no thought of getting married for many years to come. I have yet to see any man who made my heart flutter, although I like several just as pals. I can't tolerate the silly boys who think staying out all night and drinking gin is smart. I have never been petted and I don't believe in petting. I prefer reading an adventure story to being bothered by boys."[25] Perhaps she hoped to preemptively fend off any suitors of the kind that had broken into her bedroom in Germany.

American sportswriters were already calculating her possible earnings. Everyone weighed in on the lucrative offers that Trudy had missed out on by visiting Germany. She herself had commented in one her post-swim columns (again, likely written for the most part by Julia, but probably strongly reflecting Trudy's feelings) that she wouldn't be cashing in on just any old offer, and wouldn't be endorsing products about which she knew nothing. She noted that if she had accepted every offer she had gotten in the past few days, she could probably lock in a million dollars. She wanted to earn her own living, to be sure, but she wasn't going to do it by endorsing every "silly potion," cigarette, or malted beverage that offered money.[26] Westbrook Pegler, Julia Harpman's husband, published an interview with famous showman and sports agent C. C. Pyle, who dramatically bemoaned the money that Trudy was los-ing by waiting until she got home to New York to accept any offers. Pegler's article was highly critical of Dudley Field Malone's fumbled work in this area and Pegler would repeatedly attack Malone on these grounds over the next few years. By Pyle's estimate, Trudy had already lost $100,000, or $200 an hour, since she had finished the swim.[27]

Back at the Channel, Clarabelle Barrett was still hoping to make the swim. According to her pilot, she was "ready to at any time and in any weather. It takes the power of a concrete breakwater to hold her back sometimes." She made another attempt at crossing the Channel, but gave up after only two hours when she became seasick after a fierce gale wind arose. Lillian Cannon stayed as well, waiting for another opportunity, as did Mille Gade Corson.[28]

28. Homecoming

When Trudy and the rest of the entourage returned to New York City, they were greeted with a celebration the likes of which New York had never seen. Tugboats and ships blasted their horns, airplanes roared overhead, and the fireboats sprayed water in celebration. Trudy's large extended family boarded the harbor's tugboat *Macom*, which chugged out to meet the *Berangaria* in the harbor. Trudy was finally able to reunite with her mother, whom she had dearly missed for the entire summer. Sportswriter Paul Gallico wrote, "Never, that I can recall, have I witnessed as thrilling and heart-gripping a spectacle as the home-coming of Gertrude Ederle. As a spontaneous outburst of enthusiasm and affection from hundreds of thousands of loving hearts, it was unsurpassed."[1]

At the dock they were greeted by a contingent of pioneering women swimmers, among them Elsie Viets, Kathryn Brown, Claire Galligan Finney, Charlotte Epstein and more WSA women. Tension arose when the magistrate of the German United Societies tried to make a speech about Trudy's German heritage and was rounded criticized by Dudley Field Malone for not emphasizing Trudy's American heritage. The magistrate then announced that he was only making the point that Trudy was helping the country heal from the war, saying, "This demonstration may be considered as a public reunion of all the people, for it is the first time since the war that such a great and wonderful demonstration was held in which the Americans of German descent played such an important part. We are proud of Trudy, the American girl, born in this city of a father and mother who first saw the light of day in Germany."[2] But Malone didn't want anything distracting from Trudy's marketability that day.

They were all loaded into cars, with Trudy in an open car with Dudley Field Malone and the official city greeter, Grover Whalen. Massive crowds lined Broadway, pushing against the barricades to catch a glimpse of her, sometimes breaking through and impeding the progress of the parade. Paper, confetti and streamers rained down. It really was the greatest reception New

York had ever given anyone, according to the *New York Times*, "No President or king, soldier or statesman has ever enjoyed such an enthusiastic and affectionate outburst of acclaim as was offered to the butcher's daughter of Amsterdam Avenue."[3]

It had already been an intense, dramatic, and celebrity-saturated week for New York City. Heartthrob film actor Rudolph Valentino had died suddenly at age 31. Over 100,000 fans lined up to view his body lying in state at Campbell's Funeral Home, and riots between heartbroken fans erupted in the chaos.

At City Hall, Trudy was greeted by Mayor James Walker and they proceeded to the Aldermanic Chamber, where a formal ceremony took place, broadcast live on radio. As they attempted to step outside, the crowds again rushed forward, knocking over the photographers' stand and engulfing the group of dignitaries. An iron fence was knocked down by the force of the crowds and people were pushed to the ground by the surging crowds behind them. Trudy was carried back inside of City Hall by a policeman who saw that she was about to be torn to bits by the well-wishers and that the people in the crowd were in grave danger. An additional 100 policemen were called to the scene to provide assistance to the 160 already there. Trudy and her family huddled in the mayor's office while they waited for the reinforcements to arrive. When they finally did and the crowd was reasonably under control, they headed out to the cars and, with the help of a police escort, made their way north to Amsterdam Avenue. As they passed Saks and the other large department stores, representatives ran out and presented Trudy with bouquets and other gifts. As they got closer to the Ederle's neighborhood, every store and every window, it seemed, was festooned with welcome signs greeting Trudy. Thousands and thousands of people jammed the streets, craning for a glimpse of the hometown hero. When the motorcade arrived in front of their apartment building, mounted policemen had to shove open a path for Trudy to run from the car into her home where a neighborhood welcoming committee awaited her. But there was no time to relax; the entire neighborhood was calling her name, screaming it out of windows, from the streets and the rooftops. She emerged at a window, where she waved for 15 minutes to her thrilled neighbors.

For days there would be no rest. Trudy could barely leave her home, and was followed everywhere when she did. First, the family went back to the docks to retrieve some lost luggage, then to Dudley Field Malone's apartment to look over some of the financial offers that had come. Crowds stood outside her building for days.

But then, suddenly, there came some upsetting and unbelievable news. Mrs. Mille Gade Corson had swum the Channel as well. Not only had she swum it, she, too, had beaten all other existing records, aside from Trudy's. Her time was 15 hours and 29 minutes, only 67 minutes behind Trudy's incredible record. It was another victory for women everywhere, but it was a blow to Trudy.

The news came as a terrible shock. In one moment, Trudy went from reveling in her entirely unique accomplishment to knowing that it was partially eclipsed. Mrs. Corson hadn't beaten Trudy's time, but she had achieved the same astonishing swim that Trudy had, and on top of that, she was a wife and mother of two very adorable young toddlers. Trudy sent a telegram of congratulations, and issued a public statement, saying, "I am very happy that the Channel has been conquered again, and I have sent my heartiest congratulations to Mrs. Corson. But I am very proud to have been the first woman to get across and to hold the fastest record that has been made."[4]

Even worse, Mrs. Corson had made the swim without a tug, just a motor boat, and some were reviving the controversy that Trudy had been helped by the presence of the tugboat on her swim.

On August 30, Westbrook Pegler wrote in the *New York Times* that Trudy had been confined to bed on doctor's orders because she was on the verge of a nervous breakdown. It wasn't the swim that had upset her health, but the aftermath, and now, the snipes that Trudy had made the swim with help from the tug that were coming from the Corson camp. Pegler wrote angrily that Trudy, a "brave young athlete when in the water," was "utterly licked in the masculine sport of slinging mud."

He wrote, "The English Channel swim for women, conceived in sport and dedicated to the persistent idea that a woman can do anything a man can do, and do it better, is now beginning to suffer from the enthusiasm of the men. The gentlemen friends of Mrs. Clemington Corson, who swam the Channel three weeks after Trudy Ederle made it, seem dissatisfied with the grandeur of their swimmer's actual achievement, and have been endeavoring to do her additional honor by tossing aspersions on the triumphant swim of the honest kid from the soiled hem of the outskirts of Hell's Kitchen, New York City."[5]

The *Daily News*, the paper that had benefited most from Trudy's swim, plastered a headline on its front page that blared, "Trudy's Nerves Snap. Welcome Blamed."[6]

On August 31, there came even worse news for Trudy. Another person had swum the Channel, and this time, Trudy's record had been taken away. Ernst Vierkoetter, a baker from Germany, had made the swim in 12 hours and 42 minutes, slicing an entire hour and 49 minutes from the record.

That evening, another neighborhood celebration was held for Trudy. A grandstand was set up in the street, complete with a throne, and for blocks the streets were packed with screaming, enthusiastic crowds. Trudy was brought out of the house by Dudley Field Malone, Grover Whalen, and some local politicians who gave her a crown and a sash, but the ceremonial presentation was abandoned when the crowd went berserk, repeating the terrifying pandemonium that had occurred at City Hall. Police fought to keep the crowds from knocking over the grandstand or crushing women and children. "Children were trampled on and pushed against the sharp edges of the speakers platform, but no serious injuries were reported," published the *New York Times*.[7] Under the assault of screaming, music, camera flashes, and frightening crowds, Trudy simply fainted, sliding down in the throne while the crown flopped from her head to the ground.[8]

Although Trudy had turned professional, she clearly was not ready to be the kind of professional that, for example, Annette Kellerman had been. While Annette created, found, and seized opportunity with both hands, Trudy was completely unprepared to hustle in the world of contracts, advertising, and appearances that Dudley Field Malone was trying to secure for her. Some of those in the know tried to protect her, but had trouble gaining access to her. Sportswriter Bill Cunningham wrote that Trudy was being led astray by Malone and stated that "big business" was now excluding Trudy's true champions, Julia Harpman and Westbrook Pegler, keeping them away from her when they had been there all along at Cap Gris-Nez. Even worse, he intimated, Malone was pushing Trudy when what she clearly needed was to be far away from the hysterical ruckus.

Threatened with the collapse of his meal ticket, Malone downplayed the situation, saying, "She has not had a good night's rest since she swam the Channel. Every great athlete has a highly nervous system, and Gertrude has been on edge and in training for two years, with a constant ambition to accomplish her purpose. All she needs is a day of complete rest."[9]

Pegler didn't give up, though, and even if he had trouble getting close to Trudy, he clearly wrote what he felt, which was that Malone did not have Trudy's best interests at heart. The *Daily News* had delivered her promised red convertible to the docks, but Malone hadn't even let her see it until she was home at Amsterdam Avenue.

Trudy and her family finally left the city for what they hoped would be some privacy and quiet at their Jersey Shore beach house. They were greeted with another tumultuous welcome, but it was an improvement over the chaotic events in the city. Unbelievably, even more bad news followed on September 10, when a Frenchman named Georges Michel swam the channel with a time of 11 hours and five minutes, further dropping the record. On September 17, a British man, Leslie Norman Derham, swam it with a time of 13 hours, 55 minutes.

Mille Gade Corson didn't make Trudy's mistake of lingering in Europe. She returned immediately to New York, and by September 13, she was appearing at theatres in a brief-but-informative stage show that featured newsreels of her swim and a question-and-answer period, but no actual swimming. *Variety*, the entertainment industry magazine, reviewed the show, which they admitted was a "hurriedly whipped-together act," and found it extremely entertaining and likely to be a draw anywhere, although they would have liked to see her actually swimming, and speaking less, due to a slight lisp.[10] Even Clarabelle Barrett was selling out theaters on her return, at least initially.

Trudy found herself appearing at the Philadelphia Sesquicentennial, an afternoon swimming appearance at Atlantic City Beach, and making more mundane appearances, such as waving to a crowd at a football game or a boxing match for a flat fee. She was making money, but nothing like the great sums that everyone had assumed she would. *Variety* figured that she made $10,000 in her first week of appearances. She signed a contract for a touring vaudeville show that featured herself as the headliner and her friends Helen Wainwright and Aileen Riggin in supporting roles. They traveled with a portable tank, demonstrating swimming strokes and dives on small stages around the country. In May of 1927, her celebrity status was still so high that when Charles Lindbergh completed his famous flight, her telegram of congratulations was reprinted in the papers. "Heartiest congratulations from one pioneer to another. Your courageous feat is another brilliant page in history. I, too, was told it could not be done when I attempted the channel. But, youth will be served."[11] In November of 1927, she was received at the White House and met with President Coolidge. She appeared in one Hollywood film, *Swim, Girl, Swim*, a Paramount vehicle for star Bebe Daniels, in which Trudy played herself.

She spent the year touring the country with Aileen and Helen, performing in a swimming show on vaudeville stages around the country, traveling with a portable swimming tank which had previously been owned by Annette Kellerman. The tour was fun, but Trudy's hearing continued to deteriorate, making her public appearances even more stressful and strenuous. Aileen recalled, "We were in for 26 weeks, I think. We played everywhere: Toronto, Buffalo, Rochester, Chicago. Sometimes we'd stay for three weeks. We'd be held over. Wherever Gertrude went, we went along, too, just for the ride. We had a wonderful time. We would always have the neighbors greet us. We'd get off the train. We'd go right to city hall, and they'd have a luncheon. We met thousands of people on that tour because Gertrude was a national heroine. But she didn't go out and greet people. She was a very reticent, retiring person."[12]

Aileen remembered the stage show as being stressful, due to the small size of the shallow tank. "This tank made us very nervous. It was six feet deep, and just broad enough to do a swan, but you'd have to pull your arms in or you'd hit the sides, you know. And it was nerve-wracking. It was illuminated from the bottom, like a fishbowl, and it was very pretty.... Gertrude couldn't carry an act alone, really, for 15 minutes, say, because she was a swimmer. And you can just watch that for so long, you know? Gertrude would be introduced, and then they would show a bit of her channel swim on the screen, and then she'd go in for a swim. Then Helen and I would do two dives apiece. She would have changed her suit and come back again. She would give a little speech, and then we'd do two more dives."[13]

Sometimes they had three shows a day, sometimes as many as five. The stresses of performing were too much for Trudy, and the reward too little. Still, she was ready to take the tour to Europe, when doctors told her that they might not be able to save her hearing if she went. She recalled, "But then I lost my hearing altogether. I was booked to tour Europe at $2,000 a week and all expenses paid. But I was such a wreck from the American tour that I had a nervous breakdown and in a few weeks I went stone deaf. I had no choice but to cancel the tour. The doctors said I could go to Europe and never hear, or stay and maybe they could save some of it."[14]

In August of 1928, Trudy made her only attempt since the Channel swim to compete professionally. The race was the ten-mile Wrigley swim in Toronto which offered a ten thousand dollar prize to the winner. Trudy came in sixth place, 50 minutes behind the winner. Two years had passed since the Channel swim, and she had spent most of that time only demonstrating swimming on vaudeville stages. After a few years, she stopped making public appearances.[15]

Trudy did not enjoy being famous. Her experience was not a brush with fame so much as a head-on impact, and she barely survived intact. Her retreat from the limelight almost became permanent in 1933, when she suffered a broken back after falling down the stairs of her apartment building. She spent several painful years in a back brace, unable to swim, teach, or make public appearances.

Trudy's return to the public eye occurred at the famous New York World's Fair of 1939 and 1940. The fair was held in Queens and featured as one of its many awe-inspiring amusements Billy Rose's Aquacade. Rose was a theatre impresario and the Aquacade was a water-based extravaganza featuring hundreds of performers on a massive stage before an even larger pool and a five-story backdrop. The Aquacade show combined showmanship with athleticism and sex appeal.

During Trudy's seclusion, the sport of swimming had undergone many changes, along with the rest of American society. Athletic competition for women became more acceptable, and no one any longer doubted the benefit of vigorous exercise. Bathing suits were no longer used to conceal but to reveal, and advances in fabric meant that women who wanted to move in them could do so.

The featured performers of the Aquacade were Johnny Weissmuller, Eleanor Holm, and Esther Williams, all great athletes and highly attractive. The stars of the Aquacade were emblematic of how the world of swimming was becoming a foothold to a career in show business. Weissmuller had won three gold medals at the 1924 Olympics and two at the 1928 Olympics and was now in Hollywood starring in the Tarzan movies. Eleanor Holm was a Brooklyn-born swimmer who had competed in the 1928 and 1932 Olympic Games, but she was most famous for being thrown off the Olympic team for drinking and carousing on the team's trip across the Atlantic to Berlin. The expulsion only launched her further into the world of entertainment. She went on to appear in a Tarzan film herself before marrying Billy Rose. Weissmuller and Holm first appeared in the Aquacades in San Francisco.

Esther Williams, who took over for Holm when the San Francisco Aquacade show moved to New York, was a Los Angeles swimming star who missed her chance to be in the Olympics when the 1940 Tokyo games were canceled due to the outbreak of World War II. Instead, she accepted the job offer from Billy Rose, and headed to New York. There she came to the attention of MGM studios, where she became famous in a series of water-themed movies. She eventually portrayed Annette Kellerman in 1952's biographical movie *Million Dollar Mermaid*.

Trudy's role in the Aquacade was smaller, but the opportunity to be in the show gave her the inspiration to begin swimming again. She swam across the pool in each show, giving the crowd a nostalgic thrill. The name Gertrude Ederle had not been forgotten. At the end of the World's Fair, she returned to her regular life, still not interested in show business. She taught swimming at New York's School for the Deaf, and in Puerto Rico. She loved mechanical work, was known to her friends and family as a skilled auto mechanic and worked in a machine shop during World War II. She spent most of her life in Queens, sharing her home with two close female friends.

Newspaper accounts regularly appeared on the anniversaries of her swim, recapping the event and providing readers with an update on the life of Gertrude Ederle. A standard narrative developed around the Trudy Ederle story. Two facts are almost always mentioned; one, that she never married, and two, that she failed to get rich from being the first woman to swim the English Channel. Again and again it was implied that Trudy's was a cautionary tale, that she had come up short both as a woman and as a modern-day celebrity. Nothing could have been further from the truth: Trudy lived her life authentically and honestly. She knew what she wanted as well as she knew what she did not want. And although a man broke her record for time in swimming the English Channel only a few weeks after she set it, it was not until 1950 that a woman, Florence Chadwick, made the swim with a better time than Trudy.

A park in Highlands, New Jersey, is named after her, as is the amphitheatre where the Aquacade was held. The neglected pool fell into ruins and was torn down. The City of New York is now looking for funding to rebuild a pool on the site. She was inducted into the International Swimming Hall of Fame and the New York City Sports Hall of Fame and Museum. A living memorial is the Ederle Swim, which takes place annually in late October and recreates Trudy's 1925 swim from lower Manhattan to Sandy Hook, New Jersey.

Gertrude herself never had any regrets, and although she was known during her youth for her being charmingly modest, by age 80 she was vocal about her achievement. "If Hollywood plans to do a motion picture or a TV movie on my life, I wish they would do it while I'm still around."[16]

Many of the early female swimmers went on to further achievement in the field of swimming. Adeline Trapp was heavily involved in volunteer work for the American Red Cross, specifically its water safety service, her entire life. Elaine Golding taught swimming for 35 years. Charlotte Epstein was a fearless leader in women's swimming. She continued to manage the Women's Swimming Association, becoming an active representative to the AAU and the U.S. Olympic Committee. In 1935, she organized the women's swimming events of the international Maccabiah Games in Tel Aviv, Israel. The same year, she was part of a group of U.S. Olympic Committee members who publicly resigned in protest that the Americans were participating in the Olympic Games in Nazi Germany. The multi-talented Aileen Riggin toured in swimming shows all over the world, appeared in a Busby Berkeley film, was in the first incarnation of Billy Rose's Aquacade, taught swimming, was a sportswriter covering women's swimming for newspapers, and published many books and magazine articles on the sport. Alice Lord, who had participated in the 1920 Olympics, was active in the Olympic Game movement for years. She attended several Olympic Games as a chaperone and then as an official. Doris O'Mara, who had competed in the 1924 Games, served as the U.S. Olympic women's swimming team's assistant manager in 1928, organized swimming leagues for girls in Connecticut, and taught at a YMCA before moving to California. It was there that she joined her retirement community's synchronized swimming group, the Aquadettes, who for years have been performing an annual show before paying crowds. Ethelda Bleibtrey, the first American woman to win an Olympic event and the first to win three gold medals, was arrested in 1928, along with Mille Gade Corson, when they dove into the Central Park reservoir, making a statement for the International Professional Swimmers Association, who wanted the reservoir turned into a swimming pool.

The 1920s are often called the Golden Age of Sport because of the heroic accomplishments of larger-than-life figures like Babe Ruth, Jack Dempsey, and Red Grange. These individuals are all considered pioneers, and in a sense they are. But there is a different measure for the term "pioneer" when it comes to women's sports, and women who swam competitively were the ultimate trailbreakers. Although women's swimming certainly reached a pinnacle in the 1920s, when measured by the public's awareness of the sport, it was the women of earlier generations who were the true pioneers. It was women in the 1890s and 1900s who successfully fought the current of prevailing opinion that women could not take part in competitive athletics without harming themselves, their children, their husbands, or society.

Women first had to fight the prevailing attitudes for the right to be athletic, rejecting the rules on what constituted a proper activity for a girl, woman, wife or mother, and ignoring the common connotation of femininity as weak, slow, and helpless. They had to fight current notions of what was appropriate clothing. They ingeniously altered existing bathing suits, wore men's suits, and demanded swimming apparel that did not endanger them when worn in the water. They educated each other in the art of swimming and pressed for water-safety education for all, a public movement that led to personal feelings of physical empowerment for thousands of women. Once women realized they were as capable swimmers as men, they pressed to become accepted as auxiliary or full members of men's service organizations such as the United States Volunteer Life Saving Corps. The uneven levels of acceptance led them to form their own grassroots organizations, that in turn led to greater awareness of water safety and swimming education for children and adults throughout the country. The public came to accept and admire these competitive women swimmers through the very popular water carnivals, but even then the governing Amateur Athletic Union barred them from legitimate amateur competition until 1914. And, despite over three decades of proving themselves more than capable in the arena of competitive swimming, it took right up until a few months before the 1920 Olympics to convince American sport authorities of their worth on the international stage. Despite the constant official resistance to their activities, they excelled in national and international competition and became world champions, breaking records and setting new ones. It was the winning participation in the 1920 Olympic Games of America's female swimmers that cemented the role women hold as a crucial part of the American Olympic machine, and opened the Olympic Games to American female athletes in other sports. And it was Gertrude Ederle who captured the world's attention by performing a feat that had been completed by only five men, and breaking the record in the process. The great personal, social, and physical risks taken by all of these women inspired countless other girls and women, and taught the world that women could do more than anyone ever imagined.

Notes

Chapter 1

1. "How Disease Is Generated in New York," *Frank Leslie's Illustrated Newspaper*, August 20, 1870.
2. Andrew Stoddard, et al., *Municipal Wastewater Treatment: Evaluating Improvements in National Water Quality* (New York: Wiley, 2002), 19.
3. Jeff Kisseloff, *You Must Remember This: An Oral History of Manhattan from the 1890s to World War II* (Baltimore: Johns Hopkins University Press, 2000), 567.
4. *Ibid.*, 350.
5. *Ibid.*, 418.
6. *Ibid.*, 126.
7. "Coney Island," *New York Times*, July 27, 1868, 5.
8. "Law Reports," *New York Times*, August 15, 1876, 2.
9. "Local Miscellany," *New York Times*, May 22, 1877, 8.
10. "Spoilers of the Beach," *New York Times*, July 11, 1880, 7.
11. "Garbage at Coney Island," *New York Times*, August 4, 1886, 5.
12. "Want Damages from the City," *New York Times*, November 6, 1891, 2.
13. B.D. Myers, "Letter to the Editor," *New York Times*, July 9, 1925, 18.
14. "On Long Branch's Shore," *New York Times*, July 3, 1891, 8.
15. David Kaufman, *Shul with a Pool: The "Synagogue-Center" in American Jewish History, Culture and Life* (Waltham, MA: Brandeis University Press, 1999), 81.
16. Robin L. Chambers, "The German-American Turners: Their Efforts to Promote, Develop, and Initiate Physical Culture in Chicago's Public Schools and Parks, 1860–1914," *Yearbook of German-American Studies* 22 (1987): 101–110.
17. Steven A. Reiss, *City Games: The Evolution of American Urban Society and the Rise of Sports.* (Urbana: University of Illinois Press, 1989), 85.
18. Advertisement, *Brooklyn Eagle*, November 2, 1868, 1.
19. "A New Brooklyn Institution," *Brooklyn Eagle*, July 10, 1868, 3.
20. "The Park Baths," *Brooklyn Eagle*, September 17, 1870, 2.

Chapter 2

1. "Beauties at the Bath," *New York Times*, August 4, 1878, 6.
2. *Ibid.*, 6.
3. Advertisement, *The Sun*, July 4, 1880, 8.
4. "An Aquatic Exhibition," *New York Times*, September 14, 1877, 2.
5. "Lady Swimmers," *The Sun*, 1886.
6. "Mermaids Near the Park," *New York Times*, September 1, 1878, 12.
7. "Almost Young Mermaids," *New York Times*, July 24, 1884, 8.
8. "Water Nymphs at Play," *Brooklyn Daily Eagle*, August 16, 1889, 1.
9. "At Home in the Water," *Brooklyn Eagle*, April 20, 1890, 9.

Chapter 3

1. "The Board of Aldermen," *New York Times*, July 27, 1858, 5.
2. "Public Baths," *New York Times*, June 27, 1866, 2.
3. "Free Baths," *New York Times*, June 28, 1970, 2.
4. *Ibid.*
5. "The Public Baths," *New York Times*, July 2, 1870, 2.
6. "Public Baths," *New York Times*, July 5, 1870, 3.
7. "The Public Baths," *New York Times*, August 28, 1872, 2.
8. "City and Suburban News," *New York Times*, September 3, 1873, 8.
9. "Miscellaneous City News," *New York Times*, July 3, 1879, 3.
10. "Girl Swimmers Competing," *The Sun*, August 7, 1880, 1.
11. "How Poor People Bathe," *New-York Tribune*, August 14, 1881, 2.
12. "Fourteen Floating Baths," *New-York Tribune*, June 28, 1904, 7.
13. "How Poor People Bathe," *New-York Tribune*, August 14, 1881, 2.
14. "Gossip for Ladies," *Chicago Tribune*, July 8, 1877, 11.
15. "Learning to Swim," *New-York Daily Tribune*, July 24, 1900, 7.
16. "Fourteen Floating Baths," *New-York Tribune*, June 28, 1904, 7.
17. "Girl Swimmers Competing," *The Sun*, August 7, 1880, 1.
18. "Five Remarkable Swimmers," *Brooklyn Daily Eagle*, June 25, 1902, 22.
19. "Fourteen Floating Baths," *New-York Tribune*, June 28, 1904, 7.
20. "Splendid Free Swimming Pool to Be Opened in 'Hell's Kitchen,'" *New-York Tribune*, June 24, 1906, 1.
21. New York City Borough of Manhattan. Public Works Department. *Public Baths Under the Supervision of the President of the Borough of Manhattan.* New York, NY: 1912.
22. "Peeping Toms," *The National Police Gazette,* September 1, 1883, 6.
23. "Miss Kate Bennett's Resignation," *New-York Daily Tribune*, August 11, 1883, 5.

Chapter 4

1. "Captain Boyton's Swim," *New York Times*, June 14, 1875, 2.
2. "Swimming the Channel," *New York Times*, September 6, 1875, 5.
3. "The Newport Swimming Match," *New York Times*, August 23, 1879, 1.
4. "Racing for Beer Money," *New York Times*, August 23, 1880, 5.
5. "The Swimming Match," *New York Times*, July 23, 1875, 5.
6. "Butler's Long Swim," *New York Times*, August 7, 1885, 8.
7. "Stopped by the Police," *New York Times*, August 10, 1885, 1.
8. "Swimming Matches," *New York Times*, August 11, 1872, 2.
9. "Boat Racing and Swimming Matches," *New York Times*, June 22, 1873, 8.
10. "Swimming Contests," *New York Times*, July 27, 1873, 5.
11. "Swimming Extraordinary," *New York Times*, September 24, 1874, 2.
12. "Ladies Swimming Match," *New York Times,* September 7, 1873, 8.
13. "Nymphs of the Waves," *Chicago Daily Tribune*, August 27, 1874, 8.
14. "A Ladies' Swimming Match at Fort Hamilton," *New York Times*, August 31, 1874, 8.
15. "Girls to Swim the Narrows," *Brooklyn Eagle*, August 9, 1901, 2.
16. "All Beaten by a Woman," *New York Times*, August 30, 1885, 2.
17. "Swimming with the Tide," *Brooklyn Daily Eagle*, August 30, 1885, 12.
18. "A Ladies' Swimming Match at Fort Hamilton," *New York Times*, August 31, 1874, 8.
19. "Gotham," *Chicago Daily Tribune*, September 6, 1874, 11.
20. "A Woman's Swimming Feat," *Brooklyn Daily Eagle*, September 13, 1875, 2.
21. "Of Feminine Interest," *Brooklyn Eagle*, August 23, 1896, 20.
22. "Swimming Matches and Boat Races," *New York Times*, August 3, 1874, 8.
23. "Swimming for Prizes," *New York Times*, September 8, 1884, 8.
24. "Fair Swimmers Compete," *The Sun*, September 9, 1894, 6.
25. "Girl Swimmers at Brighton," *Brooklyn Eagle*, August 25, 1895, 3.

26. Ethel Golding, "Lesson No. 1," *The Evening World*, July 29, 1901, 5.

27. "The Overtrained Athletic Girl," *Modern Medical Science* 16 (1904), 631.

28. "Vaudeville Houses," *Brooklyn Eagle*, May 7, 1901, 6.

29. "Hartford Theater," *Hartford Courant*, January 30, 1912, 7.

30. "Palace Theater," *Hartford Courant*, September 30, 1914, 9.

31. "Poli Diving Girls in River Exhibition," *Hartford Courant*, June 7, 1914, 3.

32. "Give Work to Women," *Washington Post*, September 27, 1908, F11.

Chapter 5

1. "Evils of Modern Athletics," *New York Times*, December 16, 1884, 2.

2. Walter Camp, *Walter Camp's Book of College Sports*. (New York: Century, 1893), 8.

3. "Swimming for Prizes," *New York Times*, August 31, 1884, 2.

4. Andrew Sloan Draper, *Draper's Self-Culture. Volume 6: Sports, Pastimes, and Physical Culture* (New York: Ferd P. Kaiser, 1907), 220.

5. Pierre de Coubertin, "Why I Revived the Olympic Games," in *The World's Great Events*, ed., Esther Singleton (New York: P. F. Collier & Son, 1916).

6. "Ladies' Day at an Athletic Club," *New York Tribune*, March 5, 1893, 24.

7. "Day Off for Yachting," *New-York Daily Tribune*, July 20, 1910, 4.

Chapter 6

1. "Thirty Hours in the Water," *New York Times*, May 22, 1880, 2.

2. "Woman's Channel Swim," *New York Times*, September 18, 1900, 12.

3. "Women in Swimming Match," *Chicago Daily Tribune*, July 16, 1906, 8.

4. "Swim Through London," *The Observer*, August 21, 1910, 8.

5. Kellerman, *How to Swim*, p. 20.

6. *Ibid.*, p. 26.

7. Margaret A. Jarvis, *Captain Webb and 100 Years of Channel Swimming* (North Pomfret, VT: Newton Abbott and David & Charles, 1975), 22.

8. "Gay Girl Swimmer," *Boston Daily Globe*, July 30, 1905, p. SM5.

9. Kellerman, *How to Swim*, p. 30.

10. *Ibid.*, p. 46.

11. *Ibid.*, p. 47.

12. *Ibid.*, p. 183.

Chapter 7

1. "Gotham," *Chicago Daily Tribune*, September 6, 1874, 11.

2. "Four Young Heroes," *New York Times*, October 1, 1878, 8.

3. "Nan, Gil., and Ed. Eat High Pie," *New York Times*, December 29, 1878, 7.

4. "Boyton's Midnight Trip," *New York Times*, January 26, 1879, 7.

5. "The Life-Savers Disband," *New York Times*, July 14, 1879, 8.

6. "Woman in Brave Life-Saving Band," *The Republic*, June 14, 1903, 22.

7. "Volunteer Life Savers," *New York Times*, September 27, 1897, 10.

8. *Annual Report of the United States Volunteer Life Saving Corps of Rhode Island Department, Made to the General Assembly at Its January Session, 1904* (Providence: E. L. Freeman & Sons, 1904).

9. *Annual Report of the United States Volunteer Life Saving Corps of Rhode Island Department, Made to the General Assembly at Its January Session, 1907* (Providence: E. L. Freeman & Sons, 1907).

10. "Women and Girls Swim for Life Saving Corps Prizes," *Boston Daily Globe*, August 21, 1909, 2.

11. *Annual Report of the United States Volunteer Life Saving Corps of Rhode Island Department, Made to the General Assembly at Its January Session, 1906* (Providence: E. L. Freeman & Sons, 1906), 19.

12. *Annual Report of the United States Volunteer Life Saving Corps of Rhode Island Department, Made to the General Assembly at Its January Session, 1904* (Providence: E. L. Freeman & Sons, 1904), 10.

13. "The Fort Hamilton Volunteer Life Saving Corps, with Miss Florence West, One of Its Members, Who Is a Champion Swimmer," *Brooklyn Eagle*, April 24, 1902, 3.

14. "Pretty Girl in Red Ill Treated at Beach," *Brooklyn Daily Eagle*, August 13, 1901, 16.

15. "Hoodlums at Manhattan Beset Two Casino Girls," *Brooklyn Eagle*, August 18, 1901, 1.

16. "Woman Swims to Rescue of Three," *New York Times*, August 13, 1912, 18.

17. *Annual Report of the U.S. Volunteer Life-Saving Corps (Inland Waters) for the Year 1904* (Albany: State of New York, 1905), 54.

Chapter 8

1. "Coney Island Girl Swimmers," *Brooklyn Eagle*, September 5, 1887, 4.

2. "Young Girl Swims the Narrows," *New-York Tribune*, September 30, 1901, 1.

3. *Annual Report of the U.S. Volunteer Life-Saving Corps (Inland Waters) for the Year 1904* (Albany: State of New York, 1905), 62.

4. "Girl Life-Saver Tells of Test," *The Evening World*, August 5, 1904, 2.

5. "Girl Heroine of Swim Tells How to Defeat Men," *The Evening World*, August 17, 1908, 5.

6. *Ibid.*

7. *Annual Report of the United States Volunteer Life Saving Corps of Rhode Island Department, Made to the General Assembly at Its January Session, 1909* (Providence: E. L. Freeman & Sons, 1909), 66.

8. "Shocked by Bathing Suits," *Washington Post*, April 27, 1907, 3.

9. "Bare Legs Are Barred," *Los Angeles Times*, August 28, 1907, 11.

10. "Women Show Speed in Swimming Races," *New York Times*, July 3, 1911, 5.

11. William G. Wing, "Thank Her for Brief Swim Suits," *Herald Tribune*, Undated. From Adelaide Trapp Muhlenberg scrapbook, International Swimming Hall of Fame.

12. *When the Girls Came Out to Play: The Birth of American Sportswear* (Amherst: University of Massachusetts Press, 2006), 74.

13. "School Teacher Swims Hell Gate," *New York Times*, September 6, 1909, 1.

14. "Public Swimming Pool Is Popular," *New York Times*, November 27, 1910, 15.

15. "A Heroine of the Water," *New-York Tribune*, September 10, 1911, C4.

16. "Girl Swimmer Makes New Record," *New York Times*, September 4, 1911, 5.

17. "A Heroine of the Water," *New-York Tribune*, September 10, 1911, C4.

18. Letter from Boston Globe to Adeline Trapp, September 28, 1911, Adeline Trapp Scrapbook, International Swimming Hall of Fame.

Chapter 9

1. *Annual Report of the U.S. Volunteer Life Saving Corps (Inland Waters) for the Department of New York for the Year 1900* (James B. Lyon: Albany, 1901), 40.

2. "Girl of Seven an Expert Swimmer," *Brooklyn Eagle*, May 5, 1901, 29.

3. "Two Girls Swim the Narrows," *Brooklyn Eagle*, August 11, 1901, 2.

4. "Swam the Narrows," *Brooklyn Eagle*, September 17, 1900, 8.

5. "Girl Rivals Swim Narrows," *The Sun*, September 15, 1902, 4.

6. "Women Swim the Tappan Zee," *The Sun*, August 23, 1908, 2.

7. "Miss Elaine Golding Wins Swimming Race," *Brooklyn Daily Eagle*, August 23, 1908, 5.

8. "Women Swim Three Miles in Hudson," *New York Times*, August 23, 1908, S2.

9. "Twentieth Century Mermaid Champion Woman Swimmer," *Brooklyn Daily Eagle*, September 13, 1908, 9.

10. "Gives Athletes New Vigor," *New-York Tribune*, September 13, 1908, 7.

11. "Women Race in Tank," *New York Times*, September 9, 1910, 11.

12. "Miss Golding Swims Fast," *New York Times*, September 16, 1910, 10.

13. "Girls Swim from Battery to Island," *New York Times*, August 28, 1911, 5.

14. "Child Should Be Taught to Swim While an Infant," *Brooklyn Eagle*, March 21, 1937.

15. "Elaine Golding Swims the Lake," *Panama Star and Herald*, December 13, 1913.

16. "Tells How She Swam Canal," *Brooklyn Eagle*, December 27, 1913.

17. "Girls Succeed Where Men Experts Failed," *Boston Daily Globe*, July 14, 1909, 4.

18. "Rose Pitonof Swims to Boston Light," *Boston Daily Globe*, August 8, 1910, 1.

19. "Girl Swimmers' Feats Astonish," *Boston Daily Globe*, July 11, 1910, p. 9.

20. "Girl in Long Swim to Coney Island," *New York Times*, August 14, 1911, 2.

21. "B. F. Keith's Vaudeville," *Boston Daily Globe*, August 22, 1911, 11.

22. "Miss Pitonof Back," *Boston Daily Globe*, September 23, 1912, 5.

23. "Twentieth Century Mermaid Champion Woman Swimmer," *Brooklyn Daily Eagle*, September 13, 1908, 9.

Chapter 10

1. "Public Baths," *Southern Practitioner* 35 (1913): 431.

2. "Swimming Tank Is the Garden Where Girls Can Grow Beauty," *The Evening Telegram*, January 30, 1912, 6.

3. "Public Baths," *Southern Practitioner*, 431.

4. "Mermaids Hold Meet," *New-York Tribune*, August 26, 1912, 14.

5. L. de B. Handley, "The Winter Crusade to Win Women Swimmers," *The Atlanta Constitution*, November 19, 1916, A5.

Chapter 11

1. Uriel Simri, "The Development of Female Participation in the Modern Olympic Games," Stadion 6 (1980): 187–216.

2. Bill Mallon and Ian Buchanan, *The 1908 Olympic Games: Results for All Competitors, in All Events, with Commentary* (Jefferson, NC: McFarland, 2000).

3. Bill Mallon and Ture Widlund, *The 1912 Olympic Games: Results for All Competitors in All Events, with Commentary* (Jefferson, NC: McFarland, 2002).

4. James E. Sullivan, *Schoolyard Athletics: Giving Directions for Conducting Organized Athletic Activities in the Schoolyard* (New York: American Sports Publishing,1909), 25.

5. Amateur Athletic Union of the United States, *Minutes of the Annual Meeting* (No publisher, 1907), 7.

6. Amateur Athletic Union of the United States, *Minutes of the Annual Meeting*, 11.

7. "Amateur Sport Has Made Big Advance," *New York Times*, June 19, 1910, X13.

8. Mark Dyerson, *Making the American Team: Sport, Culture and the Olympic Experience* (Urbana: University of Illinois Press, 1998), 61.

9. Dyerson, *Making the American Team*, 77.

10. James E. Sullivan, *Spalding's Official Athletic Almanac for 1905, Special Olympic Number Containing the Official Report of the Olympic Games of 1904* (New York: American Publishing, 1905), 57.

11. *Ibid.*, 253.

12. *Ibid.*, 259.

13. Robert W. Wheeler, *Jim Thorpe, World's Greatest Athlete* (Norman: University of Oklahoma Press, 1979).

Chapter 12

1. "Bar Mixed Athletics," *New York Times*, July 13, 1913, S2.
2. "Hot Shot for 'Jim' Sullivan," *New York Times*, July 19, 1913, 5.
3. "A.A.U. Ban on Women," *New York Times*, January 18, 1914, S1.
4. "No Women Athletes for American Team," *New York Times*, March 31, 1914, 9.
5. "Olympic Congress Will Admit Women," *Hartford Courant*, June 16, 1914, 19.
6. "Olympic to Have Six Boxing Classes," *Hartford Courant*, June 20, 1914, 21.
7. "Bar Women from Swimming Meet," *Hartford Courant*, July 29, 1914, 16.
8. "Rye Beach Club in Bad," *New York Times*, August 12, 1914, 7.
9. Robert Korsgaard, *A History of the Amateur Athletic Union of the United States*, Dissertation (Teachers College Columbia University, 1952), 280.

Chapter 13

1. "A.A.U. Ban on Women," *New York Times*, January 18, 1914, S1.
2. "A.A.U. Lifts Ban on N. Y. A. C. Swimmers," *New York Times*, January 7, 1915, 14.
3. "Praises Miss Mehrtens," *New York Times*, February 7, 1915, 12.
4. "Action of A. A. U. Rouses Swimmers," *New York Tribune*, January 11, 1914.
5. "Women Stir Up the AAU," *New York Times*, January 5, 1915, 13.
6. "Hangs on to Prizes," *New York Times*, February 21, 1915, S3.
7. "Ladies Night Now in View for AAU," Adeline Trapp Scrapbook, International Swimming Hall of Fame, date unknown.
8. "Girl Swimmers Placed Under Ban," *New York Times*, February 12, 1915, 9.
9. Linda J. Borish, "'The Cradle of American Champions, Women Champions ... Swim Champions': Charlotte Epstein, Gender and Jewish Identity, and the Physical Emancipation of Women in Aquatic Sports," *The International Journal of the History of Sport* 21 (March 2004): 201.
10. "New Garb for Mermaids," *New-York Tribune*, February 3, 1915, 10.
11. "No Stocking Girls O.K. as Swimmers," *New York Herald*, August 4, 1915.
12. "Swim Meet for Women," *New York Times*, August 8, 1915, 31.
13. "Women Life Savers Brave Angry Waves," *New York Times*, August 15, 1915, S2.
14. "Women Swim for Title," *New York Times*, August 23, 1915, 7.
15. "Brave Suffragists Rescue 'Anti' from Sea," *New York Times*, July 18, 1915, 15.
16. "New Swimming Mark," *New York Times*, December 19, 1915, 19.
17. Metropolitan Association of the Amateur Athletic Union of the United States. *Minutes of the Annual Meeting* (1915), 43.
18. "A.A.U. Lets Down Bard for Women Swimmers," *New York Times*, November 21, 1915, A4.
19. "Woman Swimmers Want to Compete for Titles," *New York Press*, January 27, 1916.
20. "Comment on Current Events in Sports," *New York Times*, July 17, 1916, 8.
21. "Pros Retained as AAU Legislators," *New York Times*, November 21, 1916, 12.
22. "Reviews Girls' Swimming," *New York Times*, November 10, 1916, 10.
23. "Local Girl Best Swimmer," *New York Times*, October 7, 1917, 100.
24. "Laurels for Miss Boyle," *New York Times*, December 15, 1918, 21.

Chapter 14

1. *W.S.A. News*, February 1921, 2.
2. *Doris O'Mara Murphy: An Olympian's Oral History* (Los Angeles: Amateur Athletic Foundation of Los Angeles, 1988), 5.
3. L. de B. Handley, *Swimming for Women* (New York: American Sports Publishing, 1925), 145.
4. *W.S.A. News*, February 1921, 1.
5. *Aileen Riggin: An Olympian's Oral History* (Los Angeles: Amateur Athletic Foundation of Los Angeles, 2000), 2.

6. Lewis H. Carlson and John J. Fogarty, *Tales of Gold* (Chicago: Contemporary Books, 1987), 17.

7. *Aileen Riggin: An Olympian's Oral History*, 2000, 14.

8. *Doris O'Mara Murphy: An Olympian's Oral History*, 1988, 16.

9. *Aileen Riggin: An Olympian's Oral History*, 2000, 3.

10. Lewis H. Carlson, *Tales of Gold*, 15.

11. *Aileen Riggin: An Olympian's Oral History*, 2000, 18.

Chapter 15

1. *Aileen Riggin: An Olympian's Oral History* (Los Angeles: Amateur Athletic Foundation of Los Angeles, 2000), 15.

2. *Ibid.*, 16.

3. *Doris O'Mara Murphy: An Olympian's Oral History* (Los Angeles: Amateur Athletic Foundation of Los Angeles, 1988), 6.

4. Letter from the Gilliams Service to Helen Wainwright, Helen Wainwright Scrapbook, International Swimming Hall of Fame, September 24, 1919.

5. "Australians to Try for All U.S. Titles," *New York Times*, August 23, 1916, 11.

6. "Australian Yields to American Girl," *New York Times*, August 17, 1919, 19.

7. John A. Lucas and Ian Jobling, "Troubled Waters: Fanny Durack's 1919 Swimming Tour of America Amid Transnational Amateur Athletic Prudery and Bureaucracy," *Olympika* 4 (1995): 93–112.

Chapter 16

1. *Aileen Riggin: An Olympian's Oral History* (Los Angeles: Amateur Athletic Foundation of Los Angeles, 2000): 17.

2. *Aileen Riggin Soule: A Wonderful Life in Her Own Words.* International Swimming Hall of Fame, online at http://www.ishof.org/exhibits/pdf/aileen_riggin.pdf

3. *Aileen Riggin: An Olympian's Oral History*, 2000, 19.

4. *Ibid.*, 16.

5. "Olympic Games Committee Likely to Restore Decathlon to Its 1920 Program," *New York Times*, December 22, 1919, 21.

6. "Wants More Events for Female Swimmers," *Hartford Courant*, February 6, 1920, 14.

7. *Aileen Riggin: An Olympian's Oral History*, 2000, 15.

8. "Athletes Selected for Olympic Team," *New York Times*, July 16, 1920, 21.

9. "Olympic Athletes Sail for Antwerp," *New York Times*, July 27, 1920, 21.

10. Buck Dawson, *Mermaids on Parade: America's Love Affair with Its First Olympic Swimmers* (Huntington, NY: Kroshka Books, 2000), 61.

11. *Aileen Riggin: An Olympian's Oral History*, 2000, 20.

12. Leavy, Jane. "On the Playing Fields of Flanders," *New York Times*, July 14, 1996, S7.

13. *Aileen Riggin: An Olympian's Oral History*, 2000, 26.

14. *Thelma Payne Sanborn: An Olympian's Oral History* (Los Angeles: Amateur Athletic Foundation of Los Angeles), 15.

15. *Aileen Riggin: An Olympian's Oral History*, 2000, 30.

16. Buck Dawson, *Mermaids on Parade*, 62.

Chapter 17

1. "Two Girls of 14 Star in Olympic Parade," *New York Times*, October 3, 1920, 14.

2. Henry W. Clune, *I Always Liked It Here: Reminiscences of a Rochesterian* (Rochester: University of Rochester Libraries, 1983), 167.

3. "The Shower That Shattered a Mermaid Friendship," *San Francisco Chronicle*, November 27, 1921, SM3.

4. "Charlotte Boyle Married," *New York Times*, October 19, 1921, 16.

5. "Ethelda Bleibtrey's Bare Knees Ordered Off the Beach," *New York Times,* December 3, 1921, 3.

6. "Miss Bleibtrey to Turn Professional," *New York Times,* May 10, 1922, 27.

7. "Gertrude Ederle Takes Swim Race," *New York Times,* August 2, 1922, 24.

8. "Miss Ederle Sets Six World Records," *New York Times,* September 5, 1922, 23.

9. "History Made at the St. George's Aquatic Meeting," *Royal Gazette,* October 10, 1922, 1.

10. "Women Swimmers Protest A.A.U. Ban," *New York Times,* May 3, 1923, 15.

11. "W.S.A. to Compete Despite A.A.U. Ban," *New York Times,* May 12, 1923, 13.

12. "Our Girls' Trip to England," *W.S.A. News,* June 1923, 6.

13. "Aileen Riggin, Champion Diver, Dislikes Luxuries," *Hartford Courant,* August 15, 1923, 15.

14. "W.S.A. Outscored All Other Clubs," *New York Times,* November 14, 1923, 15.

Chapter 18

1. "America to Send 300 to Olympics," *New York Times,* June 19, 1923, 15.

2. "Olympic Committee Outlines U.S. Plans," *New York Times,* October 26, 1923, 20.

3. "Paddock's Records Are Again Rejected," *New York Times,* November 20, 1923, 15.

4. "Officials Appeal for Olympic Fund," *New York Times,* March 19, 1924, 25.

5. "Kirby and Hurlbert Make Olympic Plea," *New York Times,* May 20, 1924, 18.

6. "U.S. Swimming Teams Named for Olympics," *New York Times,* June 9, 1924, 20.

7. "Swim Body Ratifies 36 World Records," *New York Times,* July 12, 1914, 5.

8. "Weissmuller Wins in Swim Carnival," *New York Times,* June 15, 1924, 28.

9. *Doris O'Mara Murphy: An Olympian's Oral History* (Los Angeles: Amateur Athletic Foundation of Los Angeles, 1988), 9.

10. *Aileen Riggin: An Olympian's Oral History* (Los Angeles: Amateur Athletic Foundation of Los Angeles, 2000), 39.

11. *Doris O'Mara Murphy: An Olympian's Oral History,* 1988, 10.

12. *Aileen Riggin: An Olympian's Oral History,* 2000, 40.

13. *Clarita Hunsberger Neher: An Olympian's Oral History* (Los Angeles: Amateur Athletic Foundation of Los Angeles, 1988), 14.

14. *Aileen Riggin: An Olympian's Oral History,* 2000, 42.

15. Frank Litsky, "Aileen Riggin Soule, Olympic Diver and Swimmer, Dies at 96," *New York Times,* October 21, 2002, A17.

16. *Aileen Riggin: An Olympian's Oral History,* 2000, 42–43.

17. *Clarita Hunsberger Neher: An Olympian's Oral History* (Los Angeles: Amateur Athletic Foundation of Los Angeles, 2000), 12.

18. "Olympic Swimmers Complete Tryouts," *New York Times,* July 11, 1924, 8.

19. "U.S. Team Is Hissed by French When It Wins Olympic Title," *New York Times,* May 19, 1924, 1.

20. "Italian Foilsmen Quit the Olympics," *New York Times,* July 1, 1924, 17.

21. "Italian Fencer, Seeking Duel, Forever Barred from Olympics," *New York Times,* July 24, 1924, 9.

22. Buck Dawson, *Mermaids on Parade: America's Love Affair with Its First Female Swimmers* (Huntington, NY: Kroshka Books, 1999), 61.

23. "U.S. Team Clinches Olympic Swim Title," *New York Times,* July 19, 1924, 5.

24. "U.S. Eliminated in Water Polo, 3–1," *New York Times,* July 14, 1924, 8.

25. "U.S. Women Sweep Olympic Swim Race," *New York Times,* July 16, 1924, 12.

26. "U.S. Takes 6 Finals," *New York Times,* July 21, 1924, 6.

Chapter 19

1. Buck Dawson, *Mermaids on Parade: America's Love Affair with Its First Women Swimmers* (Huntington, NY: Kroshka Books, 2000), 85.

2. "American Girl to Try to Swim English Channel; Helen Wainwright, 19, Holds Record Here," *New York Times*, January 16, 1925, 1.

3. "Miss Ederle to Try to Swim Channel," *New York Times*, April 16, 1925, 19.

4. "Miss Wainwright to Become Coach," *New York Times*, June 8, 1925, 12.

5. "Miss Wainwright to Become Coach," New York Times, June 8, 1925, p. 12.

6. "Helen Wainwright to Get Record Pay," Newspaper Clipping, Helen Wainwright Scrapbook, International Swimming Hall of Fame.

7. "Girl Swims to Hook from the Battery," *New York Times*, June 16, 1925, 1.

8. "Miss Ederle Sails for Channel Swim," *New York Times*, June 18, 1925, 17.

Chapter 20

1. Margaret A. Jarvis, *Captain Webb and 100 Years of Channel Swimming* (North Pomfret, VT: Newton Abbott and David & Charles, 1975), 22.

2. "Burgess Swims English Channel," *New York Times*, September 7, 1911, 4.

3. "Reaches Calais Exhausted," *New York Times*, August 7, 1923, 1.

4. "Cuts Webb's Time in Channel Swim," *New York Times*, August 13, 1923, 1.

5. "Mussolini Praises Italian Conqueror of English Channel," *Hartford Courant*, August 21, 1923, 18.

6. "Channel Swim Expires Soon," *New York Times*, August 31, 1923, 12.

7. "Toth Swims Channel," *New York Times*, September 10, 1923, p. 17.

8. "Mrs. Carson Fails in Channel Swim," *New York Times*, August 8, 1923, p. 5.

Chapter 21

1. "Miss Ederle Finds Channel Waters Frigid, Says She Cannot Try Swim for Some Weeks," *New York Times*, July 6, 1925, 7.

2. "Miss Ederle Finds Channel Waters Frigid," *New York Times*, July 6, 1925, 7.

3. Alec Rutherford, "Miss Ederle in Great Swim Trial Tomorrow," *New York Times*, August 2, 1925, A1.

4. "French Girl Makes Channel Bid Today," *New York Times*, August 4, 1925, 15.

5. "Girl Swims to Portel," *New York Times*, July 3, 1925, 8.

6. "Girl Fails to Swim English Channel," *New York Times*, July 17, 1925, 1.

7. "French Girl Makes Channel Swim Today," *New York Times*, August 4, 1925, 15.

8. Rutherford, "Miss Ederle in Great Swim Trial Tomorrow," A1.

9. "Miss Ederle Goes to Town," *New York Times*, August 6, 1925, 15.

10. "Miss Ederle Resumes Training for Swim," *New York Times*, August 13, 1925, 11.

11. "Deluge of Offers to Back Miss Ederle in Channel Swim," *New York Times*, July 24, 1925, 10.

12. "Night Scared Mlle. Sion," *New York Times*, Aug 7, 1925, 5.

13. "Women Stars Delay Channel Swim," *New York Times*, August 8, 1925, 6.

14. "Want Trio in Swim," *New York Times*, August 15, 1925, 4.

15. "Miss Ederle Starts Great Swim Tonight," *New York Times*, August 7, 1925, 1.

16. "Channel Swim off Again," *New York Times*, August 10, 1925, 13.

17. "Girl Nearly Drowns Swimming Channel," *New York Times*, August 11, 1925, 1.

18. Miss Harrison Ready for Channel Again," *New York Times*, August 12, 1925, 3.

19. "Two Girls May Try Channel Tuesday," *New York Times*, August 14, 1925, 1.

20. "Nearly Loses Life in Channel Swim," *Boston Daily Globe*, August 11, 1925, 1.

21. "Ederle's Trainer Says Channel Will Win," *Chicago Daily Tribune*, August 8, 1925, 13.

22. "Two Girls May Try Channel Tuesday," *New York Times*, August 14, 1925, 7.

23. "Ederle Confident of Reaching Dover," *Hartford Courant*, August 17, 1025, 9.

24. "Gertrude Ederle Calm on Eve of Channel Swim," *Washington Post*, August 18, 1925, 3.

25. "Yankee Braves Ocean Dangers," *Los Angeles Times*, August 18, 1925, B1.

26. "Gertrude Ederle Calm on Eve of Channel Swim," *Washington Post*, August 18, 1925, 3.

27. "Miss Ederle Begins Her Channel Swim," *New York Times*, August 18, 1925, 1.

28. "Yankee Braves Ocean Dangers," *Los Angeles Times*, August 18, 1925, B1.

29. "The Start from Gris-Nez," *New York Times*, August 19, 1925, 12.

30. "The Start from Gris-Nez," *New York Times*, August 19, 1925, 12.

Chapter 22

1. Alec Rutherford, "Miss Ederle Fails in Swim," *Los Angeles Times*, August 19, 1925, B1.

2. "The Start from Gris-Nez," *New York Times*, August 19, 1925, 12.

3. "Story of the Swim from the Tug," *New York Times*, August 19, 1925, 12.

4. "Story of the Swim from the Tug," *New York Times*, August 19, 1925, 12.

5. Alec Rutherford, "Miss Ederle Fails in Swim," *Los Angeles Times*, August 19, 1925, B1.

6. "Miss Ederle Sobs as Sickness Halts Her Channel Swim," *Washington Post*, August 19, 1925, 1.

7. Alec Rutherford, "Miss Ederle Fails in Swim," *Los Angeles Times*, August 19, 1925, B1.

8. "Salt Water Made the Swimmer Ill," *New York Times*, August 19, 1925, 1.

9. "Storm Defeats Miss Ederle in Channel 6 Miles Off Goal," *Daily News*, August 19, 1925.

10. "Miss Ederle Sobs as Sickness Halts Her Channel Swim," *Washington Post*, August 19, 1925, 1.

11. Alec Rutherford, "Miss Ederle Fails in Swim," *Los Angeles Times*, August 19, 1925, B1.

12. *Ibid.*

13. "Miss Ederle Sobs as Sickness Halts Her Channel Swim," *Washington Post*, August 19, 1925, 1.

14. "Miss Ederle May Try Channel Swim Again," *New York Times*, August 20, 1925, 21.

15. "Miss Ederle to Try Channel Once More," *New York Times*, August 21, 1925, 16.

16. "Miss Ederle's New Trainer," *Hartford Courant*, August 27, 1925, 16.

17. "Miss Ederle Takes Burgess," *Boston Daily Globe*, August 20, 1925, A13.

18. "Channel Swimmers Wait," *New York Times*, August 23, 1925, 9.

19. "French Woman, Who Hopes to Swim Channel, Has Little Money for Aid," *Washington Post*, August 30, 1925, AM4.

20. "Japanese Swimmer Gives Up in Channel," *New York Times*, August 29, 1925, 11.

21. "Stormy Channel Halts Miss Ederle," *New York Times*, September 1, 1925, 11.

22. "Gale Halts Miss Ederle," *New York Times*, September 3, 1925, 25.

23. "Miss Ederle Not So Sure," *Boston Daily Globe*, September 1, 1925, A17.

24. "Jazz Band, Seasick in Channel, Won't Play for Miss Ederle Again," *Boston Daily Globe*, August 31, 1925, A6.

25. "Miss Ederle May Drop Channel Until 1926," *New York Times*, September 2, 1925, 8.

26. "Cold Defeats Helmy in English Channel: Forced to Quit When 3 1/2 Miles from Dover," *New York Times*, September 15, 1926, 1.

Chapter 23

1. "Girl Charges Trainer Halted Channel Swim," *New York Times*, September 19, 1925, 1.

2. "Miss Ederle Puts Blame on Trainer," *Hartford Courant*, September 19, 1925, 1.

3. "Girl Charges Trainer Halted Channel Swim," *New York Times*, September 19, 1925, 1.

4. "Lie, Miss Ederle Says of Charges She Didn't Train," *Washington Post*, September 20, 1925.

5. *Ibid.*

6. "Backs Miss Ederle in Blaming Trainer," *New York Times*, September 21, 1925, 20.

7. "Backs Miss Ederle in Channel Dispute," *New York Times*, September 22, 1925, 8.

8. *Ibid.*

9. "Wholesale Denials in Ederle's Behalf," *Hartford Courant*, September 22, 1925, 11.

10. "Backs Miss Ederle in Channel Dispute," *New York Times*, September 22, 1925, 8.

11. *W.S.A. News*, October 1925.

12. "Ishak Helmy Explains Saving Miss Ederle," *New York Times*, September 22, 1925, 8.

13. "Miss Ederle Gets Diamond Bracelet," *New York Times*, September 23, 1925, 10.

14. "Miss Ederle to Try Channel Next July," *New York Times*, September 24, 1925, 11.

15. Julia Harpman, "The Saga of Ederle," *Liberty Magazine*, October 2, 1926, 47.

16. "Says Crimson Will Defeat Princeton. Drugs Put in Beef Tea Cause Failure of Initial Attempt — Confident of Success Second Time," *Harvard Crimson*, October 25, 1926.

17. "Wolffe's Channel Swim," *Dover Express*, September 25, 1908, 3.

Chapter 24

1. "Gertrude Ederle to Join Pro Ranks," *New York Times*, November 4, 1925, 29.

2. *Aileen Riggin: An Olympian's Oral History*, 2000, 45.

3. "Grange Is Caught Speeding; Other Stars Are with Him," *New York Times*, January 1, 1926, 20.

4. "Skates More Appropriate Than Bathing Suit; Miss Wainwright Defers Plunge," unidentified newspaper clipping, December 29, 1925, Helen Wainwright Scrapbook, International Swimming Hall of Fame.

5. "Helen Wainwright Swims Round Isle," *New York Times*, March 24, 1926, 19.

6. Francis H. Heller, "Malone, Dudley Field" in *American National Biography* (Oxford: Oxford University Press, 1999).

7. "Social Notes," *New York Times*, January 26, 1926, 20.

8. "Financed Miss Ederle," *New York Times*, August 12, 1926, 3.

9. George Fry, "Trudie, Backed by the News, Gives Its Readers Own Story," *Daily News*, August 7, 1926, 2.

10. Julia Harpman, "Miss Ederle, Hugging Medicine Ball, Arrives for Second Try at Channel," *The Chicago Tribune and the Daily News New York* (European Edition), June 9, 1926, 8.

11. *Aileen Riggin: An Olympian's Oral History*, 2000, 46.

Chapter 25

1. "Gertrude Ederle Hopes for Luck in Channel Try," *New York Herald-Tribune*, June 3, 1926.

2. Ishbel Ross, *Ladies of the Press: The Story of Women in Journalism by an Insider* (New York: Harper, 1936).

3. "Women's Party Group Leaves for Europe," *New York Times*, May 15, 1926, 10.

4. "Dogs to Try to Swim Channel This Summer," *New York Times*, May 12, 1926, 24.

5. "Miss Cannon in Trial in Swirling Hudson," *New York Times*, May 14, 1926, 27.

6. Gertrude Ederle, "Ederle Engages Burgess to Train Her for Channel," *Chicago Daily Tribune*, June 15, 1926, 21.

7. "Cannon's Dogs Suffer from Cold; She Denies Row with Miss Ederle," *Baltimore Daily Post*, June 18, 1926.

8. Westbrook Pegler, "Old Bill Outsmarts Himself," *Chicago Daily Tribune*, August 22, 1926, A2.

9. Julia Harpman, "Trude Takes First Dip in Channel," *Boston Post*, June 12, 1926.

10. Gertrude Ederle, "Gertrude Ederle Pursued by Bull," *Boston Post*, June 14, 1926, 13.

11. W. O. McGeehan, "The Channel Swim," *New York Herald Tribune*, June 16, 1926.

12. Julia Harpman, "Where, Oh Where, Wails Wolff, Is Channel Swimmer?" *Chicago Tribune and Daily News* (European Edition), July 17, 1926.

13. "New Rochelle Girl, with Scant Resources, Will Try English Channel Swim Tomorrow," *New York Times*, July 31, 1926, 1.

14. Alex Rutherford, "Hail Miss Barrett for Channel Swim," *New York Times*, August 4, 1926, 1.

15. Alex Rutherford, "Many Offers of Aid for Miss Barrett," *New York Times*, August 6, 1926, 3.

16. "U.S. Swimmers Get Burgess for Trainer," *Atlanta Constitution*, June 6, 1926, A2.

17. "London Typist Fails in Attempt to Swim Channel," *Hartford Courant*, July 25, 1926, B7.

18. "Danish Girl Ends 153-Mile Swim," *New York Times*, September 9, 1921, 21.

19. "Mrs. Corson Self Trained," *New York Times*, August 29, 1926, 3.

20. David Darrah, "Beats Men's Record," *Chicago Daily Tribune*, August 29, 1926, 1.

21. Gertrude Ederle, "Ederle Seeks Crackers for Lively Fourth," *Daily News*, July 2, 1926.

22. Gertrude Ederle, "Ederle Meets Former Trainer," *Chicago Tribune and Daily News* (European Edition), July 13, 1926.

23. Gertrude Ederle, "Gertrude Plans to Eat Salad in Channel Swim," *Chicago Daily Tribune*, June 27, 1926, A4.

24. *Daily News*, August 2, 1926, 1.

Chapter 26

1. Gertrude Ederle, "Gertrude Plans to Eat Salad in Channel Swim," *Chicago Daily Tribune*, June 27, 1926, A4.

2. Buck Dawson, *Mermaids on Parade: America's Love Affair with Its First Women Swimmers* (Huntington, NY: Kroshka Books, 2000), 80.

3. Gertrude Ederle, "Four Mile Swim Is Sunday Drill for Miss Ederle," *Chicago Daily Tribune*, June 28, 1926, 15.

4. Buck Dawson, *Mermaids on Parade: America's Love Affair with Its First Women Swimmers*, 80.

5. Julia Harpman, "The Saga of Ederle," *Liberty*, October 9, 1926, 20.

6. Julia Harpman, "How Gertrude Made the Swim," *Boston Post*, August 7, 1926, 10.

7. Harpman, "The Saga of Ederle," 23.

8. Harpman, "How Gertrude Made the Swim," 10.

9. *Ibid.*

10. *Ibid.*

11. "Big Bonfires," *The Scotsman*, August 7, 1926, 9.

12. Harpman, "How Gertrude Made the Swim," 10.

13. *Ibid.*

Chapter 27

1. Paul Gallico, "Rushed to Hub by Steamer and Airplane," *Boston Post*, August 15, 1926.

2. "Mrs. Ederle Taught Gertie Endurance," *New York Times*, August 8, 1926, 3.

3. Julia Harpman, "'Trudie's' New Heroine Role Disliked By Her," *Atlanta Constitution*, August 8, 1926, A4.

4. *Ibid.*

5. "Miss Ederle Returns to France Amid Wild Acclaim," *Chicago Tribune*, August 8, 1926, 1.

6. Julia Harpman, "Trudie Ederle Swims Channel, Father Wins Bet of $175,000," *Bosto Post*, August 7, 1926, 1.

7. Julia Harpman, "Ederle Cheered on Both Sides of the Atlantic," *Chicago Daily Tribune*, August 8, 1926, A1.

8. William Burgess, "Burgess' Story of Epic Swim," *Chicago Tribune and Daily News* (European Edition), August 9, 1926.

9. Bill Cunningham, "Trudie Had Her Many Troubles," *Boston Post*, August 26, 1926.

10. Alec Rutherford, "Return to France Cheered," *New York Times*, August 8, 1926, 3.

11. "Ederle Given Reception in Calais," *Washington Post*, August 12, 1926.

12. "Germany Greets Ederle by Songs, Parades, Bands," *New York Times*, August 13, 1926, 15.

13. "Lionising Miss Ederle," *The Observer*, August 15, 1926, 13.

14. "Miss Ederle Hears of Death of Aunt," *New York Times*, August 14, 1926, 5.

15. "Begging Cranks Pester Trudy," *Boston Post,* August 16, 1926.

16. "Singing German School Children Greet Trudie at Grandmother's Home," *Chicago Tribune and Daily News* (European Edition), August 15, 1926.

17. "Begging Cranks Pester Trudy," *Boston Post*, August 16, 1926.

18. "Lionising Miss Ederle," *The Observer*, August 15, 1926, 13.

19. "Trudie Did Jolly Well, but Jove, How It Irks the English," *Chicago Daily Tribune*, August 16, 1926, 21.

20. "English Press Knocks Ederle," *Chicago Tribune*, August 17, 1926, 6.

21. "Friends Make Affidavits on Ederle's Swim," *Chicago Daily Tribune*, August 17, 1926, 19.

22. "Miss Ederle Hurls Challenge at World for Channel Swim," *The Atlanta Constitution*, August 18, 1926, 10.

23. "American Admirers Attack Europeans," *The Atlanta Constitution*, August 18, 1926, 10.

24. "Gazette Advances Another Alibi for Ederle's Success," *New York Times*, August 17, 1926, 11.

25. "Flock of Offers Come to Trudie," *Boston Post*, August 10, 1926.

26. *Ibid.*

27. Westbrook Pegler, "Trudy Wastes $100,000 Since Humiliating Channel — Pyle," *Chicago Daily Tribune*, August 25, 1926, 19.

28. "Miss Barrett Held by Channel Storm," *New York Times*, August 16, 1926, 5.

Chapter 28

1. Paul Gallico, "Sporting Chatter," *Chicago Tribune and Daily News* (European Edition), September 10, 1926.

2. "Harbor Welcome Rivals the Lands," August 28, 1926, 3.

3. "City's Throngs Give Greatest Welcome to Gertrude Ederle," *New York Times*, August 28, 1926, 1.

4. "Miss Ederle Cables Praise," *New York Times*, August 29, 1926, 3.

5. Westbrook Pegler, "Women Swim Channel, Men Wade in Talk," *Chicago Daily Tribune*, August 30, 1926, 23.

6. *New York Daily News*, August 30, 1926, 1.

7. "Neighborhood Roars Welcome to Trudy," *New York Times*, August 31, 1926, 3.

8. "Queen 'Trudy' Faints on Throne, Ending Great Fete by Neighbors," *The World*, August 31, 1926.

9. "Ederle Is Threatened by Nervous Collapse," *Washington Post*, August 30, 1926.

10. "Mille Gade Corson," *Variety*, September 15, 1926, 24.

11. "Miss Ederle Sends Congratulations," *New York Times*, May 22, 1927, 2.

12. *Aileen Riggin: An Olympian's Oral History*, 2000, 47.

13. *Ibid.*, 46.

14. Tony Kornheiser, "It's Been 45 Years — But Memories Still Vivid," *Newsday*, August 6, 1971.

15. "Ethel Hertle First in Marathon Swim," *New York Times*, August 30, 1928, 1.

16. "Gertrude Ederle Wants Her Movie Now," *Queens Daily News*, February 13, 1983, 40.

Bibliography

Books

Camp, Walter. *Walter Camp's Book of College Sports*. New York: Century, 1893.

Carlson, Lewis H., and John J. Fogarty. *Tales of Gold*. Chicago: Contemporary Books, 1987.

Clune, Henry W. *I Always Liked It Here: Reminiscences of a Rochesterian*. Rochester: University of Rochester Libraries, 1983.

Costa, D. Margaret, and Sharon R. Guthri. *Women and Sport: Interdisciplinary Perspectives*. Champaign, IL: Human Kinetics, 1994.

Dahlberg, Tim, Mary Ederle Ward, and Brenda Greene. *America's Girl: The Incredible Story of How Swimmer Gertrude Ederle Changed the Nation*. New York: St. Martin's, 2009.

Dawson, Buck. *Mermaids on Parade: America's Love Affair with Its First Olympic Swimmers*. Huntington, NY: Kroshka Books, 2000.

Draper, Andrew Sloan. *Draper's Self-Culture. Volume 6: Sports, Pastimes, and Physical Culture*. New York: Ferd. P. Kaiser, 1907.

Dyerson, Mark. *Making the American Team: Sport, Culture and the Olympic Experience*. Urbana: University of Illinois Press, 1998.

Gallico, Paul. *The Golden People*. Garden City, NY: Doubleday, 1964.

Handley, L. de B. *Swimming for Women*. New York: American Sports Publishing, 1925.

Jarvis, Margaret A. *Captain Webb and 100 Years of Channel Swimming*. North Pomfret, VT: Newton Abbott and David & Charles, 1975.

Kaufman, David. *Shul with a Pool: The "Synagogue-Center" in American Jewish History, Culture and Life*. Waltham, MA: Brandeis University Press, 1999.

Kellerman, Annette. *How to Swim*. New York: George H. Doran, 1918.

Kisseloff, Jeff. *You Must Remember This: An Oral History of Manhattan from the 1890s to World War II*. Baltimore: Johns Hopkins University Press, 2000.

Korsgaard, Robert. *A History of the Amateur Athletic Union of the United States*. Dissertation, Teachers College Columbia University, 1952.

Mallon, Bill, and Ian Buchanan. *The 1908 Olympic Games: Results for All Competitors, in All Events, with Commentary*. Jefferson, NC: McFarland, 2000.

Mortimer, Gavin. *The Great Swim*. London: Walker, 2008.

New York City Borough of Manhattan. Public Works Department. *Public Baths Under the Supervision of the President of the Borough of Manhattan*. New York: 1912.

Phillips, Ellen. *The Olympic Century: The Official 1st Century History of the Modern Olympic Movement. Volume 8. The VIII Olympiad*. Paris 1924, St. Moritz, 1928. Los Angeles: World Sport Research and Publications, 1996.

Reiss, Steven A. *City Games: The Evolution of American Urban Society and the Rise of Sports*. Urbana and Chicago: University of Illinois Press, 1989.

Ross, Ishbel. *Ladies of the Press: The Story of Women in Journalism by an Insider*. New York: Harper, 1936.

Stoddard, Andrew. *Municipal Wastewater Treatment: Evaluating Improvements in National Water Quality*. New York: Wiley, 2002.

Stout, Glenn. *Young Woman and the Sea: How Trudy Ederle Conquered the English Channel and Inspired the World*. New York: Houghton Mifflin Harcourt, 2009.
Sullivan, James E. *Schoolyard Athletics: Giving Directions for Conducting Organized Athletic Activities in the Schoolyard*. New York: American Sports Publishing, 1909.
_____. *Spalding's Official Athletic Almanac for 1905: Special Olympic Number Containing the Official Report of the Olympic Games of 1904*. New York: American Publishing, 1905.
Warner, Patricia Campbell. *When the Girls Came Out to Play: The Birth of American Sportswear*. Amherst: University of Massachusetts Press, 2006.
Wheeler, Robert W. *Jim Thorpe, World's Greatest Athlete*. Norman: University of Oklahoma Press, 1979.

Articles

"Big Bonfires." *The Scotsman*, August 7, 1926.
Borish, Linda J. "'The Cradle of American Champions, Women Champions ... Swim Champions': Charlotte Epstein, Gender and Jewish Identity, and the Physical Emancipation of Women in Aquatic Sports." *International Journal of the History of Sport* 21 (March 2004): 197–235.
Chambers, Robin L. "The German-American Turners: Their Efforts to Promote, Develop, and Initiate Physical Culture in Chicago's Public Schools and Parks, 1860–1914" *Yearbook of German-American Studies* 22 (1987): 101–110.
Coubertin, Pierre de. "Why I Revived the Olympic Games," in *The World's Great Events*, ed., Esther Singleton, New York: P. F. Collier & Son, 1916.
Dyreson, Mark. *Icons of Liberty or Objects of Desire? American Women Olympians and the Politics of Consumption. Journal of Contemporary History* 38 (2003): 435–460.
"Elaine Golding Swims the Lake." *Panama Star and Herald*, December 13, 1913.
Gallico, Paul. "Rushed to Hub by Steamer and Airplane." *Boston Post*, August 15, 1926.
"Gertrude Ederle Wants Her Movie Now," *Queens Daily News*, February 13, 1983.
"Give Work to Women." *Washington Post*, September 27, 1908.
Golding, Ethel. "Lesson No. 1." *Evening World*, July 29, 1901.
Handley, L. de B. "The Winter Crusade to Win Women Swimmers." *The Atlanta Constitution*, November 19, 1916.
Harpman, Julia. "The Saga of Ederle." *Liberty*, October 2, 1926.
_____. "The Saga of Ederle (Part II)." *Liberty*, October 9, 1926.
_____. "The Saga of Ederle (Part III)." *Liberty*, October 16, 1926.
Heller, Francis H. "Malone, Dudley Field" in *American National Biography*, Oxford: Oxford University Press, 1999.
"History Made at the St. George's Aquatic Meeting." *Royal Gazette,* October 10, 1922.
Hollander, Daniel B., and Edmund O. Acevedo. "Successful English Channel Swimming: The Peak Experience." *The Sport Psychologist* 14 (2000): 1–16.
"How Disease Is Generated in New York." *Frank Leslie's Illustrated Newspaper*, August 20, 1870.
Kornheiser, Tony. "It's Been 45 Years — But Memories Still Vivid." *Newsday*, August 6, 1971.
"Lionising Miss Ederle." *The Observer*, August 15, 1926.
Lucan, Jon. "The Hegemonic Rule of the American Amateur Athletic Union 1888–1914: James Edward.
Lucas, John A., and Ian Jobling. "Troubled Waters: Fanny Durack's 1919 Swimming Tour of America Amid Transnational Amateur Athletic Prudery and Bureaucracy," *Olympika* 4 (1995): 93–112.
"Mille Gade Corson." *Variety*, September 15, 1926.
"The Overtrained Athletic Girl." *Modern Medical Science* 16 (1904): 631.
"Peeping Toms." *The National Police Gazette*, September 1, 1883.
"Public Baths." *Southern Practitioner* 35 (1913): 431.
"Queen 'Trudy' Faints on Throne, Ending Great Fete by Neighbors." *The World*, August 31, 1926.
"The Shower That Shattered a Mermaid Friendship," *San Francisco Chronicle*, November 27, 1921.

"Sullivan as Prime Mover." *The International Journal of the History of Sport* 11 (December 1994): 355–371.

"Swim Through London." *The Observer*, August 21, 1910.

Welch, Paula D., and Harold A. Lerch. "The Women's Swimming Association Launches America into Swimming Supremacy." *The Olympian* (March 1979): 14–16.

"Woman in Brave Life-Saving Band." *The Republic*, June 14, 1903.

Periodicals

Boston Daily Globe, 1890–1920.

Brooklyn Eagle, 1860–1930.

Chicago Tribune, 1924–1926.

Hartford Courant, 1870–1920.

Los Angeles Times, 1924–1926.

New York Herald Tribune, 1924–1927.

New York Times, 1860–1930.

New York Tribune, 1860–1924.

The Sun, 1860–1920.

W.S.A. News, 1919–1927.

Amateur Athletic Union of the United States. Minutes of the Annual Meeting, 1900–1918.

Annual Report of the United States Volunteer Life-Saving Corps (Inland Waters). (Albany: State of New York) 1900–1911.

Annual Report of the United States Volunteer Life Saving Corps of Rhode Island Department. (Providence: E. L. Freeman & Sons) 1904–1910.

Oral Histories

Murphy, Doris O'Mara: An Olympian's Oral History (Los Angeles: Amateur Athletic Foundation of Los Angeles, 1988).

Neher, Clarita Hunsberger: An Olympian's Oral History (Los Angeles: Amateur Athletic Foundation of Los Angeles, 1988).

Riggin, Aileen: An Olympian's Oral History (Los Angeles: Amateur Athletic Foundation of Los Angeles, 2000).

Sanborn, Thelma Payne: An Olympian's Oral History (Los Angeles: Amateur Athletic Foundation of Los Angeles).

Soule, Aileen Riggin: A Wonderful Life in Her Own Words. International Swimming Hall of Fame, online at http://www.ishof.org/exhibits/pdf/aileen_riggin.pdf

Index